Empowerment and Participation in Youth Work

Titles in the Series

To order, please contact our distributor: BEBC Distribution, Albion Close, Parkstone, Poole, BH12 3LL. Telephone: 0845 230 9000, email: **learningmatters@bebc.co.uk**. You can also find more information on each of these titles and our other learning resources at **www.learningmatters.co.uk**

Empowerment and Participation in Youth Work

ANNETTE FITZSIMONS, MAX HOPE, CHARLIE COOPER AND KEITH RUSSELL

Series Editors: Janet Batsleer and Keith Popple

LearningMatters

First published in 2011 by Learning Matters Ltd

British Library Cataloguing in Publication Data
A CIP record for this book is available from the British Library.

ISBN 978 1 84445 347 4

This book is also available in the following ebook formats:
Adobe Ebook: 9781844457830
EPUB: 9781844457823
Kindle: 9780857250322

Cover and text design by Code 5 Design Associates Ltd.
Project management by Newgen Publishing and Data Services
Typeset by Newgen Publishing and Data Services
Printed and bound in Great Britain by Short Run Press Ltd, Exeter, Devon

Learning Matters Ltd
20 Cathedral Yard
Exeter EX1 1HB
Tel: 01392 215560
info@learningmatters.co.uk
www.learningmatters.co.uk

Contents

Foreword from the Series Editors

Youth work and community work has a long, rich and diverse history that spans three centuries. The development of youth work extends from the late nineteenth and early twentieth century with the emergence of voluntary groups and the serried ranks of the UK's many uniformed youth organisations, through to modern youth club work, youth project work and informal education. Youth work remains in the early twenty-first century a mixture of voluntary effort and paid and state-sponsored activity.

Community work also had its beginnings in voluntary activity. Some of this activity was in the form of 'rescuing the poor', while community action developed as a response to oppressive circumstances and was based on the idea of self-help. In the second half of the twentieth century, the state financed a good deal of local authority- and government-sponsored community and regeneration work, and now there are multi-various community action projects and campaigns.

Today, there are thousands of people involved in youth work and community work both in paid positions and in voluntary roles. However, the activity is undergoing significant change. National Occupation Standards and a new academic benchmarking statement have been introduced and all youth and community workers undertaking qualifying courses and who successfully graduate do so with an honours degree.

Empowering Youth and Community Work Practice is a series of texts primarily aimed at students on youth and community work courses. However, more experienced practitioners from a wide range of fields will find these books useful because they offer effective ways of integrating theory, knowledge and practice. Written by experienced lecturers, practitioners and policy commentators, each title covers core aspects of what is needed to be an effective practitioner and will address key competences for professional JNC recognition as a youth and community worker. The books use case studies, activities and references to the latest government initiatives to help readers learn and develop their theoretical understanding and practice. This series then will provide invaluable support to anyone studying or practicing in the field of youth and community work, as well as a number of other related fields.

Janet Batsleer
Manchester Metropolitan University

Keith Popple
London South Bank University

About the Authors

Annette Fitzsimons is programme director for Youth and Community Work, in the Department of Social Sciences at the University of Hull where she teaches undergraduates and postgraduates. Her research interests are in gender and equalities where she has published extensively.

Annette has extensive experience of working with community and voluntary sector organisations particularly those engaged in delivering support services to vulnerable young people. Her current research reflects this experience and focuses upon current issues in youth work, in particular, policies directed at social exclusion and notions of young people's resilience.

Max Hope is a Lecturer in Education and Social Inclusion at the University of Hull. She has extensive grassroots experience in the community and voluntary sector, including young people's projects, HIV organisations and women's centres. She has a keen interest in democracy and participation and in particular, about how the leadership and management of organisations can enhance these processes.

Charlie Cooper is a professionally-qualified housing practitioner and youth worker. In the 1970s and 1980s he largely worked in the community and voluntary sector with Women's Aid and community-based housing associations. Since the 1990s he has worked in higher education, teaching and researching in the areas of housing, tenant participation, education, social policy, and community and youth work.

Keith Russell is the Coordinator at The Warren, a voluntary youth project in Hull, UK.

Introduction

Every Child Matters (2003) and *Youth Matters* (2005) focus on the participation of young people in decision making at all levels, thus ensuring that participation occurs in an empowering environment and with empowered individuals, which is a key requirement for this legislation. The book seeks to provide concrete explanations, arguments, suggestions, reflections and ideas on how young people can be empowered to participate in both social and political life effectively. It begins with an examination of competing definitions of the concept of empowerment. It proposes a working definition and explores the contradictions of using this approach in youth work settings. The concept of participation is examined in a similar way in Chapter 3, and a case is made for a view of participation which is based on a model of empowerment. The elements that are needed for young people to feel empowered are thus a central theme of the book and the notion of resilience, outlined in Chapter 5, is introduced as a strategy for a strengths-based perspective within youth work practice.

The Warren, a young people's community and resource project, is a unique agency working with a very clear empowerment philosophy and policy of participation for over 20 years. The results of this approach are described in Chapter 2 with the aim of demonstrating the achievements of a youth work practice with a clear philosophical and ethical underpinning for their work with young people. The discussions of empowerment and participation draw on the real experiences and difficulties faced by youth workers who work with current governmental agendas of youth development.

As facilitating quality youth work requires a number of complex skills including reflection and facilitation of people and resources, Chapters 4 and 6 guide the reader through these issues and challenges. The first of these addresses some central issues within organisations. This is not a 'how to' guide to management. Instead, it takes a fresh look at key aspects of organisation theory – in particular, leadership, the development of organisational structures and cultures, models of decision making and the management of staff – to find ways to ensure that these are consistent with empowerment. The aim is to explore how the *values* of youth and community work can be aligned with leadership and management practice. In essence to find ways to ensure that organisations can be effective and yet still be empowering.

Empowering practitioners need to be reflective, and Chapter 6 is focused on exploring what this means and how workers might develop these skills. Reflection is about introspection, decision making and action in the real work of practice. Critical thinkers are able to appraise situations, act purposefully and evaluate their actions. In addition, youth workers play a crucial role in supporting young people to develop their reflective capacities, and the possibilities – and challenges – of this are explored. It is concluded that not only must youth workers be reflective practitioners in themselves, but they must also work to support young people in becoming reflective too. This is central to empowering practice.

Critical reflective practice involves the following:

- Being pro-active, flexible and adaptable in the face of changes in policy, law and organisational structures.

- Being articulate about and acting upon professional values including a commitment to tackling oppression in practice.

- Being accountable to appropriate stakeholders.

- Being able to take decisions in conditions of uncertainty.

- Being capable of working on their own initiative and with others.

- Being self-evaluative and self-critical and taking responsibility for personal and professional development.

Chapter 7 explores different models of citizenship and argues for a 'rights' approach which recognises the social inequalities experienced by groups of young people. The aim here is to equip youth workers with a vigorous emancipatory approach to projects on citizenship which work towards positive social change.

The theoretical underpinnings to youth work practice are explored in the final chapter. Here, the account of the models of youth work practice, both historically and present day, is linked to key sociological theorists to trace the links between theory and practice, which shape so much of the theoretical underpinnings of youth work practice.

Chapter 1

What is empowerment?

CHAPTER OBJECTIVES

This chapter will help you meet the following National Occupational Standards:

1.1.2   Enable young people to work effectively in groups

1.4.1   Provide information and support to young people

1.1.5   Support young people in taking action and to tackle problems

It will also introduce you to the following academic standards as set out in the QAA youth and community work benchmark statement (2009).

5.1.2   Fostering democratic and inclusive practice

The aim of this chapter is to explore empowerment – a term which is currently used in youth and community work and throughout the caring professions as a strategy for including people into the decision-making processes of organisations and communities. The extent of this inclusion can refer to participation on committees, to influencing decision making or to the control of resources. It is also an internal process, whereby individuals develop and change their self-concept, perhaps by improving their levels of confidence. These two processes are interconnected; individuals may not be able to participate in empowering organisational processes unless they perceive themselves as being able to do so.

CASE STUDY

Empowering process?

Susie is an active member of the local youth club. She attends most drop-in sessions and has recently started helping out as a volunteer.

The youth centre is recruiting new staff members. They have developed a process for ensuring that young people are genuinely involved in the interview process. Susie is invited to be on the interview panel. She will be interviewing the candidates along with three other young people and one worker.

On the day, Susie is very quiet. When asked her opinion, she waits for others to speak. She goes along with what others say. She does not seem to know what she thinks. The workers are not sure whether she agrees with the final decision, although she says that she does.

Has the youth club been empowering? Which aspects of empowerment have they focussed on?

The term 'empowerment' has been increasingly used by social and healthcare professionals, researchers and activists since the 1970s and though historically its roots are radical and revolutionary, it is used increasingly in liberal and consumerist and managerialist discourse (see Quinn and Davies, 1999), thus producing conflicts and contradictions for practitioners.

A series of literature reviews of the term (see, for example, Perkins and Zimmerman, 1995; Page and Czuba, 1999) point out the ways in which the term increasingly lacks clarity and precision. Indeed, the majority of writings on the term begin with the problem of definition (see Rappaport, 1984; Servian, 1996; Payne, 1997; Adams, 2003; Thompson, 2007). These critical accounts are very useful, in that a number of issues are beginning to emerge through this work, which can help practitioners to begin applying the concept with increasing confidence.

So what is empowerment? How can it be measured and evaluated? Is it a set of values or a series of outcomes? Does it only pertain to an individual or can a group or an organisation become empowered? And if so, how do you know that this has happened and how can you help groups and individuals to achieve this? To address these questions, this chapter seeks to explore some of the issues which emerge in attempting to define the term. One of the first problems encountered in the literature is that empowerment is referred to as a theory, as a process and as a concept. It might be useful to consider the difference between a theory and a concept before we embark on an exploration of the term.

Empowerment: theory, concept or process

A theory is an explanation of some phenomenon or event, whereas a concept is a part of this explanation. A theory is composed of a series of concepts which are linked in a logical fashion to provide an explanation of a 'thing'; for example, the theory of internal combustion. There are a number of concepts (parts), such as engine parts, oil, air filters and fan belts, which need to be placed together in a certain pattern in order for the theory to operate, or in this case, for the car to start. The process would be the operation of the car, the technology at work. Although this example relates to a machine, and empowerment is anything but mechanistic, it is useful in illustrating the distinction between theory, concept and process. Rather than considering empowerment as either a theory or a concept, it is perhaps more useful to consider it as a process by which groups and individuals feel empowered to achieve, to participate and to overcome their lack of power and control.

The term began to appear in the 1970s in literature on development and gender. It then began to be used by academics in psychology, sociology, educational and organisational research as a strategy for the development of individuals, communities and organisations. Throughout this literature, the key terms that empowerment is posed against are 'oppression', 'powerlessness', 'control' and 'marginalisation', and it can be viewed as *A process of increasing interpersonal or political power so that individuals can take action to improve their life situation* (Gutierrez, 1990, page 149).

The core of the term empowerment is this contrast to the operation of power and many studies attempt to explore the complexity of empowerment by outlining theories of power (see Thompson, 2007).

'Power' is a useful starting point, as is an understanding of the different insights which alternative definitions provide. Power is commonly conceptualised as pertaining to politics, politicians and governments who make laws and exercise control over citizens. When a parent forbids their child to do something, or an employer reprimands a worker, this too is an exercise of power. Power, just like empowerment, is a difficult subject of study as it is an *essentially contested concept*. This means that there are different ways of conceptualising power, that definitions are disputed and usually depend on the theoretical approach adopted by the writer. So the following sections will explain the work of some of the key writers on the topic, beginning with the work of Max Weber (1864–1920).

Power and authority

In contemporary society, it is important to differentiate between power and authority. Past societies can be identified which operated with one or the other, but this clear cut distinction is blurred in the organisation of current liberal democratic nation states. The distinction between authority and power is used by Weber to refer to authority as legitimised power. For him, the idea of power without authority is: *The probability that one actor within a social relationship will be in a position to carry out his* (sic) *own will despite resistance, regardless of the basis on which this probability rests* (Weber, 1947, page 152).

Authority exists when citizens give their consent and accept the authority of others as legitimate. This exercise of power is based on legitimate authority and not on coercion. Max Weber explores three sources of legitimacy for authority and power.

- Traditional authority, which is an established belief in authority of, for example, the 'divine right of kings'.

- Charismatic authority, which can be obedience to an exceptional individual as they are deemed to possess inspirational characteristics, for example, Jesus Christ, Chairman Mao. Such people acquire positions of authority over others on the basis of their personal qualities.

- Rational legal authority, where power is given to those who uphold an office or position, for example, a traffic warden, a judge, a manager. The exercise of power is not based on the personal qualities of the person but on the legitimacy of the office.

So, in Weber's view the rational exercise of power is based on legitimate authority. Is this, however, the only way power operates in society?

ACTIVITY **1.1**

Spend a couple of minutes thinking about your organisation.

Who has power? Who is powerful?

Is it the manager? The Management Committee? The staff team? The volunteers? The young people? The funding body? The local residents?

Where does their power come from? Do they have authority? Does it fit with Weber's three sources of legitimacy? Can you think of any other ways that power might operate?

Foucault's Concept of Power

Foucault's (1926–1984) analysis of the relationship between power, discursive practices and subjectivity provides a number of conceptual tools from which to reformulate theories of power. These theoretical resources can contribute to the debate on empowerment and help with a clearer definition. His analysis of power is in contrast to one that views power as something that is possessed, something that *some* people possess, and *not* others. Foucault says of conceptualisations of power such as these, that

> *it allows power to be only ever thought of in negative terms: refusal, delimitation, obstruction, censure. Power is that which says no. Any confrontation with power thus conceived appears only as transgression. The manifestation of power takes on the pure form of 'thou shalt not'.*

(Foucault, 1979, page 53)

Arising from his critique of this way of formulating power in society, Foucault outlines a different way of thinking about power. If power is always about domination, it is posed

*only in terms of constitutions, sovereignty etc., hence in juridical terms;
(and) on the* Marxist *side, in terms of the state apparatus. (Then) The way
in which it was exercised concretely and in detail, with its specificity, its
techniques and tactics was not looked for; one contented oneself with
denouncing it in a polemical and global manner, as it existed among the
'others' in the adversary's camp: power in soviet socialism was called
totalitarianism by its opponents, and in Western capitalism it was denounced
by Marxists as class domination, but the mechanics of power were never
analysed.*

(Foucault, 1979, page 34)

Rather than concentrating on the negative, repressive aspects of power, Foucault
argues that if this was the only story about power, it cannot explain what he terms
the productivity of power – the way power *produces things ... induces pleasure ...
forms knowledge ... produces discourse* (1979, page 36). Foucault's critique and
analysis allows a more liberating or emancipatory analysis of power, which is a
central dimension of empowerment. Rather than viewing power as a possession,
Foucault views power as running through the social network; producing effects;
as productive, rather than negative. He says that:

*What gives power its hold, what makes it accepted, is quite simply the fact
that it does not simply weigh like a force which says no, but that it runs
through, and it produces, things, it induces pleasure, it forms knowledge
[savoir], it produces discourses; it must be considered as a productive network
that runs through the entire social body much more than as a negative
instance whose function is repression.*

(Interview in Morris and Patton, 1979, page 36)

This includes the recognition that whenever two or more people are engaged
in some activity, power conflicts and struggles are involved. This means, however, that young people, socially excluded groups or marginalised individuals
are also involved in the exercise of power. Rather than viewing power with
unease, or simply in terms of control, as coercion, as a negative concept, the
fact that everyone has and exercises power means that power cannot simply
be located with particular groups in society. Foucault's 'new' concept of power
provides the possibility of enabling a productive discourse on power, which
could be used to explore the empowerment in ways that can be progressive and
liberating.

ACTIVITY **1.2**

Do you think that power can be liberating?

Can you find examples within your practice to back up this perspective?

What, for you, are the connections between power and empowerment?

Nancy Fraser (1989) also puts forward a positive reading of Foucault on power, arguing that his analysis enables power to be analysed at the micro level, at the level of everyday practices, and turns the focus away from power as residing with the state or with the economy. Jana Sawicki (1991) makes similar points in her discussion of Foucault and power. She analyses the ways in which his concept of power differs from traditional conceptions, which concentrate on power as dominance, as repression, and discusses the exercise and productivity of power in relation to identity, sexuality and the body.

Foucault's work has been hugely important for the reformulation of the place of the individual/subject within structures of power and dominance. One important theme is the notion of resistance to the imposition of power and the impetus for empowerment. What determines individual resistance and complicity is very difficult to analyse, and with the development of psychoanalytic theory it is clear that one cannot address this problem only in terms of sociological theory. The questions of desires, identity, fantasy, resilience and fear all have to be addressed, as would the ways in which individual personal histories intersect with both structures and discourses. In this way subjectivity and agency are marked with difference.

Based on this formulation, it is possible to explore the effect of a number of discourses in the production of empowerment in practice. This is an alternative approach to theorising empowerment, which can provide a contrast to the accounts of power that pose the problem in terms either at the level of the economy, the State, or the individual. Rather than deny the power of these structures – as Foucault says 'I don't want to say that the State isn't important', rather,

> The State is superstructural in relation to a whole series of power networks that invest the body, sexuality, the family, kinship, knowledge, technology and so forth. True these networks stand in a conditioning-conditioned relationship to a kind of 'meta-power' which is structured essentially round a certain number of great prohibition functions; but this meta-power with its prohibitions can only take hold and secure its footing where it is rooted in a whole series of multiple and indefinite power relations that supply the necessary basis for the great negative forms of power.

> (Foucault, 1979, page 39)

This dimension to Foucault's theory of power is often overlooked. The focus is on his discussion of the individual exercise of power, power at the micro level rather than at the macro level of the operation of power throughout society. If all elements of Foucault's writings on power are taken into account, then it cannot be contrasted with Weber in any simplistic way. One of the important insights into the operation of power that Foucault provides is the account of power operating throughout society and as located not only in the state but also in the individual. The work of another theorist can be used as a way of combining all of these facets of power.

Steven Lukes in his book *Power: A Radical View* (1974) argues that there are at least three dimensions or ways of analysing how power is exercised in modern societies. The first dimension Lukes defines as:

> *the ability of A to prevail over B in formal political decision-making (normally in government) on one or more key issues; where there is a direct and observable conflict between A and B over outcomes.*

(1974, cited in Cox et al., 1985, page 32)

Power here is taken to mean the ability of one formal office holder to shape the final outcome of government. This definition of power corresponds to a pluralist view of power, and it is based on the assumption that:

- Power is diffuse, held by many groups.

- Groups compete for power.

- Different groups exercise power in different areas.

- Groups are open to new members and outside influence.

- The state (administrative apparatus) is a neutral arbiter between different groups.

Pluralists do not compare the relative power of different groups or the degree of influence they have on the state.

Lukes' (1974) second dimension is defined as:

> *the ability of A to prevail over B in determining the outcomes of observable conflicts of interests in formal decision-making and also in determining what is to count as a formal issue, where there is a conflict of interests over policy preferences and observable grievances over these preferences outside the political system.*

(1974, cited in Cox et al., 1985, page 32)

All decisions are likely to be of importance to some group or interest in society. However, some groups are strategically placed so that they can ensure that all issues which threaten them are resolved in their favour. In other words, elite groups in society either inside or outside the political system can continuously use their influence or presence in the system to determine the outcome of those issues that are important to them.

- Power is concentrated in the hands of a few.

- Dominant group is unified by background and beliefs.

- This group makes all the important decisions.

- This group is closed to new members.

Power in this second dimension is not seen as flowing directly from the public through to government. Instead power is exercised by those in the top positions of major institutions in society. This formulation corresponds to the elite theory of power. The two 'founders' Vilfredo Pareto (1848–1923) and Gaetano Mosca (1858–1941) together with Robert Michels (1911) would insist that the idea of a classless society or of participatory democracy are simply idealist delusions. So they divide society into key social institutions such as parliament, civil service, judiciary, church, armed forces, business, finance, press and universities; each of these is run by an elite who have developed excellence in these particular areas, and these elites substantially control the political process.

Before exploring Lukes' third dimension, it is relevant to bring in theory from C. Wright Mills, an American sociologist who produced an analysis of power entitled *The Power Elite* (1956). In this, it was argued that the three dominant spheres of influence in American society are the political, the military and the industrial and that these areas are increasingly interdependent on each other. This interdependence is reinforced by the fact that the top staff of these elites are drawn from a common social and education background and are often connected by kinship and marriage. Interchange of top personnel between each sector means there is a power elite dominating in the three areas. Similar studies by Ralph Miliband of the British state (1982, 1983) demonstrate the connections between elite groups, which are strengthened through intermarriage, shared cultural background, activities and education.

Power here is conceived much more in terms of a division between the 'haves' or the 'have nots', though C. Wright Mills (1956) argues that below these elites (see Figure 1.1) lie competing interest groups and then the disempowered masses.

The simplicity of Mill's view is attractive, but it denies the majority of people any power at all.

Let's now turn to Steve Lukes' (1974) third dimension of power which he defines as:

> *the ability of A to prevent B from realising his (sic) 'real' interests or from articulating them effectively due to the mobilisation of bias resulting from the institutional structure of society.*

(1974, cited in Cox et al., 1985, page 32)

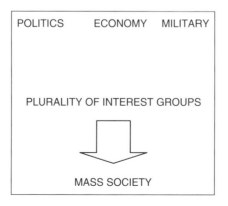

Figure 1.1 Power elite

In this view, power is equated not just with who decides but with the way in which the economic and social structure of capitalist society conditions human thought and action, so that individuals never understand their 'real' interests. In this formulation, power can only be analysed by first asking the question of where people's ideas of reality and their desires come from, which directs one to the underlying structure of the capitalist system. It is this structure which predetermines individual thought and action such that fundamental threats to the system are not only contained but also that people are incapable of realising that they could either want to change the system, or indeed to actually change it. This third dimension corresponds to a Marxist analysis of power, in that the class which holds the material resources of production also control mental production (creation of intellectual ideas) as explained by the following passage:

> *The ideas of the ruling class are in every epoch the ruling ideas, i.e., the class which is the ruling material force of society, is at the same time its ruling intellectual force. The class which has the means of material production at its disposal, has control at the same time over the means of mental production, so that thereby, generally speaking, the ideas of those who lack the means of mental production are subject to it.*

> (Marx and Engels, 1965, page 60)

This approach maintains that there is a class structure whereby the owning classes dominate the working classes and that politics and the state reflect this structure. It argues that elite theorists inadequately analyse this fundamental structure, because it is not simply a question of elites but a question of a ruling class. The State, which is the instrument of this ruling class, is the real basis of power relations. Parliamentary politics or workplace democracy would be viewed as 'ideologically' significant rather than being of any fundamental significance as it gives the illusion that people can exercise real political choices and power.

Thus, there are distinct theoretical approaches suggested by Lukes' (1974) analysis of power, which could, for simplicity, be categorised as liberal, pluralist and socialist/Marxist.

The concept of discourse

There are a number of approaches to the study of discourse; and the terms 'discourse' and 'discourse analysis' will have very different meanings depending upon the theoretical approach of the writer. Rather than discourse analysis, the concept of discourse that is used here is the one that is based on Foucault's view of discourse as knowledge.

For Foucault, discourses are anything that can carry meaning. Language, images, stories, scientific narratives and cultural products are, therefore, all discourses; but also social practices like constructing 'youth' as a time of transition, freedom to explore, the idea that youth is about freedom, mobility, an ideal time, a fantasy of having a good time in contrast with adult state of responsibilities. In Foucault's account, discourses are not a reflection of already existing differences between people but the means by which these differences are produced. Our subjectivities are formed out of the self-understandings that we gain from encountering these publicly available discourses. For Foucault, not only does the scope of discourse expand beyond that of language, the discourses we have available to us, regarding, for example, masculinity or femininity, are multiple, contradictory and subject to variation and change. Think of the multiplicity of discourses of masculinity and femininity: hysterical woman, women governed by hormones, superwoman, mother, whore, feminist woman, butch dyke, strong black woman; rational man, repressed man, violent and dominating man, gentle father, new man, queen, real gentleman, loyal husband. These discourses are dynamic and our identities are constituted from negotiating them along with others, for example, Irish woman, working class grammar school girl, lesbian, African, socialist, musician, and so on. In this negotiation for Foucault, young people participate in the production of discourses and thereby in the production of themselves.

For Foucault, discourses are tied to power. He understands power not only in the sense of state and structural power but also as something which is pervasive and operates throughout all relations within society via discursive understandings. So, for example, certain gender discourses make possible and reinforce power relations between men and women, discourses for example which construct men as stronger or more rational. In the negotiation of our identities via public discourses, however, we do not always adopt those which are most dominant. Wherever there are discourses promoting certain relations of power, there will, for Foucault, also be *resistant* discourses produced, which enable different kinds of subjects to be produced.

ACTIVITY **1.3**

Think about a young person you know well.

What sort of discourses might have influenced the way that they are?

For example: Do you know a young man who thinks that he has to behave in a certain way in order to 'be a man'? What sort of language would he use about himself?

What are the 'discourses' that might have affected him?

The notion of discourse provides the means for interpreting the practices which structure people's understanding of themselves in relation to the world and suggests how subjectivity is constructed and negotiated by individuals. However, this subjectivity is *precarious*, contradictory and constantly in process, continually being reconstituted in discourse each time people think and speak. So, while this notion of discourse helps to explain the contradictions, shifts and changes, there appears to be no way of determining why or how some discourses are more powerful and more marginal than others. It is here that Marxism does appear to help to explain why some discourses are more powerful than others. Althusser (1984) advances an idea of 'subjects' as constituted in and through ideology. An article by Trevor Purvis and Alan Hunt (1993) contrasts the concept of discourse with the concept of ideology by suggesting that:

> if 'discourse' and 'ideology' both figure in accounts of the general field of social action mediated through communicative practices, then 'discourse' focuses upon the internal features of those practices, in particular their linguistic and semiotic dimensions. On the other hand, 'ideology' directs attention towards the external aspects of focusing on the way in which lived experience is connected to notions of interest and position that are in principle distinguishable from lived experience.

(Purvis and Hunt, 1993, page 476)

Althusser (1984) had moved the concept of ideology from a crude and simplistic understanding of ideology as false consciousness or as a set of ideas which are imposed in a simplistic manner on the working classes by the bourgeois class to one which is much more complicated and contradictory. Ideology for Althusser was not a set of mistaken beliefs or lies: it represented a particular understanding of the world – a particular interpretation which legitimated a particular view of society. Ideology in Althusser's work represents a shift from a strict determination of the economic base to the notion that ideologies have an autonomy and are only determined in the *last instance* by economy relations. Althusser's (1984) concept of ideology helps us to understand how sets of ideas – for example, ideology of gender of masculinity and femininity – are linked to a system of power and control. However, despite the notion of autonomy, the concept still retains the notion that these ideas are imposed (even if that imposition is consensual rather than coercive) and that ideologies act on people rather than people acting on ideologies. The human subject is passive rather than active in this theoretical framework, and this means that it is difficult to explain shifts and changes in ideologies. How, for instance, can the notion of an ideology of masculinity explain many different masculinities rather than masculinity in the singular? The concept of discourse helps one to examine this plurality. It also provides a framework from which to trace historical changes in discourses.

Though there are a number of tensions in Foucault's work, what is offered here is the suggestion that his notion of discourse when linked with his concept of power can be used to elaborate the dilemmas and contradictions of the process of empowerment. Foucault's notion of power provides an escape from the notion that power is simply an imposition, a form of coercion, and allows the possibility of power being productive, collective and personal. The emphasis is on the practices of discourses that produced 'discursive regimes' of knowledge/power, or power in discourse. Posing the concept of discourse in this way allows one to ask, how does discourse serve, explain, assist in an understanding of – in this case – empowerment.

The linkage Foucault makes between discourse and power means that discourses have effects and implications for social processes as well as social practices. This means that his ideas can be used to situate empowerment as relational to the constitution of the subject within a specifically local context.

ACTIVITY **1.4**

It is useful to think about identity and subjectivity as part of how a person makes his or her way in the world. So, for example, some people have an identity shaped by their ethnicity, say, an Irish woman. This identity is shared with other women who are also Irish. However, each woman will bring her own subjectivity, her own sense of self, personality, experiences and so on, to bear on this identity. Thus, in this way, though there are discourses about women and about Irishness, each Irish woman will negotiate her way through these stories – thus negotiating with the discourses.

What is your identity? How is it similar, or different, from other people in your life? Can you see how your own self, personality, and personal experiences have influenced this identity?

Empowerment discourse

The concept of empowerment is used in these distinctive ways and is shaped by these ideological and theoretical disputes. The problem with using a 'simple', 'clear', 'useful' definition of empowerment is that the ideological underpinnings can be ignored and dismissed. There is not one approach or definition which can be used to cover up or mask these differences. Rather it is only through the process of critical reflective working that reveals at which level the activities, interactions or outcomes are operating.

ACTIVITY **1.5**

What do you think that 'empowerment' is?

Do any of the following statements fit with your definition?

- *Empowerment is about encouraging deprived people to seize power in society.*

- *Empowerment is about individuals developing the skills to fit into society.*

- *Empowerment is important because every individual has a right to influence what happens in the world.*

Is your personal definition influenced by a particular political perspective? What are the ideological underpinnings? Would everybody agree with your definition?

Another difficulty is that, at times, it may be important (or the only available option) to operate at the level of a liberal approach to empowerment, for example, the basic level of allowing individuals a choice. Who determines the choice may not be an issue.

To achieve another outcome it may be essential to regard the power to set the agenda as a critical element in the process of empowerment. This would allow a wider range of individuals to become more involved in the workings of power, for example, they set the agenda rather than simply making a choice between set agendas.

It may be impossible or impractical for workers to operate at the level of structure.

Thus, there can be practical and pragmatic reasons why the type of empowerment on offer is curtailed or contained. There is another reason, however, why the process of empowerment can be stifled or restricted and this can be related to how the workers view their role.

The discourse of professionalism

The development of empowerment can create problems for workers depending on how attached they are to the notion of their role as professionals and how much power and control (expertise and knowledge) they invest in their role. The dilemma and tension may be that they acquire authority through their status as a professional yet they may have to lose this in the process of empowerment.

CASE STUDY

What is best?

Mark is employed by a community project with a good reputation. He is funded to support young people on work placements with a view to helping them find employment. His success will be measured by how many people manage to get jobs which last for at least three months.

Mark has a dilemma. His 'professional' head tells him to find out what sort of job opportunities are available locally and to offer training so that his work placements have the best chance of getting these jobs. He has a great deal of knowledge and experience, which will help him to do this successfully.

His 'youth worker' head is directing him towards finding out what the young people want, and how they want to use the placement opportunity. This means supporting them to develop their self-confidence and to work out what to do with their lives. To do this effectively, Mark has to let go of any feelings of 'knowing what is best' and of being an 'expert'.

At its worst it may mean that some workers may seek to modify the process so that they can maintain control, in effect, curtailing empowerment to the limits in which the worker feels comfortable. It may be that this is an unconscious rather than a conscious act on their part. It may be that the worker is faced with the dilemma that in order to be seen to be 'working' he or she needs to demonstrate expertise and authority. It could also be that the worker is actively resisting the radical and revolutionary basis of empowerment as a way of protecting his or her status. The important point here is that different ideological positions will try to create their own version of the process of empowerment, and because these positions can only be analysed at the level of underlying theoretical positions, this is quite often perceived as an unnecessary over-complication of a simple process. The argument here, however, is that empowerment is not simple and a simple definition will not suffice, rather that analytical work needs to be ongoing in order for a model of empowerment to operate effectively in an organisation. The unclear ideological base, which can be part of the empowerment philosophy, is both a challenge and a danger for workers and for the process of empowerment.

One of the central contradictions in pursuing the goal of empowerment is the relationship between the individual and society. While all definitions are agreed on the ability of individuals to make decisions, control and guide their own lives, the extent to which this ability is constrained is less likely to be agreed by practitioners. An understanding of the structural constraints imposed on an individual again is dependent on the ideological stance of practitioners and how they see the relationship between structure and agency. One of the problems is that the ideological weight given to individualism and individual choice in consumer capitalism usually means that there is a blurring of the relationship between structure and agency among practitioners. Thus, the process of empowerment is viewed as working with people to increase their confidence, knowledge and skills. The structural constraints imposed by capitalist power relations, which can stop or hinder opportunities, are not addressed nor is the goal of empowerment, which has as its radical core the liberation for a collective rather than for an individual or a group. How are these dilemmas and contradictions to be resolved?

For Askheim (2003), the process of consciousness-raising as outlined in Freire (1993) can be used for groups

> to overcome a purely individualistic analysis of their problems and to realise how social and structural factors affect or create their difficult life situation. In other words, the goals of such a process are to establish a comprehension among the users of the relationship between their personal situation and social structures.
>
> (Askheim, 2003, page 233)

The necessary prerequisites for the process of empowerment is that the professional has to shift from the notion of 'expert' to work with individuals and groups in ways that enable them to actively reflect and analyse their experiences. For Askheim:

> A relationship between the user and the professional characterised by collaboration, openness, respect and trust is therefore at the core for professional work within an empowerment tradition.
>
> (Askheim, 2003, page 233)

For this writer and some others (see discussion in Askheim, 2003) this ability to communicate, even with groups who may not have verbal skills, is a fundamental part of the process. For another writer, Natorp (1920, 1922, cited in Askheim, 2003), these skills are not in themselves sufficient. Workers also need to be able to critically reflect on the theoretical basis for their practice. This reflection, however, has to be conducted with the user groups taking the leading role in developing theory and practice. So, professionals must be prepared to be constantly adapting to challenges by users to existing theories, and they also need to understand the relationship between structural constraints and individual needs and desires. If these dimensions are ignored then empowerment is reduced to a new therapeutic tool in the hands of the professionals (Askheim, 2003, page 235).

Thus, the ways in which workers interpret their role and their understanding of politics and state power are critical to the process. The process of empowerment is also dependent on the opportunity for workers to exercise this approach in an organisational setting. If the agency does not have the analytical framework which is needed for the work, then they are working within these limitations. To put these elements into another framework provided by Foucault, this is the notion of competing discourses, all of which will impact on the process of empowerment. One of these discourses has been discussed, that of the professional; others include the discourses of power and participation.

These varieties of discourses shape the available positions for subjects to take up and produce choices, though these may not be simple or conscious. Discourses do not stand alone; they can only be abstracted for the purpose of study and analysis but in practice there is a wide network of discursive fields that overlap and intermingle.

The problem of definition

This chapter ends as it began with the problem of definition. The preceding discussion has emphasised the need for an awareness of the theoretical underpinnings. Zimmerman (2000) suggests in his study that it is useful to differentiate between three levels of analysis: empowerment values, empowering processes and empowered outcomes. Lee Staples (1990) links process and outcomes by using the metaphor of an empowerment spiral (see figure 1.2).

Individuals when participating in groups acquire skills and resources, which strengthen the group's confidence in widening their goals and increasing their contribution to their local community.

Though I have resisted definitions, it might be useful to note some.

Wallerstein and Bernstein (1994, page 380) state:

> *Empowerment is a social action process that promotes participation of people, organisations, and communities in gaining control over their lives in their community and larger society. With this perspective, empowerment is not*

Figure 1.2 Empowerment spiral
Source: www.servalt.com/teamspirit/spiral.html

> characterized as achieving power to dominate others, but rather power to act
> with others to effect change.

> (Wallerstein and Bernstein, 1994, page 380)

Parsloe, in her text entitled *Pathways to Empowerment*, writes:

> *No definitive definition of empowerment is offered here because the concept is
> still evolving and it means different things to different people… It may be seen
> as a way to reduce professional power or a ploy used cynically by professionals
> to protect their status and power. Its purpose may be to promote the personal
> growth of those empowered, to raise the quality and appropriateness of social
> services or to give the disadvantaged members of society some influence which
> may lead to their attaining greater political power.*

> (Parsloe, 1996, xvii on page 27)

Thompson (2007, page 21) states: *Empowerment can be defined as helping people gain greater control over their lives and circumstances. It is therefore closely
linked to the notion of power*.

Rather than continue to list more definitions it may be useful to consider the notion
of powerlessness. According to the text on *Surplus Powerlessness* by Michael
Lerner:

> *When we feel powerless for any extended length of time, we tend to become
> more willing to accept parts of the world we would otherwise reject. We act in
> ways that go counter to our best visions of who we are and who we can and
> want to be.*

> *Powerlessness corrupts.*

> *Powerlessness corrupts in a very direct way: It changes, transforms, and
> distorts us. It makes us different from how we would otherwise want to be.*

We look at our world and our own behaviour, and we tell ourselves that although we really aren't living the lives we want to live, there is nothing we can do about it. We are powerless.

(Lerner, 1988, page 2)

C H A P T E R   R E V I E W

- Empowerment as a strategy for including people in decision making is interconnected with empowerment as an internal process for individuals.

- Empowerment is a process, rather than a theory or a concept.

- Power is a useful starting point and is a contested concept.

- Max Weber offers three sources of legitimacy for authority and power.

- Foucault's analysis of power includes a liberating and emancipatory perspective.

- Steven Lukes proposes three dimensions on analysing power in modern societies.

- The power elite are the military, political and economic spheres of society. This illustrates a distinction between the 'haves' and the 'have nots'.

- Ideological underpinnings of definitions of empowerment should not be dismissed.

- Discourse of professionalism creates a dilemma for workers.

- Discourse analysis is a way of understanding the ways in which people live, think and speak.

- Empowerment can be seen in terms of values, processes and outcomes.

FURTHER READING

Lerner, M (1988) *Surplus Powerlessness: The Psychodynamics of Everyday Life and the Psychology of Individual and Social Transformation.* New York: Humanity Books.

Thompson, N (2007) *Power and Empowerment.* Lyme Regis: Russell House Publishing.

Chapter 2

Empowerment in practice – case study of an agency

CHAPTER OBJECTIVES

This chapter will help you meet the following National Occupational Standards:

4.8.1   Understanding organisations.

4.8.2   Management and leadership in community-based projects.

4.8.3   Multi-disciplinary and multi-agency working.

It will also introduce you to the following academic standards as set out in the youth and community work benchmark statement (2009 QAA):

5.1.1   Understanding, developing and managing their professional role. An understanding of and the capacity to apply and integrate theoretical frameworks and key concepts relevant to practice in youth and community work.

The Warren – origins

With the massive growth in youth unemployment in the late 1970s and early 1980s, Humberside Youth Association (HYA) met with Hull City and Humberside County Councils to see what could be done to provide support and activities to those young people who were out of work, living in poverty, homeless and facing many other issues. HYA undertook to do research, and two workers interviewed 100 young people on the streets of Hull asking what kind of provision they would like in the city centre. Other research took place within HYA, which ran a training scheme as well as youth activities, and had been involved in setting up 'Club East', based in a church hall on Holderness Road, the city's first project for the young unemployed. From all the research, the councils suggested that HYA be the lead body in setting up a Young People's Community and Resource Centre, and it was duly opened in 1982. I had organised Club East as part of a HYA Youth Training Scheme and I became The Warren co-ordinator in 1987.

On moving into premises once owned by the city council but then 'privatised' to Yorkshire Water, at 100 Alfred Gelder Street, the name 'The Warren' was created because of the myriad of corridors and rooms. Strangely enough when the project had to move premises, after a £220,000 partnership bid with the city council to central government to make good and equip our current premises at Queen's Dock Avenue, the most noticeable thing on the first inspection visit by young people, apart from pigeons occupying the top two floors, was that the layout of the building certainly warranted the retention of the name, The Warren. In 1988, The Warren became independent of HYA and became a registered charity and company limited by guarantee in its own right.

What is 'empowerment'?

At this time in The Warren, the forum for discussions of activities and projects centred on the Daybook, a daily meeting, for volunteers and paid workers only, and had been imposed on The Warren by the Manpower Services Commission as a condition of some funding. The actual daybook was a large diary where in return for funding the staff team told, on a daily basis, how many young people had used the project, what issues had arisen, what activities had taken place and what the weather was like. Frequently, on rainy days, the daybook recorded that it had 'thatchered down'; there were descriptions of clouds on a par with Wordsworth and Mayokovsky. However, while there was a discussion, it was clear that the three paid workers made the running, and it was at these meetings that the terms of the struggle for empowerment were set.

An early example of the lack of young people's participation and some of the many contradictions that reared up can be gleaned from the following incident. The agency received a cheque for £1,000 as a donation; I asked volunteers at a Daybook meeting, 'How do you want to spend this money'? Knowing that some young people wanted to engage with music activities, I wanted to hear their ideas. Nobody said a word. I asked the meeting about whether there was a consensus to start a music project. One of the volunteers said, 'They won't let us'. I asked who 'they' were and got an answer of 'You know, them', so I stated that as a coordinator, I did not know who 'them' were and ventured the opinion that from now on 'they are us', or to be more specific you are 'them'. As a piece of oratory, or even logic, it wasn't the best, but after working out what the hell had I meant, we agreed that I was apparently saying young people would now be making the decisions about the future of The Warren. The meeting erupted and then evenly split on this revolutionary intention. I was accused of betraying The Warren, undermining tradition that had been established in the last five years since it had opened. All of this was part of my wider subversive left-wing agenda for taking over The Warren. A volunteer on 'my side' pointed out that as I had been appointed co-ordinator maybe I had already taken over The Warren, and if there was anything subversive, it was that he wanted to give his power away to young people. At one point, an 'anti'-volunteer shouted at me, 'And how will we make all these decisions?' I reflected for a moment and then said, 'By debate … and then issues can be put to a vote. It's called democracy'. More uproar. I added a further spontaneous thought, 'And whilst I think paid workers can and should speak in debates, only young people should be able to vote.' One staff member hit the roof at this idea, while the other roared with laughter and gave me a sympathetic look of 'keep going'. The meeting went on well into the evening. At one point, I got so emotional that I picked up the cheque from a local parochial church council and started to tear it just a little bit. As I carried out this gesture, I quickly lectured them on the traditions of radical democracy in Britain – bits about Wat Tyler, the Levellers and Diggers, the Chartists, the suffragettes, the trade unionists, the socialists, the women's movement, the struggles of blacks and Asians, the struggles of gays and lesbians – they got the lot and just before I was going to widen the history of struggle to the whole world, I suddenly remembered to stop tearing the cheque and said, 'Either you take responsibility for making decisions or I send the cheque back and I will look to leave The Warren as soon as I can'. Emotional blackmail to win the argument for empowerment! Fortunately, one of the volunteers spoke up and berated me about the cheque ripping melodramatics, and after asking who the hell was Wat Tyler and what had he got to do with empowerment, went on to say that he had changed his mind and he would support young people such as himself debating and voting on issues as long as I said unequivocally that I was being 'genuine' and not just being some kind of 'manipulative slimy politician'. This speech effectively turned the meeting as I made the pledge to be genuine and not to be slimy.

The next day after dealing with reports and being on the phone a lot, I left my office to go to the cafe. The first person I met on the stairs was a regular user. He said, 'Are you he? Are we them? Who are they?' and walked past me laughing. In the cafe at the counter a volunteer, who had not been at the meeting the night before, picked up a leaflet and began to tear it down the middle, 'to tear or not to tear'? I quickly found out that the whole project, or at least the hardcore regulars along with all the volunteers, was discussing what had happened the previous night.

By the end of the week, a group of volunteers went off to purchase some music equipment. I would love to say that I had developed a strategy, written a well-thought out paper, deliberated and reflected in tranquillity. No that wasn't the way at all. My 'introduction' of empowering processes was bungled, ideas thought of in the middle of red-hot debates, influenced by the flow of arguments or what one young person says that doesn't appear to get picked up but has a kernel of real insight. It is, of course, possible to prepare papers in advance, at least get some bullet points on a flipchart, but somehow I still feel that the best ideas and outcomes come from live discussions where the individual and collective intellects and emotions are engaged in resolving some problem or creatively seeking the best way of doing some activity.

As we discussed which room now would become the base for the new music project, I was again guilty of thinking aloud at a Daybook meeting by suggesting we make other room changes. Top of my list was to change the location of the 'Women's Room – a barely used cold, dark, damp cell in the bowels of the building where it was best to approach the gas fire as if you were a member of a bomb disposal unit. Symbolically, the only resource in the room was a splendid old Singer sewing machine. When women did use the room, I had discovered, they were frequently mocked by their boyfriends and others who thought it was funny to interrupt any session with their wit and scorn. The young women who supported the idea of a move suggested it be next to my office and this might offer more security and reduce the interruptions. Our only woman worker opposed the moves, as did she when I raised the question with her and others of why were our volunteers overwhelmingly male – there was only one female volunteer! These and other debates raged and very quickly the volunteers took on 'democracy' and saw that their votes mattered as changes were made, and there was a general feeling that the project was improving.

But all of this beggared the question of those young people, the vast majority of users who were not volunteers – how did they get a say? Interestingly, the only other people who seemed to be thinking about this apparent contradiction were a small group of skinheads who had been, and were still suspected of being, National Front sympathisers, who were, nevertheless, hard core 'Warrenites' and were very good at informing young people new to the project about what was expected of everyone in terms of their behaviour. On more than one occasion, they had helped me, and others, to deal appropriately with young men who were behaving aggressively or were in some way 'out of order'. The technical term for this is, as you know, 'peer group pressure'. This group engaged me in several discussions in the cafe about how almost every day they were being told about the Daybook discussions from the previous evening, held when The Warren had closed to users. And yet they themselves as regular users could play no part in deciding what went on. I agreed with them but said at the present time, it might be difficult to go beyond the current Daybook.

This inadequate answer was blown away by events or actually one event – I got a phone call from HYA headquarters that the owners of the building wanted to double the rent (and the city council were unable to make any more contribution) or Yorkshire Water would sell us the building for £250,000. Further bad news, in the same call, disclosed that a senior youth officer at the County Council had said it was going to be very difficult for funding to The Warren to continue. Both threats had very severe time limits. At the time, the only Warren reserves consisted of £200 (rainy day money) from the £1,000 donation and a loan of £4,000 from HYA. The last words of the HYA officer had been, 'I'm sorry Keith but we think The Warren will have to close unless you can come up with some answers'. Within minutes, I demonstrated a less than admirable ability of going straight from utter bewilderment to utter panic. I flapped around the building, slightly reminiscent of the Scottish character in Dad's Army in that I might have well have been shouting 'we're doomed, we're all doomed'. Some volunteers and users thought I had just run out of cigarettes but others listened and acted as I urged everyone to assemble in the cafe. Some 20 minutes later, apart from counsellors who kept a skeleton crew on duty, about 100 young people were crowded in the cafe.

I have noticed over the years that whenever I have to get up and make some dramatic statement about The Warren, there always appears at my side a flipchart stand and paper. In the heat of my excitement or panic, I have never thought to get one set up, but they always appear. I'm half convinced that this is a mystical process for the alternative is that someone on the staff team, or maybe a volunteer, can tell before I do that the situation demands a flip chart and there are always new marker pens.

Anyway, stood next to the aforesaid stand I wrote a summary of what I had been told on the phone. We broke into open discussion. This gave me time to think. I thought there were four options:

1. We could just close;

2. We could close the building but try to carry on the project out on the streets and wait for better days;

3. We could organise and lobby for The Warren to have a new building, and continued (possibly increased) funding;

4. As our building was across the street from the city council's Guildhall, and even though they were completely innocent, we could get publicity for our cause by allocating the £200 on food and provisions and occupy the building until Yorkshire Water and the County Council saw sense.

Needless to say, after much debate, the vote for Option 4 was almost unanimous. I then realised that I had been guilty, perhaps, of what used to be called in my activist days 'ultra leftism'. I urged the meeting to hold Option 4 in abeyance and that really we should go for Option 3, but it was no use voting for it if people weren't going to get really involved.

Over the next few weeks, we trained young people and ourselves in media techniques, such as how to do interviews, how to lobby effectively but politely, how to do press statements and so on. We leafleted everywhere we could and delegations of young people went and spoke to councillors, officers and a range of other organisations. We got good media coverage and even a supportive editorial in the local newspaper.

We took a group of about 40 young people to successfully lobby the county council where I knew the councillors were going to support us by the ever-deepening scowls on the face of the senior youth officer. And the city council really came to our rescue, finding money for extra posts as well as agreeing to be a partner in looking for funds to get new premises.

We quickly came to the conclusion that a joint bid to the government's Inner Area Programme would be the best bet. The council appointed one of their architects to work with us. I asked him to attend meetings of young people where they would decide what the new building would look like internally, what projects there would be and where they would be based. And using the lessons I had learnt during a weekend conference at Ken Livingstone's Greater London Council (GLC), I also asked him not to speak unless there was a question directly to him or he had some technical knowledge that would prevent the young people from making poor deci-sions – such as he pointed out at the subsequent initial meeting that it was best to have a photographic darkroom near an existing water supply. Thankfully, the officer was more happy to do this and really enjoyed the experience, as did we all, as we discovered through sheer hard work that empowering processes actually worked. As an interesting aside when it came to voting for allocation of rooms, a large turnout was almost unanimous in voting for the women's room to be next to the co-ordinator's office.

So began a practice that continues to this day that young people at The Warren vote what projects we do; that, for example, all potential bids for new projects have to be approved and voted on.

Of course, the crisis resolved for us the whole question of whether users should be involved in the decision-making process. Their contribution to not only the survival but also the development of the project was absolutely outstanding. If particular meetings did not go well, we learnt that it was because we, as facilitators, had failed on the whole to make the processes clear to everyone. Our slogan became, 'Trust the young people, trust the process'; do both of these and the tasks will be achieved or at least we won't fail because of lack of effort or thought, and in trust-ing in the process, we could gain a wider and deeper range of outcomes than we had originally intended. All kinds of positive developments, big and small, collec-tive and individual, could arise. We thought we could meet daily, but young moth-ers pointed out that it was difficult for them to make a lot of meetings because of their child care responsibilities (this didn't seem to affect young dads so much!), and by the way, in the new building, they said, we want a crèche. Carried.

So we moved to a weekly meeting. The name 'Daybook' was redundant, so we sought another. I worked with a small group of young people on this whose job was to make recommendations to the wider body. Members of the group at one particular meeting were discussing a recent trip to the Viking Museum in York. Casually being a keen reader of history, I mentioned that the Vikings used to call their assemblies 'The Thing'. No one listened as I boringly went on to say that 'The Thing' was also the term used by William Cobbett to describe government corrup-tion in the early nineteenth century. I noticed that I had lost the audience for they were having their own discussion about 'The Thing', Viking name for meeting. That was it! Despite my opposition, where I was firmly told that my opinion was interesting, but it didn't really matter because I had no vote, they took it to the wider meeting who voted for 'The Thing' as the name of our weekly 'parliament'.

Over the next period, a series of decisions were taken whereby young people increasingly debated and voted on what the agency should be doing. In 1989, another element of an empowering process was added: it was agreed by young people and the management committee that interview panels for posts should consist of the co-ordinator (or representative) and three or four young people and an equal-opportunities observer. By 1991, at the instigation of the then chair of the Management Committee, Don Major (had been manager of the HYA YTS before retirement and was in the 1950s and 1960s a prominent local trade unionist), I was urged to create and submit a Warren Empowerment Policy. This I did with active involvement of young people. The document was then debated and agreed by young people, the staff team and the committee.

The most useful part of the document and the bit that has got most comments from external people and agencies is our attempt at defining empowerment.

1) *At The Warren empowerment is about facilitating each young person to have control over their own lives by developing the skills, knowledge and information so that they can make their own informed choices.*

2) *We aim in all of our activities and services to create processes to maximise the involvement of young people and that they should make the decisions about how the agency works and develops.*

3) *We recognise the inequalities of power and resources in our society and will actively support all young people who wish to join together to address such matters.*

4) *We understand that our attempt to develop empowerment is an ongoing, often contradictory and, at times, conflictual process; but, whatever the struggles, our core values of supporting young people to have control over their own lives informs all debates and actions.*

(From The Warren Empowerment Policy)

'Empowerment' as a term wasn't as such particularly important to us. I had first come across it on a training day organised by the Manpower Services Commission (MSC) when I worked on HYA's YTS and after accusing the facilitators, almost from the word go, of using the term to skilfully manipulate people to do what you wanted them to do (e.g. empower your staff to work harder, empower your staff to be happily made redundant and empowerment means workers can see unemployment as a fresh opportunity and other business school-induced gobbledygook) and thus being asked to leave the course and missing what appeared to be a lunchtime buffet. No, what was interesting, and still is, I think, about the term, is that right in the middle of the word is 'power' which, of course, is of crucial significance in all human relationships, politics and certainly in youth work. 'Empowerment' for me never allows 'power' to go unnoticed. It is at times a trendy word and concept, but in the right hands, it can be a real tool for unlocking a whole host of issues that really need to be constantly addressed. I concede that it is a term forever to be contested, but it helped us at The Warren to find a conceptual way of linking work with individuals to working with individuals in groups, the latter maybe being one of the most striking characteristics of good youth and community work.

At the same time, I came across the following quote which was, and remains, a very important statement with so many implications.

When we feel powerless for any extended length of time, we tend to become more willing to accept parts of the world we would otherwise reject. We act in ways that go counter to our best visions of who we are and who we can and want to be. Powerlessness corrupts.

Powerlessness corrupts in a very direct way: It changes, transforms, and distorts us. It makes us different from how we would otherwise want to be. We look at our world and our own behaviour, and we want tell ourselves that although we really aren't living the lives we want to live, there is nothing we can do about it. We are powerless.

(Lerner, 1991, page 2)

For staff and volunteer training purposes and for visitors to the project, we developed the following statement that tries to sum why we chose the path we did.

Why empowerment?

When we introduced a formal policy of empowerment, as well as being keen to avoid tokenistic versions of participation, we sought an approach that could work consistently and coherently at different levels of the agency's operation. We needed an approach that:

- *allowed us to work on a one-to-one basis with all young people (such a method had to be as consistent as possible with our person-centred [Rogerian] approach in our counselling work);*
- *encouraged and facilitated group and collective ways of working with young people (where we could put an equal emphasis on process, task and outcome);*
- *covered the whole organisational structure and processes of the agency and allowed for practices such as the relative autonomy of projects/workers within the overall accountability of the agency (such structures and processes to be constantly checked against our values base);*
- *provided a value base for working with external agencies, including making bids, developing and entering into formal partnerships, organising collaborative work and campaigns as well as taking an active part in externally based local and national strategies. (We needed this values 'benchmark', so that young people can have some standards by which to understand and judge whether we should get involved or not.)*

And those core values – including respect; the right for the voices of young people to be heard; developing anti-oppressive awareness and practice; developing democratic decision-making processes including voting and working for consensus; that young people's involvement should be voluntary, that is, based on their choice – is not exactly revolutionary. But then again, in the aggressive political and economic climate we now live in, maybe even seeking respect and tolerance with and for those marked so negatively by our national politicians and most of the media, such values are becoming increasingly radicalised and revolutionary.

The growth of religious fundamentalism (and their associate youth organisations, often sadly to be found in the voluntary sector), whether of the Christian or Islamic variety, has also, by their lies and distortions, made a society based on respect, tolerance and understanding less and less achievable. As nearly all funding bids nowadays include an obligatory statement about respecting equal opportunities, it is hard to see why these groups have been so successful given their position on women, gays and lesbians. But to be empowering is to be open to being challenged, and to welcome the debates with young people requires such values, and these are the values we should unashamedly offer as virtues for living.

There are three other Warren practices, which I think influence the way we work with young people and thus impact upon our empowering processes.

1. The Warren has always been an 'Open Door' agency (no membership). It was, and is, important that there be no impediment to young people just coming in when they want to. A positive off-shoot of this policy is that The Warren never gets 'possessive' or territorial about the young people who use its facilities and services. We are always keen to let young people know what else is going on in the city and we never feel that we are 'losing someone' if a young person then decides to go somewhere else.

2. Offering all our activities for free is a key recognition of the socio-economic position that the majority of young people who use The Warren find themselves in, and we would definitely say that this is through no fault of their own. This reinforces our philosophy of not having a 'deficit model' attitude towards young people.

3. Working alongside young people in empowering ways means demystifying knowledge and power; it means to be open to showing young people how we work. At The Warren, there are very few hours in the week when we do not have young people present. We do not use the traditional sessions of traditional youth work. Rather we chose deliberately, even when we only had three workers, that young people can come into our offices, that they can help if they want to and they don't need to be formal volunteers to do this, and when those occasions rise when a worker needs to be able to concentrate on a bid or a workshop programme, then they negotiate their space with young people just as we would with colleagues. This, at times, can put extra strains on workers, but overall and even on a daily basis, this willingness to share the whole project helps young people to feel a genuine sense of ownership. If a team is having a planning meeting, they encourage young people to come as well if they wish to but negotiate what the meeting needs to do, agree common ground rules for all. Allied to this is the right of young people to be left alone within the project; if they wish to sit all day in the cafe that is up to them. There will undoubtedly be attempts by workers and volunteers to encourage them to get involved in an activity or course but no more than that. Sitting in the cafe just chatting, being quiet and alone, but being safe within the company of others, may be exactly what that young person needs to be doing for themselves.

As leading writers on youth work have said, for many years, the basis of our approach is conversation. It is through this that we build the mutual respect and trust that allows further developments to occur. Added to this, at The Warren, it is our effort to establish genuine empowering ways of working with young people, so that they start to get involved in making decisions about what The Warren does. As their confidence and skills increase, it is hoped that they begin to apply the same level of skills and belief in taking, in so far as circumstances allow, ever increasing control of their own lives.

In the process of doing this for themselves, we hope to engage young people in sufficient interesting experiences for them to consider their responsibilities to others, whether they be of a close personal relationship or more widely as fellow citizens in a shared society and world.

So we have been trying to build genuine models of empowerment for a very long time. I have indicated above some of the pressures on staff when working within a process. You have to allow for my own bias here as the manager of The Warren, but I think the most important thing I've learnt about empowering processes with young people is that the organisation has to empower its own staff. We use the term 'relative autonomy'. If we seek young parents using the child care project to get really involved in what goes on, then our child care workers have to have the freedom to be able to make decisions with the young people about what they are going to do. But, of course, part of the knowledge and skills that workers have to develop is understanding the 'relative' bit of autonomy in that they are not only accountable to other staff members but through The Thing equally accountable to all the young people who use the project. And they have a responsibility to explain this to the particular individuals and groups they work with as we all, staff, volunteers and users, need to get a full grasp of how our individual wishes and desires cannot dominate over the needs of the rest. Doing this with young people enhances both their understanding of their own rights and their responsibilities towards others. So, in a project, like so many others having limited resources, and where decisions are crucial about making best use of the resources, young people, like the staff team, have to think about and decide what the key priorities are. This leads, we believe, in our own micro-society to people getting used to be realistic, thinking about the needs of others and also developing 'political' skills in terms of making a case and learning to negotiate before making a decision maybe based more on a wider and deeper perspective than would otherwise be the case.

We make the same kind of points when discussing at The Thing or elsewhere the levels of public monies we get from such bodies as Hull City Council or the local National Health Service. We educate ourselves to understand that there are many demands on these limited resources, and, of course, we think, as do the young people, that we should get more funding to do more things, but we are obliged to spend such funding as carefully as possible. We should be sure that we always offer value for money and that all the support we get really does go towards making a real difference in the lives of young people of Hull. Over the years, I have become less suspicious of setting targets and outcomes because they can be useful tools within the empowering process for making best use of resources. Maybe we have been lucky because when negotiating with our key funders, I feel that they have been genuine negotiations between partners. The trick, I think, is to make sure that all the administrative record-ing and evaluations do not dominate the working lives of the workers and thus have a demoralising influence on their work with young people. For a period in our exist-ence, we had 14 different funders all of whom had different administrative systems to monitor our work by and record the progress of young people.

Workers and Empowerment

I have worked at The Warren for 19 years, which is a long time, but the memories of working in the private sector prior to this are still very vivid. The reason for this is that the way of working in The Warren, within a philosophy of empowerment, is completely unheard of in the private sector, or it was when I worked there. To work at The Warren is a privilege, although at times it is very challenging. Working within such a philosophy is very exciting, rewarding and demanding all at the same time. The organisation allows and encourages workers to get involved at so many levels of its work, but alongside of this we are accountable to the young people who use the project as well as to each other. There are often contradictions in that, because of such a philosophy and approach, some workers find this fairly unstructured and find it difficult to take on board that many decisions, about the organisation, their individual work, etc. are not made hierarchically, but rather openly and collectively. I have found that these views can change over time and empowering ways of working are embraced and cherished, or simply the workers leave, because empowerment, and its demands, is not for them.

For me I have to say that I have embraced and cherished this way of working, it would now be extremely difficult for me to work for an organisation that did not work under such a philosophy, that encourages relative autonomy, creativity, choice and the individual.

Janet Kent; Finance Officer

I grew up with limited resources and little to no money, I have a background where it's normal to be told what to do and how to do it and was given very little space to explore my life.

It was only when I came to The Warren and spent the rest of my younger years volunteering I really started to gain some identity and become an individual, an individual with choices. As I mentioned this was not normal for me.

It's actually quite amazing to be honest, to look back on myself 12 years on, the changes in me, and my life have moved considerably. I can now say I am a very confident person, unlike my younger days I have grown in so many ways that telling what I had to go through can still mesmerize me and I just give myself a gentle pinch to check that it's really true. I have worked at The Warren for 8 years on and off, and to be truly honest I could not see myself working in another organisation unless they truly believe in empowerment not only for themselves but the whole of the project – young people, staff and all.

I now can say I have a set of values and beliefs, and have skills and knowledge and the space to be creative, spontaneous and adventurous. I never thought that one place could change a person so much and that's why I believe in empowerment because I've lived through it.

To work as an empowered worker gives you so much freedom to do the work that matters, having the space and time to develop relationships and build on the important things; and told that you are believed in by colleagues and others gives you enthusiasm and energy that no one other place can provide.

What's also important is having the relative autonomy within a team. This supports being creative and where we can with young people make decisions and find answers to problems quickly.

Lee Andrews – Learning Activist; Can Do Project.

My experience of working at The Warren is that it inspires you to constantly challenge – to reflect adapt and develop on the personal histories of self and others – offering an alternative way of seeing and believing and yes ultimately living. This is crucial if you are to support those who are struggling to cope with the pressures placed upon them by others and society.

Lisa Wedgner – Can Do Coordinator

I grew up in the 80s on a council estate in east Hull. When I left school I became a bricklayer and carried on with this, when I finished my apprenticeship, for about seventeen years and then I left to become the main career for my parents who both were old and becoming increasingly dependent. Then a friend, who at that point worked at The Warren, suggested I volunteer there because she thought I might enjoy it and knew I was looking for a change of career. At this point in time I don't think I had ever heard of the word empowerment and thought it was just another buzzword being bandied about and never really meant anything. I volunteered there for a year or so doing training, working with young people and the staff, being taught new things whilst not really realising that I was learning. Then I started getting bits of tutoring work and then gaining full-time employment. Obviously this is a very condensed version of the last thirteen or so years, but being empowered by the workers, young people and the whole Warren way of working has changed my life and enabled me to achieve so much, through being listened to, treated with respect, given a *voice and still learning what empowerment is; that it is a true process, not a tokenistic buzzword. And all this gives the confidence to offer the same things to young people.*

Paul Leonard – Project Worker

Farage Busara. Me and The Warren

My story

My name is Farage Busara aka Hekima. I am a father and a musician. I came to Hull around April 2004. Like any other ethnic minority I struggled to fit in this alien environment. I had a few African friends who were my only sense of belonging at the time. The only point of reference I had to the city was the story of William Wilberforce who I read about back when I was at school in Africa. I kept myself to myself and spent most of my time writing lyrics or reading books I borrowed from the city library. The library was one of the few places I felt at ease.

When I started college I made friends with a few locals who became my guide. I told them that I wrote lyrics and I was looking for a studio where I can record a demo. After a long search I was introduced to The Warren by one of college friends.

At The Warren I was given a warm welcome by the staff and the young people. Even though my intention was to record a demo I could not help noticing how peaceful it felt in there. In my two years in Hull I had never walked into a building full of locals and felt like that! I felt like The Warren was more than just a recording studio but at the time I could not put into words what else it was. All I could remember after leaving the building was that, for the first time since I have been in this city I felt like I was genuinely welcomed by the locals. I had to revisit The Warren.

I started going to The Warren on regular basis. During this time I got to record my demos and also made new friends; even the people who didn't take much notice of me still showed respect and made me feel welcome. That meant everything to me. At the time I was reading a biography of Mahatma Gandhi which I had borrowed from the library. It spoke about how he helped organise the ethnic minorities in Africa and helped them to gain a sense of belonging in an alien environment. Even though the situation in Hull is no comparison to what was going on in South Africa, I could not help it referring it back to The Warren because for some strange reason I felt like I had a sense of belonging there.

Spending most of time in The Warren recording studio, I started to learn that there is a lot more to music than just writing lyrics and recording demos. I learnt a lot from the staff and the young musicians who became my close friends. I learnt a lot about studio operations. I even started to learn how to play the guitar. After a short while I decided to become a volunteer so I can help other young people especially around the music area. I felt like I owed this to The Warren.

I learnt so much from The Warren in such a short period of time I felt like I needed to go back to college in order to clarify and arrange all this information in an orderly manner. I went back to college and enrolled on a music course. This time my experience at college was different or rather better than before. I felt much more relaxed and confident. I felt like no matter what happened I had The Warren as a Refuge to go back to.

Everything I learnt at Hull College I practised at The Warren and everything I learnt from The Warren I passed it on to my fellow Africans. I decided to join The Warren tutor bank and started teaching the young people about studio operations which I am still doing to this day.

Even though I always saw myself as a Rapper and was a member of a hip hop crew, The Project Feenix, I always dreamed of starting a live band. I simply wanted to connect with my roots more. I could never imagine this dream coming true until I started getting involved with The Warren. Me and Stewart (who is staff at The Warren and also a brilliant musician) managed to put together a multicultural band called 'Hekima and the Bongoflava'. The Warren gave us a chance to perform at the Refugee Week. It was my very first time to perform with a band and being the front man I was very nervous but we got a very good response from the crowd. Then we got a chance to perform at the Love Music Hate Racism alongside some of the big names from London. We have just finished recording our first album titled 'The Sunrise' which is due for release 10 September on Freedom Festival this year. I still cannot believe it is happening! To this day the reality of it is yet to sink in.

The aim of the band is to bridge the gap between the First and the Third World by raising awareness in our unique music style which is combination of Africa roots, Hip hop and reggae, etc. We call it 'The cocktail'. The idea is to pass on everything I have learnt in the first world to my people in the third world and vice-versa. Our music is meant to reflect the people through our individual experiences.

The future is looking bright for the Bongoflava and I owe it all to The Warren.

Current projects

We have been lucky and worked extremely hard over many years to develop the current projects at The Warren. The oldest project is the Counselling, Information and Advocacy that offers one-to-one counselling either in a 'crisis' situation or on an ongoing basis. The model is based on Carl Rogers' person-centred approach. We also offer sexual health as part of this project.

Our Health Beat project was initially funded by the Lottery's Healthy Living Centre funding but is now supported by NHS Hull. This team aims creatively and without any lecturing to work on health issues with young people. There have been a number of interesting challenges around health and empowerment as traditionally health is perceived and was carried out in a top-down 'we know what's best' way. Finding alternatives to such an approach has been really exciting at times. The most recent project is a cookbook by young people delicately entitled 'For Cook's Sake'. A key part of Health Beat is the cafe that offers increasingly healthy meals at an affordable price.

The Child Care project includes a crèche and various initiatives at increasing creative play between parents and children. Young parents have been particularly attacked by the gutter press over the years and a lot of work goes into challenging the stereotypes and helping to build self-esteem. Child protection has been an important element of this project's work and requires a very clear analysis of how empowering processes can work. It also depends on building excellent relationships with young parents as well as being able to deal well with other agencies who may have very different viewpoints on key issues around a child's welfare. The child always comes first.

Can Do is our informal learning project. It has demonstrated time and time again that 'socially excluded' young people who did not do well at school can really benefit from a 'second chance'. Young people constantly show determination to learn this time around and it was the young people's decision at The Thing for us to sign up to a partnership with the National Open College Network, so that we could offer accredited courses. As well as the wide range of courses, carried out in creative ways, such as '24 hour learning challenges', we run a wide range of activities like currently renovating a Land Rover for the Victoria Climbie School in Ivory Coast, building a dj booth and running classes in music theory. We put a lot of emphasis on numeracy and literacy skills, the acquisition of which is probably one of the most self-empowering actions a person can take. At the time of writing, we are waiting for news from the National Lottery as to whether this stunning project will continue. It has proven to be a really good way of offering alternative activities to crime, anti-social behaviour and boredom. The project lends itself to young people getting involved and the quarterly programme is discussed, negotiated and finally voted on at The Thing.

The sports' project – run by a part-time worker – has proven, like Can Do, to offer exceptional alternative activities to crime and anti-social behaviour. In particular, the football team has helped many young men to stay out of prison, helped them combat drugs and alcohol abuse, and provided structured activities that help them on a weekly basis to see that they can make changes if they wish to their lives.

Music and Arts is also a very important part of the work we do with young people. We have a recording studio, a midi room and a rehearsal space. Our latest venture is setting up a film and animation project. Before that we launched, thanks to a fortunate gift from a Channel 4 Secret Millionaire, our own record label. Find out about Warren Records on the website under its own name. Six albums have been currently released, and we need to sell them to produce the next few.

One of the key activities over the last few years is the growth of partnerships, which has allowed us to do a range of large-scale activities. In addition to gigs for National Refugee Week, a Rock The Vote project, around the last general election where we put on gigs in local venues attracting 2,000 people and where we asked them to make sure they were registered to vote, the biggest action has been around the annual FREEDOM FESTIVAL where the city council, and its other partners, invited us to put on a live gig in gardens right in the heart of the city. With the grant, we got into partnership with the national Love Music Hate Racism organisation as well as with Hull Youth Council to put on fantastic anti-racist, celebrate Hull gigs drawing attendances of between 10,000 and 15,000 people. We also put up a FREEDOM Tent where we distributed educational materials on issues like racism, violence against women, positive stuff about health and so on.

On campaigns, there is usually at least one campaign going on at The Warren at any one time. Recently a long campaign to secure the refugee status and then full citizenship of an Afghani asylum seeker, Gholam Nazary, was successful. This campaign was led by young people who had formed the Coalition of Hull's Young People (CHYP) (supported by The Warren and Hull Youth Council) – initially formed to oppose dispersal orders in the city centre (successfully). Over 2000 signatures were collected and presented at No. 10 Downing St by Gholam and CHYP members.

The current campaign is called FRESH and is a young women's group fighting domestic violence. Recently on a Million Women Rise march, a group of young women were invited by the organisers to speak about their project to thousands of women in Trafalgar Square. This was brilliant but spare a thought for the current writer who knows by marching so many times around the square in his youth and into early middle age every pigeon who resided there between 1968 and about 1989 and never, not just once, was he invited to share his thoughts and wisdom. These young women on their second demo have photographs of them speaking. The group is currently working on a pamphlet on the issues (also showing photos of Trafalgar Square), and the two workers at the time of writing have spoken about the work with the group and the wider Warren work to a government and EU conference in Hungary on crime and community cohesion.

At times in our work, we have felt very isolated. While we had links with some of the very good youth workers in the city council we rarely ever worked in partnership despite our many efforts over the years to do so. We hope that partnership working can be more developed and certainly given the current government's attacks on young people and youth work we need alliances to be built as quickly as possible. Our main youth work partners have been Hull Youth Council and the Rights and Participation Project, in which we played a major role with the council and Save the Children in setting up. All three of us were heavily involved in establishing the Hull Young People's Parliament.

A view of The Warren by Nickie Johnson, Voice and Influence Manager, Children and Young People's Services, Hull City Council

The Warren is at the forefront of participation work with disadvantaged young people. Their developed culture of empowerment enables young people, from a variety of backgrounds and experiences, to participate in decisions that affect their lives and work together in the planning and direct delivery of projects and activities within the project. Opportunities for participation are many fold, promote choice and have a real impact on the skills and confidence of young people taking part.

This is clearly evident when listening to young people talk about The Warren and the impact the project and its staff has had on them. The Warren are fundamental partners in the development of participation work across the city, including the work of the Hull Youth Council and the Hull Young People's Parliament, advising on best practice, guiding and co-delivering developmental work to enable young people to raise and act on their issues.

Despite a long tradition of local and national excellence, The Warren never rests on its laurels but continues to reflect, challenge and develop its work to best meet the changing needs of young people within the context of difficult and often contradictory government agendas.

Example of partnership work – active citizenship: Hull Young People's Parliament

The Hull Young People's Parliament started in July 2006, as a partnership of The Warren, The Hull Youth Council, The Rights and Participation Project and Hull City Council. In our initial proposal we argued for the maximum involvement by a wide range of young people and that all agencies desist from being tokenistic. Including the latest 13th Parliament, there have been a total of 2,024 children and young people attend. 160 agencies, from across the statutory and voluntary/community sectors, have sent representatives (67 Schools, 2 Colleges, 19 BME groups and 72 youth organisations) addressing themes chosen by children and young people, including negative media images of young people, crime, racism, health, education, bullying and the environment.

Children and Young People debate in groups and then put forward resolutions for the plenary debates in the Council Chamber. These sessions are divided in two by age group to enable better participation. For the older young people there have been so many resolutions that we have now introduced compositing as a regular feature, whereby each group elects one representative to do this and the compositing session adds yet another useful set of skills to those already being learnt by the young people.

Successful resolutions (of which there have been 101 out of 160 debated) are passed direct to the Children's (and Young People's) Trust Board for action. However, we think it would be fertile ground if, in addition, the parliament had a direct link to the Council's Cabinet.

A very positive development has been Local Action Points, whereby Hull Youth Council staff give support as required to groups of children and young people who have raised specific local issues at the parliament. The representatives have raised action on 124 locally based issues. The potential for the parliament as a dynamic body for young people's active citizenship is immense. However, it does need to be properly resourced.

Liz Lesquereux: Institute of Community Cohesion Associates

'Big Society and Hull' – visit to The Warren, Hull, 30 September 2010

I visited The Warren as part of the team reviewing Hull's readiness for the 'Big Society' (through the Institute of Community Cohesion). I was enormously impressed by what I saw ... a unique facility for young people up to the age of 25 years, where young people can be supported through very difficult times in their lives, where they can gain qualifications, and gain the confidence and skills required for adult life.

The services provided are free to the young people and are supplied by staff and volunteers [who] are highly rated by the young people.

The Can Do project runs courses, activities and trips and encourages young people to get involved in programme planning and designing and running campaigns (such as anti-racism and domestic violence).

The Warren also runs a very successful music studio, and young people get involved with local music festivals, building skills and confidence as they go. The Warren really helps with computers, stamps, envelopes, CV writing, applying for jobs, budgeting, cookery, benefits and housing advice, how to pay bills, interview skills, how to change a light bulb, counselling and health services ... All the skills a vulnerable young person needs when moving into their own flat or starting a job.

The young people I met were articulate and considered in their questions to me about the Big Society. They are concerned about the benefits being cut and 'enforced' volunteering; that funds for The Warren may be cut, and that there is no alternative provision for them.

They are concerned about fairness and injustice in society, where footballers and bankers get paid huge amounts of money while they are expected to survive on £50 a week, in a part of the country where there are very few jobs.

I was enormously moved by some of the stories I heard from young people about the challenges they have faced – and are still facing. The Warren provides more than just advice – it provides a point of stability, friends, competent adults, and a lifeline for many young people.

Towards a conclusion

So we have been trying to work in an empowering way for over 20 years. We still have not got it right. Applying our values and practices across a wide range of projects and initiatives constantly gives us issues and problems to confront. A lot of these are difficult but can also be fun to work through, and as long as we 'trust the young people, trust the process', we seem to get solutions that most people can live with, and we can see the positive differences that this makes to young peoples' lives.

As with all youth and community work, the dynamics of organisations and the relationships between people are forever changing and shifting. A few new young people start coming to our weekly The Thing, and what seemed a very settled atmosphere last week has now become edgy but sometimes can be exciting. Every time a young person in The Warren gets what they and we would call a 'proper job' there is widespread cheering and clapping but then usually a silence descends as people think 'if only it had been me'. The young people of Hull, the so-called no hopers, the 'socially excluded', the benefit cheats, the scroungers, the asylum seekers, the unmarried mothers and on and on we could go outlining the reper-toire of the British media, show, as do similar young people across the country, Europe and the world, an amazing patience, a generosity of spirit, a willingness to work, to learn, to train that no prime minister in this country, certainly since the dark days of Thatcherism and probably before, has shown the slightest inclination to understand or properly support. Generation after generation of young people have not only been let down by governments but by us in the wider society, those of us adults who collude with the media and politicians in stigmatising young peo-ple and blaming young people for being unemployed, homeless, poor and so on. Blaming the victims is now the staple part of television sitcoms and other shows where ex-pubic schoolboys and Oxbridge graduates gloat in the misery of many young people. Our political leaders with their unquestioning faith in the mysteries and superstitions of nineteenth-century political economy continue to serve the very rich and the very powerful. The media, on the whole, feed the ideas that there is no alternative, that what is, is and it's almost some kind of natural order of things that social inequalities become ever wider; the rich deserve to be rich and the poor deserve to be poor. The media encourages apathy and cynicism, although politicians contribute as best they can to this at time, which pervades much of our society. And I would argue that apathy and cynicism are just as potent as sexism, racism and homophobia in adding to the cocktail of perspectives informing the parties of the right whilst never aiding the voices arguing for justice, freedom and democracy. It is a sad reflection on the political achievements of humanity that nowhere as yet have we managed to develop an economics, a political economy, that is democratic. And with the environmental challenges facing us, and whether the big battalions of corporate capital yet to decide that saving the planet is really in their interest, we may not get a good chance to do so.

In the most difficult circumstances, I continue to be optimistic because I have seen time and time again what ordinary people can achieve and in The Warren's case what ordinary young people can achieve. We have seen countless acts of courage such as the women who survive rape and abuse; the young man whose teachers and parents told him he was 'thick' and a 'waste of space' gets more accredited courses under his belt and now plans to go to college; the youngster with a disability who gets up on stage and performs at a live gig; and the stories never end. It's such a pity that our society does not recognise these young people in a positive way; does not see them as having so much untapped potential but rather they are; because of their poverty and class background to be seen as an ongoing threat; to be treated accordingly with laws and practices that are ever more authoritarian and bring into question whether we truly live in a civilised society. Who knows whether we can all find creative and democratic ways that will match the needs of all peoples?

I conclude with a longish quote from Edward Bernays, the founder of Public Relations, nephew of Sigmund Freud, who wrote, perhaps, the most honest expose, *from the inside*, of what our rulers do in order to hold and stay in power.

> *The conscious and intelligent manipulation of the organised habits and opinions of the masses is an important element in a democratic society. Those who manipulate this unseen mechanism of society constitute an invisible government, which is the true ruling power of our country.*

> *We are governed, our minds moulded, our tastes formed, our ideas suggested, largely by men we have never heard of. This is a logical result of the way in which our democratic society is organised. Vast numbers of human beings must cooperate in this manner if they are to live together as a smoothly functioning society.*

> *They govern us by their qualities of natural leadership, their ability to supply needed ideas and by their key positions in the social structure. Whatever*

attitude one chooses toward this condition, it remains a fact that in almost every act of our daily lives, whether in the sphere of politics or business, in our social conduct or our ethical things, we are dominated by the relatively small number of persons who understand the mental processes and social patterns of the masses. It is they who pull the wires that control the public mind, who harness old social forces and contrive new ways to bind and guide the world.

Bernays, 2005, page 37

RECOMMENDED READING

Ali, T (2002) *The Clash of Fundamentalisms*. London: Verso.

Berman, M (1993) *All That Is Solid Melts into Air*. London: Verso.

Bernays, E (2005) *Propaganda*. New York: IG Publishing.

Bryson, V (2003) *Feminist Political Theory*. London: Palgrave Macmillan.

Davies, B (2005) A manifesto for our times. *Youth and Policy* Issue 88 Summer.

Foot, P (2005) *The Vote*. London: Viking.

Herzog, D (1998) *Poisoning The Minds of the Lower Orders*. New Jersey: Princeton University.

Hind, D (2007) *The Threat to Reason*. London: Verso.

Keane, J (2009) *The Life and Death of Democracy*. London: Simon & Schuster.

Klein, N (2007) *The Shock Doctrine*. London: Penguin.

Kundnani, A (2007) *The End of Tolererance*. London: Pluto Press.

Rees, S (1991) *Achieving Power*. Sydney: Allen & Unwin.

Rowbotham, S (1974) *Hidden From History*. London: Pluto Press.

Spender, D (1983) *Women of Ideas (and What Men Have Done to Them)*. London: Arc.

Chapter 3
Youth participation and emancipation

CHAPTER OBJECTIVES

- To make the case for an authentic emancipatory model of youth participation.
- To set out the contemporary context for youth participation in England.
- To theorise on what an authentic emancipatory model of youth participation might look like.
- To consider how an authentic emancipatory model of youth participation might be applied in practice.

The chapter will help you meet the following National Occupational Standards:

1.1.5   Support young people in taking action and to tackle problems.

1.3.2   Encourage young people's involvement in the design of youth work activities.

1.4.2   Enable young people to access information and to make decisions.

2.1.1   Ensure that the rights of young people are promoted and upheld.

3.1.2   Assist young people to express and to realise their goals.

It will also introduce you to the following academic standards as set out in the QAA youth and community work benchmark statement (2009).

5.1.2   Fostering democratic and inclusive practice including the following:

- The ability to foster participation and support for young people and adults in playing an active role in their communities, increasing their voice and influence in contexts and on issues that affect them.

- The ability to create inclusive environments and to identify and counter oppressive attitudes, behaviours and situations, at both interpersonal and systemic levels.

- The capacity to build practice on an understanding of issues of power, empowerment and the complexity of voluntary relationships.

The case for youth participation

A central tenet throughout this chapter is that youth participation has a vital role to play in enhancing the well-being of young people. There is a wealth of evidence pointing to a decline in young people's social well-being in the United Kingdom since the 1990s, particularly among the most disadvantaged (Child Poverty Action Group, 2009; Collishaw et al., 2004; New Economics Foundation, 2009; The Primary Review, 2007; UNICEF, 2007). What is proposed here is that social policy measures designed to address this decline are more likely to succeed if they are conceived in response to wants and needs expressed by young people themselves. Moreover, facilitating this expression will require allowing young people opportunities to engage in authentic participatory techniques which

- allow the full socio-cultural context shaping their expectations, life chances and experiences to be revealed;

- allows them to identify possibilities for change; and

- allows them to develop the capacity to take part in collective action in pursuance of such social transformation (Cooper, 2010).

The main objective of this chapter is to theorise on what such a model of youth participation might look like and how it might be applied in practice.

The chapter starts by describing the background to the contemporary context shaping youth participation practice in England before then exploring the purpose of mainstream citizen engagement practices for powerholders. Arguably, citizen participation allows the powerful to claim that different views have been considered and democracy prevails. However, measured against the ideal of supporting young people to attain well-being, such practices remain fundamentally flawed because, as Beck and Purcell argue, they have been organised 'according to the hegemonic needs of powerful institutions … [d]espite the rhetoric surrounding youth and community work practice that suggests we are engaged in empowering people' (Beck and Purcell, 2010, page 8). Community and youth work practice continues to be embedded within an administrative approach designed to achieve centrally defined, predetermined targets aimed at tackling 'dysfunction' – that is, specifically in relation to young people, their deficient sexual mores and attitudes to schooling and work ethic; their (ab)use of drugs and alcohol and their 'anti-social' and 'criminal' behaviour. At the same time, there has been little attempt at 'any systematic analysis of structural problems within society' (Beck and Purcell, 2010, page 5), which means that the effects of structural inequalities based on class, 'race', gender, sexuality and disability have remained beyond scrutiny in mainstream youth participation practice.

Youth work practice at the Octagon Youth Club, Redfield DC

The author worked as a youth work student placement throughout the summer of 2010 at the Octagon Youth Club, Redfield DC (an east midlands' town in England). The club was located in one of the most socially deprived areas in England. The philosophy of the club was to provide 'strictly-managed fun activities that would engage young people' (personal communication with lead youth worker). There was also a strong emphasis on meeting performance-related accredited outcomes through work targeted on the five Every Child Matters outcomes. There were few existing mechanisms within the club for engaging its members in decision making beyond asking them what summer activities they wanted to engage in from a pre-determined menu of choices. The youth work approach at the Octagon was consistent with the managerialist audit culture described by Bradford when he argued

youth work has become fundamentally managerialised in order to secure the accountability of youth work and youth workers. Rather than engaging with young people in ways that young people themselves partially determine, youth workers now operate in a range of pre-set targets, standards and performance indicators.

(Bradford, 2010, pages 65–6)

Early on in the placement, the author introduced some of the young people there to a consultation tool designed to stimulate dialogue – a laminated neighbourhood map upon which they were invited to place sticky notes expressing what they liked about their neighbourhood, what they didn't like, and what they would like to change. Such techniques are described by Drysdale and Purcell (2001) as having 'the benefit of helping people identify what are the important areas of their lives, what might be the potential problems or concerns, who is important to them and what kind of support/threat might be expected from them' (cited in Beck and Purcell, 2010, page 100). This activity and the subsequent conversations it spawned allowed a number of key factors and concerns to be revealed. These included the following:

- *Things the young people liked: 'friends and family'; 'easy access to town'; 'places to go'; 'the diversity of the area' and 'local amenities – shops, clubs, park'.*

- *Things the young people didn't like: 'those living in the homeless shelter – scary!', 'vandalism', 'too many vicious fights after school', 'bullying at my school', 'disrespectful teachers who label me', 'lack of qualifications – no hope of getting a decent job', 'black people don't have same rights', 'kiddy-fiddlers by the park', 'treatment of Muslims and war on terror' and 'affording to buy/do things'.*

- *Things the young people would like to change – for example, 'just more to do', 'make the area nicer' and 'more advice and support about careers and schooling'.*

CASE STUDY *continued*

The names of the Octagon Youth Club, Redfield DC and the people working at and attending the club have been changed to protect the confidentiality of anyone named.

ACTIVITY 3.1

How might you respond if these concerns were revealed in conversations held in your own youth work setting? Can you identify generative themes appropriate for further analysis?

The model of youth participation ultimately advocated in this chapter emphasises an approach that allows young people to critically explore their experiences collectively and to identify possibilities for change. It draws heavily on radical critiques of citizen participation, which emphasise building critical consciousness and counter-hegemonic collective strategies for achieving social transformation. The need for radical critique in community and youth work practice is easy to justify. As Beck and Purcell argue

> *There is no such thing as a neutral position, and it has to be recognised that youth and community work is about taking sides. The National Occupational Standards for Community Development Work recognise this and identify promoting social justice as a core value underpinning practice. As the great American community organiser Saul Alinsky commented, this means taking the side of the have-nots, those who are left out and overlooked.*

(2010, page 77)

Therefore, the key objective of this chapter is to advocate a model of youth participation that will make a significant contribution to enhance the well-being of the have-nots rather than the haves.

The contemporary context for youth participation in England

There has been growing support over the last 30 years for user participation in public service provision in Britain. The contextual framework for this development has been shaped by ideological, economic and social imperatives, supplemented by human rights legislation and ethical concerns.

Ideologically, encouragement for user participation reflects the rise to predominance throughout this period of neo-liberalism and the new managerialism in

British politics and social policy, and the desire to achieve greater cost-effectiveness in the delivery of public services alongside privatisation. User engagement since the 1980s has been primarily fostered to achieve management efficiencies and cost savings through making service providers more accountable to their 'customers' – for example, by involving service users in the evaluation of those services (Williams, 2010) or privatisation strategies. The participation approach adopted here is one inherited from the world of business ('customer satisfaction') and is intended to challenge the previous monopoly of control held by professionals and welfare bureaucrats throughout the post-war Keynesian welfare state period – a system of control viewed as inherently inefficient by the political right.

While there was little interest in the 1980s to extend developments in user engagement to young people, this began to change by the end of this decade. The motor behind this change was Article 12 of the United Nations Convention on the Rights of the Child (UNCRC). This states that

> *children have the right to participate in the decision making processes that may be relevant to their lives and to influence decisions taken in their regard, within the family, the school or the community.*

> (UNCRC, 1989, cited in Podd, 2010, page 21)

The UNCRC gave impetus to the notion that young people should be allowed greater involvement in decision making about public services.

At the same time, there had been a growing concern about the 'state of youth' throughout the 1980s stemming from social unrest involving many young people in a number of major cities from the early part of that decade. Industrial decline alongside rising youth unemployment and poverty was said to have caused a sense of alienation among working-class and black youth, resulting in a renewed interest in developing local youth councils – which had first emerged in the 1940s – in some areas as a means of engaging these 'disaffected' young people (Podd, 2010). Participation here is seen as an effective management tool for dealing with a perceived social problem.

However, it was a further rights-based determination, the incorporation of the European Convention on Human Rights (ECHR) into British law through the Human Rights Act (HRA) 1998, which had significant implications for citizens – young and old alike. Now, young people are permitted to challenge any domestic law or policy, which they feel breaches any fundamental right they enjoy under the ECHR (Maguire, 2009). This measure added legislative support for acknowledging:

> *... the need to ensure young people become involved in decision making about public services as this, in turn, ensures that the services are better tailored to meeting their needs collectively and at an individual level.*

> (Maguire, 2009, page 73)

45

While acknowledging the need to recognise young people's rights, Maguire's comment here also restates the managerialist imperative of generating greater efficiency in service delivery. Beyond such necessities, however, it can also be argued that there are strong ethical grounds for facilitating user engagement in decision-making processes. Arguably, youth participation is central to professional youth work practice and essential if young people are to determine their own development (Roberts, 2009). Consequently, 'participation' is an underpinning value throughout the youth work and community development National Occupational Standards (Beck and Purcell, 2010).

Despite this support for participation in public service provision today, 'participation' itself remains a contested concept with very different meanings and purposes for different people. In the next section, we explore these different meanings and intentions and the implications of these for young people.

Concepts and purposes of 'participation'

The most common approach to conceptualising 'participation' since the late 1960s is that based on Sherry Arnstein's influential typology of citizen participation. Arnstein's classification is arranged in a ladder pattern with each rung representing the degree of influence held by the community in decision-making processes. Her model is based on her research into anti-poverty and urban regeneration programmes in the United States in the 1960s. In attempting to overcome the empty rhetoric that often accompanies such notions as user involvement in social programmes, Arnstein begins by defining what citizen participation should be:

> *My answer to the critical* what *question is simply that citizen participation is a categorical term for citizen power. It is the redistribution of power that enables the have-not citizens, presently excluded from the political and economic processes, to be deliberately included in the future. It is the strategy by which the have-nots join in determining how information is shared, goals and policies are set, tax resources are allocated, programs are operated, and benefits like contracts and patronage are parcelled out. In short, it is the means by which they can induce significant social reform which enables them to share in the benefits of the affluent society.*

> (1969, page 17 – emphasis in original)

Arnstein's definition poses a radical agenda for citizen involvement in social policy. For Arnstein,

> *… participation without redistribution of power is an empty and frustrating process for the powerless. It allows the powerholders to claim that all sides were considered, but makes it possible for only some of those sides to benefit. It maintains the status quo.*

> (1969, page 17)

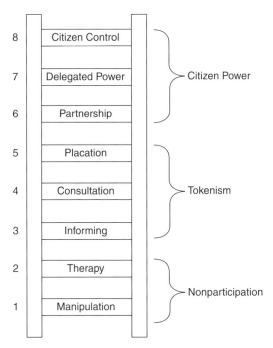

Figure 3.1 Eight rungs on a ladder of citizen participation
Source: Adapted from Arnstein (1969)

As will be shown throughout this chapter, this is what has been happening in mainstream community participation programmes throughout the past four decades in British social policy – including community and youth work projects.

Arnstein's typology (Figure 3.1) contains eight levels of participation, which distinguish between what she defines as types of participation and 'non-participation'. This was subsequently adapted by Roger Hart (1992) as a ladder of young people's participation with similar descriptions for the rungs.

The bottom rungs of the ladder correspond to forms of 'non-participation', which Arnstein says are contrived by agencies to represent genuine involvement but in reality are intended to manoeuvre ('manipulation') or treat ('therapy') a 'problem' – for example, 'disaffected youth' (as occurred in Britain in the 1980s – discussed previously).

Further up the ladder, we witness degrees of tokenism where citizens are provided with information ('informing') and listened to ('consultation'), but with no assurance that this will affect decision making. One step up from this is to include citizens on advisory panels or boards of trustees but without changing the existing majority power base ('placation'). In all these cases, the status quo remains intact and participation is used to serve the interests of agencies. The top three rungs of the ladder describe types of participation which Arnstein argues represent the degrees of empowerment which allow citizens genuine influence. Here, citizens may be offered opportunities to negotiate with powerholders – for example, through community representatives being elected on to planning committees ('partnership'). At a higher level, citizens may be handed devolved authority over aspects of particular budgets or projects ('delegated power'). Then finally, at the top of the ladder, citizens may be given the power to run their own projects ('citizen control').

CASE STUDY

Youth Participation in Redfield DC

Local authorities have a statutory requirement to engage with young people. This is set out in Para 5, Section 507B, of the Education Act 1996.

In Redfield (the midlands' town where the author worked at a youth club – described earlier), the local District Council established nine local area youth forums where young people aged between 11 and 19 could be elected as youth councillors to their local forum through their school or youth club. Local forums were given the remit of discussing how to improve the local neighbourhood. Youth councillors who wanted to get more involved in decision making townwide were encouraged to attend the town's Youth Council meetings. Being a youth councillor means volunteering on average for about 15 hours a month, and they are expected to be role models in their communities. In return, the town council promise accredited training opportunities and lots of fun.

During the author's time working at the club, he attended one of the local Youth Council meetings with a fellow worker, whose tasks included being the Youth Engagement worker for the local area, and two young people from the neighbourhood. The meeting focused on determining what information should be included on a new website for young people and how to encourage young people to participate in a new online questionnaire survey exploring their issues of concern. The session was directed and controlled by adults. A Youth Council questionnaire prepared by council employees was offered to the young respondents attending the meeting to survey what issues of concern they had. This was presented to them as a predetermined list of issues to 'tick' – issues that largely related to managing young people's attitudes and their behaviour in relation to education, training, work, leisure activities and volunteering. In addition, the council's strategy on getting young people to engage in the new online questionnaire survey emphasised offering some kind of reward (such as a loyalty-card points scheme) commensurate with how many times a respondent went online.

ACTIVITY **3.2**

Where on Arnstein's ladder would you place Redfield's approach to youth participation and why? Think of an approach or approaches to youth participation you have experienced – where on Arnstein's ladder would you place this/these and why?

Arnstein herself identifies a number of limitations with her own typology. For example, she acknowledges that the model simplifies the relationship between the powerful and the powerless, characterising both as homogeneous blocs in opposition to each other. In reality, each side may well encompass divergent points of view (e.g. on one side, radical community workers working within 'conservative' agencies to a different agenda; on the other side, significant cleavages within communities based on 'race', class, gender and age). Overall, the typology fails to offer any analysis of barriers to community empowerment based on racism, sexism, homophobia and socio-economic disadvantage. In addition, as Cooper and Hawtin have argued in relation to resident involvement, conceptualising community involvement as a ladder could be misinterpreted:

> *For instance, the lower rungs of the ladder may not necessarily imply a lack of control: they may offer opportunities for residents to get involved at a level appropriate to their needs and wishes. It could also be argued that some of the examples of involvement identified by Arnstein as empowering communities (such as partnership approaches) may be designed to placate or manipulate troublesome communities, or to undermine the power base of local authorities.*

> (1997a, page 85)

Partnership approaches in the delivery of services that have traditionally been provided by the public sector are now widespread. However, this does not mean that there has been an increase in citizen control as 'it is typically the relatively powerful players in a particular situation who shape the agenda' (Marsh and Murie, 1996, cited in Cooper and Hawtin, 1997a, page 85). This use of power is particularly evident in respect of youth engagement. As Beck and Purcell argue, mainstream approaches to participation merely perpetuate a myth of 'classlessness and equality of power' practiced by 'representatives' who 'are seldom representative of anything other than a small constituency' (Beck and Purcell, 2010, page 93). In such a context, existing power relations remain intact even at the higher levels of engagement on Arnstein's ladder. This is clearly evident currently in the case of the Conservative/Liberal Democratic coalition's proposals for 'The Big Society'.

David Cameron's plan for 'The Big Society' was set out in his speech at Liverpool Hope University on 19 July 2010. In this, he defined 'The Big Society' in radical terms as

> *.... a huge cultural change – where people, in their everyday lives, in their homes, in their neighbourhoods, in their workplace – don't always turn to officials, local authorities or central government for answers to the problems they face but instead feel both free and powerful enough to help themselves and their own communities.... It's about liberation – the biggest, most dramatic redistribution of power to the man and woman on the street. And this is such a powerful idea for blindingly obvious reasons.*

> (Cameron, cited in McSmith, 2010, page 1)

Cameron's rule of government would aim to unleash community engagement through social action, public service reform and community empowerment (McSmith, 2010). To achieve this, Cameron identified three techniques:

1. Decentralisation of power from central government to local government, communities and individuals – for example, new powers for local communities to take over the running of parks, libraries and post offices.
2. Empowering people by providing them with the information to call services to account and, if necessary, to take action themselves – for example, establishing neighbourhood watch schemes, youth clubs or after-school clubs in response to concerns about crime and disorder.
3. Finance – both public service funding and by connecting private capital investment to social projects, including using funds in dormant bank accounts to establish a 'Big Society Bank' to finance social enterprises (McSmith, 2010).

In summing up his scheme, Cameron stated, 'This is a big advance for people power. The people power I have spoken about for years. And the big change this coalition government wants to bring' (Cameron, cited in McSmith, 2010, page 5).

The implementation of the scheme is to be detailed in a localism bill that will pave the way for parents, council employees and community groups to compete with local authorities and private companies to run services. The bill will create the following:

- A community *right to buy* local buildings in competition with other groups including private sector companies;

- A community *right to challenge* and take over a local service;

- A community *right to build* allowing homeowners to add extensions or build new homes as long as a simple majority in the area votes in favour.

Eric Pickles, the communities secretary, argued: 'This powerful series of measures puts new rights in law for people to protect, improve and even run important frontline services. For too long people have been powerless to intervene as vital community resources disappear'.

(Cited in Curtis and Ramesh, 2010, page 22)

On the surface, these measures seem radical and would appear to take community empowerment to the top of Arnstein's ladder – 'citizen control'. However, 'The Big Society' project has to be understood in the context of the coalition government's sweeping cuts in public expenditure – cuts that will particularly hit young people. Local authorities face losing 27% of their budgets over four years with the bulk of the cuts (a half) front loaded in 2011/12. Research by the Special Interest Group of Municipal Authorities (SIGoMA) suggests that the worst hit authorities include some of the most deprived areas in Britain (Curtis, 2010, page 22). The Conservative-controlled Local Government Association (LGA) predicted 140,000 local government job losses in 2011/12 (Wintour, 2010). Overall, unemployment is expected to reach 9% (over 2.5 m) in 2011 with youth unemployment rising most significantly. Meanwhile, welfare benefits are expected to be cut by 2% per annum due to increases now being related to the Consumer Price Index. In addition welfare support for children and young people will be eroded due to the closure of Sure Start and Connexions' services; the abolition of the pregnancy grant, child tax credit for under-ones and the child trust fund; the rise in cost of childcare and loss of education maintenance allowance for the poorest teenagers. Devolving power to the local level – local authorities, communities and individuals – requires local tax raising powers, which the coalition government are not prepared to concede (McSmith, 2010).

As Sir Stuart Etherington, chief executive of the National Council for Voluntary Organisations, argues, 'The Big Society' ambition is threatened by grant cuts to voluntary organisations and charities, which will 'have a detrimental effect on the services received by some of the most vulnerable people' (cited in Watt, 2010, page 4).

In such a context, the notion of 'citizen control' is a somewhat vacuous one. This seems borne out by Eric Pickles' admission that 'The Big Society' was 'unashamedly about getting more for less' (cited in Watt, 2010, page 4).

Arguably, 'The Big Society' represents continuity with the previous government's efforts to stimulate the role of civil society and civic engagement in Social Policy. New Labour actively sought to encourage the community and voluntary sector to participate in service delivery (e.g. through engagement in local strategic partnerships) and to advance the active involvement of citizens in local decision making (e.g. community safety initiatives). This active encouragement was influenced by Amitai Etzioni (1993) and his brand of communitarianism that called 'for people to live up to their responsibilities and not merely focus on their entitlements, and to shore up the moral foundations of society' (cited in Packham, 2008, page 31). What we have seen since 1997 has been the acceleration of a move 'towards the community and voluntary sector carrying out what have previously been the roles of the welfare state' (Packham, 2008, page 33), and, through such measures as the Communities and Local Government Empowerment White Paper (2008), an enhanced role for citizen involvement and volunteering in initiatives aimed at solving 'shared problems' (Packham, 2008, page 37).

These interventions, however, have generated tensions between, on the one hand, the political rhetoric of participation and empowerment and, on the other hand, structural barriers to effective community participation caused by unequal power relations. As Packham argues, government intervention in the community and voluntary sector has done little to empower that sector's autonomy or its ability to work creativity in pursuit of social justice. 'Rather it has sought to influence and control it, and use community and voluntary organizations as a deliverer of its services' (Packham, 2008, page 39). In addition,

> *in relation to citizens, the government has become involved in areas which were usually determined by individual citizens. Through the development of*

volunteering, much of which is no longer freely chosen (for example as part of the school citizenship curriculum or activity undertaken as part of a community service order), and through the development of a set curriculum for active citizenship, the government can be seen to be seeking to control the role of individuals in civic and civil society.

(Packham, 2008, page 39)

Such forms of civil and civic involvement do little to change the relations of power that underpin social inequality and injustice. This is largely because, as Garratt and Piper (2008) argue, 'behind the official rhetoric of local citizen participation and community partnership is frequently a concern to impose centrally determined and authoritarian structures on problematic neighbourhoods' (cited in Packham, 2008, page 8). And despite claims about the need to redistribute power, Arnstein's typology, still cited by many as the key to understanding models of participation in community and youth work (e.g. Batsleer, 2008; Beck and Purcell, 2010; Freeman et al., 1999; Hart, 1992; Packham, 2008; Patel, 2010; West, 1998), fails to address the issue of structured power relations and how these might be challenged at each and every level.

Having said this, Arnstein's ladder does alert us to the purpose of citizen engagement for the powerful and how it had evolved in US urban policy throughout the 1960s (and subsequently in Britain in the late 1960s in the guise of the Community Development Projects). In the United States, New Deal policies – that is, social democratic measures designed to achieve full employment and improved access to decent housing – were abandoned by the late 1940s in favour of the 'Great Society'. This development deepened socio-economic divisions (particularly based on 'race') and exacerbated social struggles, led by newly emerging social movements, over municipal services, housing, employment and demands for civil rights. 'The explosion of political and social unrest in the northern cities in 1966 and 1967 was a critical factor underlying the rapid expansion of direct federal urban policies in the mid-1960s and early 1970s' (Florida and Jonas, 1991, page 366). New measures included the Civil Rights Acts of 1964 and 1968 providing legal protection for black people in relation to employment and housing. The Model Cities programme provided federal funding available for neighbourhood regeneration and community development. Federal aid to disadvantaged urban areas rose dramatically throughout the 1960s. However, despite this increase, there 'was no attempt to build new institutions or sets of social relationships designed to address the structural roots of income poverty and unemployment' (Florida and Jonas, 1991, page 368). State-led community development continued to prioritise 'bolstering the conditions for capital accumulation, while providing some marginal assistance to disadvantaged groups in the context of greater social control' (Florida and Jonas, 1991, page 370).

Similar concerns have been expressed about the impact of the 'Great Society' and 'The Big Society' on the democratic process. Much of the federal funding made available under the 'Great Society' was allocated directly to neighbourhoods, thereby bypassing the scrutiny of the city authorities. This raised concerns at the time about democratic accountability (Florida and Jonas, 1991), something that has been brought up more recently in Britain with regard to 'The Big Society'. The coalition's plans to transfer power to local communities and outsource public services to charities and the private sector led to Gus O'Donnell, head of the civil service, calling for an investigation into the democratic impact of such large-scale devolution. In *The Guardian* of 22 January 2011, Polly Curtis suggests that on top of the erosion of local democracy, children's services and doctors' practices might finish up outside the scope of the Freedom of Information Act (Curtis, 2011, page 6).

Around the time of the Great Society, in the United Kingdom similar concerns in urban political analysis emerged alongside similar policy solutions. In parallel with the collapse of the New Deal in the United States, in Britain:

> *The ideological hegemony of the post-war welfare state began to break down in the 1960s as it became increasingly evident that the state was failing to deliver the goods. The 'rediscovery of poverty', rising unemployment, slums and homelessness, flawed public housing schemes and unpopular private-sector office developments led to a number of urban protest movements seeking major changes in the way urban services were delivered.*
>
> (Cooper and Hawtin, 1997a, page 99)

The British government responded to these developments by drawing on the example of the Model Cities programme in the United States:

> *[T]he Community Development Projects (CDPs), initiated in 1968 in the aftermath of Enoch Powell's 'rivers of blood' speech and growing urban tensions, can be seen to represent an attempt by government to pre-empt further urban problems by achieving social cohesion through community participation.*
>
> (Cooper and Hawtin, 1997a, page 99)

As initially conceived, the CDPs approach was based on a positivist understanding of urban problems and the flawed pathology of area-based 'problem communities' in need of treatment or manipulation – a corollary of which was that the structural underpinnings of urban disadvantage were underplayed, allowing the status quo to remain intact.

From the 1970s, however, the CDPs adopted a Marxist critique of urban problems and prescribed a solution that required 'the redistribution of wealth and power achieved through the politicization of working-class communities and through broader social, political and economic restructuring' (Cooper and Hawtin, 1997b, pages 285–6). This view was one shared by the Association of Community Workers (Harris, 1994) and informs the values and beliefs about the role of community and youth work held by this author. More specifically, it can be argued that the moral imperative for community and youth workers is to create opportunities for communities and young people to discover the true nature of social disadvantage and to be supported to explore possibilities and avenues for engaging in collective action for positive social change. The next section will describe a model of participation that offers the possibility for this vision of community and youth work to be realised.

A model of emancipatory youth participation practice

Traditionally throughout modernity, the 'voice' of young people has been marginalised and young people have largely been treated as passive recipients of 'expert knowledge' (France, 2007). Moreover, social policy responses to the 'problem of youth' have continued to be dominated by neo-positivist interpretations of youth as somehow 'in deficit' (Cooper, 2009). A key recent influence here, for example, is the work of the Local Well-being Projects (LWPs) under the guidance of Richard Layard at the London School of Economics. Layard advocates the practice of cognitive behaviour therapy (CBT) to enhance the 'emotional resilience' of young people to deal 'more constructively' with difficult circumstances (The Young Foundation, 2008). Under the previous Labour government, youth policy (Department for Education and Skills, 2005, 2006) increasingly focused on targeted interventions aimed at incentivising young people 'at risk' to become more accountable for their own social development by overcoming their 'cultural deficits' – that is, their flawed attitudes to work, schooling and training and their 'risky'/'anti-social' behaviour. What these approaches lack, however, is acknowledgement of the broader sociocultural context within which young people strive to attain well-being in post-industrial Britain – a context that has become increasingly unsupportive under neo-liberalism (Cooper, 2009, 2010; Wilkinson and Pickett, 2009).

ACTIVITY **3.3**

A technique the author has used with community and youth work students to facilitate critical scrutinising of contemporary mainstream accounts of the 'problem of youth' is to show two media clips from YouTube:

1. *The first, a poem 'No Respect' by Laura Walsh, available at www.youtube.com/ watch?v=JfxA9Bp6ds4 (at the time of writing).*

2. *The second, a talk on youth and restorative justice by Phil Gatensby, available at www.youtube.com/watch?v=9xFG2t5JIFU (at the time of writing).*

These convey competing perspectives on the nature of the problem. Laura Walsh's poem is a powerful, highly emotive presentation backed by techno music and fast-moving images portraying vandalism, verbal abuse, thieving, guns and knives, drug use, and devils and hell fire. Walsh is from Liverpool and she states that her

---

poem 'illustrates some of the facts of current gang culture and [highlights] the futility of such behaviour and suggests an alternative path from a lifestyle of drugs and violence'. The essential message is that youth crime and deviance is caused by a lack of self-control and free choice, and cannot be linked to educational disadvantage and social deprivation. Young people needed to be more responsible for their own actions. In contrast, Phil Gatensby, a restorative justice activist in Canada, focuses less emotively on the responsibility of adults to do more to address the underlying societal problems young people face and not merely react to the symptoms (i.e. drug use and crime). In the course of critically reflecting on these two clips, students invariably see beyond mainstream discourses on youth crime and engage with broader understandings that give greater recognition to the social and its interrelationship with dominant power structures (Cooper, 2010).

Look at the two clips with others in the context of your own youth work setting and then debate what each clip adds to our understanding of the 'problem of youth' in contemporary times and how society might best respond to this.

In parallel with this development, there has been a growing appreciation within the sociology of childhood in respect of young people's competence as social actors (James et al., 1998) and acknowledgement of the need to listen to young people and to recognise their agency. Established views about the abilities of young people to participate creatively, to reassess their world and to engage in collective action to transform unjust social relations have been redefined (Dentith et al., 2009). Such reconsiderations are leading to a repositioning of young people towards the centre of social enquiry through the adoption of models built on participatory action research (PAR) (Nieuwenhuys, 2004) or, more specifically, youth PAR (Dentith et al., 2009).

Youth PAR seeks to permit young people to explore, reflect and act upon their social world and in doing so strengthen their capacity for self-determination. PAR involves a dialogical approach where the researcher/youth worker and research population/young person co-investigate dialectically the object of concern – a process Paulo Freire (1996) described as 'conscientisation'. Young people are fully involved in the process while themes are discussed in the context of power relations and their structural manifestations. As Giroux (2000) argues, such an approach is particularly appropriate to enquiries with disadvantaged young people increasingly exposed to the commercial pressures of consumerist society because it presents genuine opportunities for fostering what C. Wright Mills (1959) called a 'sociological imagination' and the means to perceive more clearly what is happening to us and to discover alternative avenues for self-development. It allows the fatalism (described by Freire [1996], drawing on Marx, as 'false consciousness') often apparent in the statements of the oppressed to be exposed and countered (Mayo, 2004). It offers an opportunity to address what Lukes (1974) sees as an inhibited oppressed unable to mobilise in pursuit of their own interests due to having their understanding and perceptions manipulated by powerholders. It offers a strategy for countering what Gramsci (1971) describes as hegemonic domination – that is, the way 'commonsense' belief systems are generated by the dominant culture and how these shape (false) consciousness and understanding.

A toolbox for unravelling false consciousness has been described elsewhere by the author (Cooper, 2005, 2008, 2010). This draws on Niels Åkerstrøm Andersen's (2003) synthesis of the discourse analyses of Michel Foucault, Reinhart Koselleck, Ernesto Laclau and Niklas Luhmann. Andersen combines the theoretical contributions of these writers to offer a practical means to deconstruct normative understandings and subject these to critical scrutiny. In doing this, possibilities emerge for arriving at more meaningful insights into the natural order of things and alternative ways of being.

- Foucault's (2005) *Archaeology of Knowledge* offers a framework for critically analysing moral interpretations of 'social reality' by raising such questions as: who determines what is 'good' and acceptable (and, as a consequence, what is 'bad' and unacceptable)? And what knowledge sources ('discourses' – ideas and ways of representing 'truths') have been included in making such determinations (and what sources have been excluded)? And how are the 'subjects' of these determinations represented (e.g. deserving or undeserving?) and what are the consequences (e.g. inclusion and welfare support, or exclusion and criminalisation?). Finally, who gains most from these discursive practices? And who loses out?

- Foucault's ideas on exposing excluded knowledge sources is consistent with Koselleck's (Brunner et al., 1990) exploration of the history of concepts. Here, Koselleck identifies a terrain upon which counter positions to dominant discourses and representations can be forged. By emphasising the contestability of ideas, Koselleck focuses attention on to their ambiguity – that is, concepts can never be a true representation of reality, otherwise they would not be concepts. Consequently, there is always the possibility of formulating counter-discourses and concepts around which alternative representations and understandings can be formulated. There are always possibilities for resisting dominant discourses and the concepts these are based on through presenting counter-discourses and alternative concepts.

- Foucault's and Koselleck's notions are supported by Laclau (and his work with Mouffe) in *Hegemony and Socialist Strategy* (2001). Laclau explores hegemony in action – that is, the way that power is acted out and reinforced throughout society via social institutions, thereby sustaining the interests of the status quo. Through this investigation, Laclau identifies possibilities for organised resistance. Because hegemony is always contingent – that is something which has to be constantly strived for in a 'battle of fixating' – hegemonic consent can never be fully secured. As a consequence, there is always potential, therefore, for counter-hegemonic projects to emerge. This is also close to Foucault's (Morris and Patton, 1979) notion that 'there are no relations of power without resistance' and that there is always the potential for social change through 'reverse discourse'. Possibilities always exist for counter-hegemonic projects to develop wherever dominating discourses seek to impose their discipline and order.

- Finally, Luhmann's (1995) thesis on social systems offers a framework for scrutinising the motives of social institutions and bringing them to account. He defines social institutions (e.g. scientific, political, social, economic, judicial and the media) as the 'function systems' of society and argues that we need to examine how they observe and explain 'social reality'. Luhmann describes how such observations always involve the selection of distinctions – that is, we cannot observe social phenomena without first having selected a means of distinguishing the way we see and name. Ways of distinguishing will always accord with particular predetermined value judgements, and therefore, what is seen and named will always possess characteristics that are not indicated because other ways of distinguishing were not chosen. In brief, all observations will have blind spots. The task, therefore, is to illuminate these blind spots through what Luhmann calls 'second-order observations'. Second-order observations reveal the way social institutions only observe and represent what their choice of distinction permits them to see, and therefore, what is presented as 'social reality' is only a partial portrayal.

In short, Andersen's framework offers an appropriate toolbox for academics and community and youth workers to both research and work with young people in ways that facilitate: (a) the unravelling and scrutinising of dominant discourses (to appraise the 'commonsense' notions of 'truth' they stake claim to, and whose interests are being served); (b) the generation of counter-discourses (that expose contradictions within dominant discourses and allow alternative 'truths' that serve the interests of a broader constituency to be told); (c) the identification of possibilities for counter-hegemonic projects and the potential sites of conflict for engaging in these and (d) the development of strategies for exposing the limited assumptions underpinning the activities of social institutions and calling these to account.

Applying these tools to PAR in practice will require the researcher/youth worker to adopt a less directive role than in more conventional research/practice and instead play the part of 'intellectual mediator' – facilitating an open dialogue in which various values and positions can be mapped out, evaluated and challenged. As a mode of enquiry, this approach is close to Pierre Bourdieu's concept of 'reflexivity' where the researcher/practitioner strives to avoid imposing their own objective position on to the object of their research/work.

> *Bourdieu discusses how observers and analysts … project their own vision of the world onto their understandings of the social practices that are the object of their studies … Thereby, they unconsciously attribute to the object of their observations characteristics that are inherently theirs and those of their own perception and comprehension of the world.*
>
> (Deer, 2008, page 201)

As developed by Bourdieu, reflexivity becomes a critical practice that seeks to 'unveil the un-thought categories of thought that predetermine and delimitate what is thinkable' (Deer, 2008, page 204). It is an approach that aims to highlight the questions we don't ask to reveal 'the unknown mechanisms of the established order, or *symbolic violence*' (Deer, 2008, page 208, emphasis in original) that maintains conditions of domination and suffering. Systems of domination, argues Bourdieu, are not solely maintained by brute force (e.g. violent policing). Following Durkheim, he sees power being exerted through a 'logical conformism' with

> ... a **consensus** on the meaning of the social world, a consensus which contributes fundamentally to the reproduction of the social order. 'Logical' integration is the precondition of 'moral' integration.

> (Bourdieu, 1991, page 166)

This comes close to Freire's (1996) notion of 'false consciousness'. Indeed, Bourdieu argues that the dominant culture contributes not only to the integration of the dominant class (by distinguishing them from others):

> ... it also contributes to the fictitious integration of society as a whole, and thus to the apathy (false consciousness) of the dominated classes ... [O]ne class dominates another (symbolic violence) by bringing their own distinctive power to bear on the relations of power which underlie them and thus by contributing, in Weber's terms, to the 'domestication of the dominated'.

> (Bourdieu, 1991, page 167)

For Bourdieu, what largely underpins existing power relations is people's 'belief in the legitimacy of words and of those who utter them' (1991, page 170) – leading, in turn, to the maintenance of social inequality and suffering (symbolic violence). Inter alia, Bourdieu focused on suffering and symbolic violence in the French education system and in processes of consumption.

In respect of education,

> This system marginalized many members of the working classes at the same time that it served to reproduce class hierarchies in postwar France. The institution of a supposedly meritocratic system – and the credentials that it bequeathed – resulted in symbolic violence against those left behind by it. Not only did pupils suffer as a consequence of their marginalization, they were taught that their failure to perform well academically and to reap the benefits of academic success were a result of their own lack of natural talent.

> (Schubert, 2008, page 185)

Blaming 'dysfunctional' working-class children and their parent(s)/carer(s) in this way legitimates the existing social order.

In respect of consumer culture, Bourdieu observed how conditions of domination are maintained not only in relation to the means of production but also by consumption processes. He discounts the notion of personal preference or taste, arguing instead that our inclinations and likings are not only socially constructed but also used to maintain conditions of domination:

> *Taste classifies, and it classifies the classifier. Social subjects, classified by their classifications, distinguish themselves by the distinctions they make, between the beautiful and the ugly, the distinguished and the vulgar, in which their position in the objective classification is expressed or betrayed.*

> (Bourdieu, 1984, cited in Schubert, 2008, page 191)

Consumption processes, therefore, are structured by our *habitus* – that which drives 'our ways of acting, feeling, thinking and being' (Maton, 2008, page 52). They represent culturally determined daily practices or taken-for-granted habits. In the context of neo-liberal globalisation, these culturally determined practices have increasingly been shaped by the expansion of Westernised/Americanised global images impacting on identities in both the 'developed' and 'developing' world. Moreover, the representations of lifestyles, body image and fashion required for 'self-esteem', 'success' and 'sexual attractiveness' proffered by these images are having profoundly harmful consequences for the well-being of those young people who strive to live up to these styles – particularly in relation to their health and the pressure they feel to consume.

The next section explores the application of emancipatory youth participation in practice in a way that scrutinises the 'commonsense' understanding behind symbolic violence in the British state education system and allows a counter discourse offering alternative understandings and possibilities to begin to emerge.

A framework for generating a counter discourse in the education system

The author has illustrated elsewhere how the state education system in Britain has retained a role in sustaining dominant power relations (Cooper, 2002). Between 2009 and 2010, the author was involved in a Children's Workforce Development Council's Practitioner-Led Research project that set out to explore the effects of exclusion from mainstream education on young people who were, at the time, being educated outside schools in Hull (Spooner, 2010). The research involved seven young people, aged between 15 and 19 years, undertaking training in PAR over one weekend. Five were members of Hull's Young Advisors (a body of young people who engage in social action with other young people), and two were from a pupil referral unit (PRU) in the city. Because the approach seeks to maximise the expression of views and interpretations from a range of perspectives informed by different contexts, PAR does not have a distinct set of methodologies but instead draws on tools conducive to the type of wide-ranging dialogue it seeks to facilitate (Nieuwenhuys, 2004). In the case of this project, the training introduced the young people to the following techniques:

Spider diagram

A subject or an issue is written in large letters in the middle of a piece of flipchart paper and participants write around the word definitions, feelings and emotions that are connected with the subject. The tool is often used as a good introduction to a subject and the responses provide a basis for further exploration of utilising other tools.

Timeline

Individuals draw a line on a piece of flipchart paper from one end of the paper to the other. Participants then chart on the paper significant events in their lives on the timeline up until the present day. On the other side of the paper, participants are asked to outline their thoughts on how things may develop in the next 10 or 20 years. The tool can be used on an individual, group or organisational basis and is an excellent method of stimulating reflective practice, alongside providing a platform for charting aspirations/action planning.

Body mapping

One participant lies on a large piece of lining paper taped to the floor while another participant draws an outline of them. All participants then proceed to write/draw emotions/feelings on that part of the body where a specific issue may affect them. This tool is fun and interactive and is useful in exploring health-related issues.

Mapping exercise

Participants draw on a piece of flipchart paper the area in which they live, highlighting on the map areas of specific interest/significance to them. Participants then list three changes that they would like to make to their local area. This tool is good in planning/consulting on any physical changes communities may wish to make/proposed planned changes to an area.

Cause and impact diagram

Similar to the Spider Diagram, this diagram revolves around a central theme/issue written in the centre of a piece of flipchart paper. Writing at the top of the paper 'Cause', participants write what they think are the causes of a particular issue. At the bottom of the page is the word 'Impact' where participants write/

draw some of the effects that the issue has. This tool is a good method of determining the reason why things happen and the effect this can have on individuals/
communities.

Impact ranking table

This involves a simple table/grid on a flipchart sheet with rows going across the
paper and columns going downwards. The columns highlight the differing impact
different courses of action will have, while the rows highlight the differing ease
in which to apply the different courses of action. Using 'sticky notes', participants
post possible solutions to a problem on the table/grid, placing them in correl-
ation between effect and their difficulty to implement. This provides participants
with a visual representation of a potential solution to an issue which, undertaken
within a group, can provide an interesting platform for discussions (Spooner, 2010,
Appendix 2).

Following the training, of the initial seven, five (including the two attending the
PRU) went on to undertake fieldwork with nine participants (aged between 13 and
15 years and mixed by gender) who also attended the PRU. The aim of the fieldwork was to explore the participants understanding of exclusion from mainstream
education in terms of who is excluded and how, and how this impacts on perceptions of self-identity, relationships with family and peers, and aspirations for the
future. The study also sought to evaluate the utility of PAR for exploring such views
with young people.

Through a selection of the techniques described previously, respondents revealed
internalised feelings of failure in relation to exclusion as well as difficult domestic
and personal circumstances. At the same time, however, they also recognised
structural determinants of exclusion reflected in neighbourhood deprivation,
poverty, unemployment and a lack of amenities and linked these to the dimensions of 'race', class, age, sexuality, gender, (dis)ability and religion. It was also
clear that the effects of exclusion on self-identity and interpersonal relationships
had been extremely damaging – for example, the young people were left with
feelings of being different, disappointed, isolated, angry, injustice, heartbroken,
lonely and depressed. Despite these difficulties, most retained clear yet modest
ambitions (to study at college and get a job; to find a home and settle down to
family life) – a modesty of expectation identified in previous studies with disadvantaged young people (Ridge, 2003). Finally, the participants stated how
they had gained valuable research skills throughout this project, including learning different ways of interpreting and expressing the respondents' responses.
They had also grown in confidence and learnt how to speak in a 'professional
way'. A key implication of this project for practice is the benefits to be derived
from actively engaging young people in the design, delivery and evaluation of
youth services. This proposition is consistent with the findings from Bostock
and Freeman's (2003) PAR with young people in Northumberland, which led to
young people's views becoming routinely engaged in local decision making. It

just requires recognising young people as competent social actors rather than as being somehow in deficit (Spooner, 2010).

ACTIVITY 3.4

Some argue that we are heading towards 'an increasingly homogenized popular culture underwritten by a Western "culture industry"' (Steger, 2009, page 72), what Ritzer calls the 'McDonaldization of Society' – that is, the advancement of a bland, dehumanised uniformity in Westernised societal relations (Ritzer, 1998). Behind the 'globalisation' of culture in contemporary times lays the power of a Westernised/Americanised global corporate media empire:

> Saturating global cultural reality with formulaic TV shows and mindless advertisements, these corporations increasingly shape people's identities and the structure of desires around the world. The rise of the global imagery is inextricably connected to the rise of the global media.
>
> *(Steger, 2009, page 78)*

The transnational expansion of Westernised/Americanised global images is over-powering the ability of individuals and communities to take control of their own localities and lifeworlds. This development threatens people's capacity to make choices and their competence to act as a 'crucial source of innovation in the world' (Ritzer, 2007, page 210) – a situation that is arguably leading to the impover-ishment of the domain of culture and pushing us nearer towards what Marcuse (1964) conceived as the creation of One-Dimensional Man.

The following activities and discussions are designed to facilitate scrutiny of the relationship between consumerism, body image and well-being.

- *At the time of writing, the following YouTube clip explores the relationship between consumer culture and women's body image:*
  www.youtube.com/watch?v=hMxtBL8lHbU&feature=related

Discussion: how does consumer culture influence women's body image and what are the implications for young women's health and well-being?

- *At the time of writing, the following YouTube clip explores the relationship between consumer culture and men's body image:*
  www.youtube.com/watch?v=sj3De6s3ZjQ

Discussion: how does consumer culture influence men's body image and what are the implications for young men's health and well-being?

- *At the time of writing, the following YouTube clip explores the relationship between the media, consumerism and youth identity:*
  www.youtube.com/watch?v=v3gEFwQo_7k

Discussion: how does the media influence the way young people have become judged in contemporary times and what is the implication of this for young peo-ple's well-being?

- *At the time of writing, the following YouTube clip, produced by young people themselves, critically explores the role of the media and consumerism in shaping youth identity. This might stimulate other young people to generate similar clips.*
  www.youtube.com/watch?v=4vFrZHZWJHA&feature=related

Both Activity 3.4 and the Children's Workforce Development Council's Practitioner-Led Research project described earlier are pertinent to concerns raised during the author's neighbourhood mapping exercise with young participants at the Octagon Youth Club, Redfield DC (described in Activity 3.1). Both achieve the aims of Andersen's (2003) toolbox for scrutinising dominant mainstream understanding – in these cases, recognising (a) young people as competent social actors and (b) the social harms experienced by young people at the hands of the global corporate media industry – and possibilities for developing different meanings.

Having arrived at a more meaningful (proportionate) understanding and possibilities for alternative ways of being, the next task for emancipatory youth participation practice is to support young people to translate this new found conscienciousness into collective action for positive social change. Andersen's (2003) framework offers one means of achieving this by stressing a need to focus on sites of conflict and calling powerholders to account. Similarly and specific to youth work, Bamber and Murphy's (1999) model of critical youth work practice outlines an approach built on Freirean critical pedagogy. Having developed a group's critical awareness about an issue and their shared commitment to deal with it, the next stage would be to debate and assess what course of action is realistically possible and, where there is a consensus to pursue this, plan and mobilising people behind that action.

ACTIVITY 3.5

Mobilising collective action for social change – during the author's time working at the Octagon Youth Club, Redfield DC (described in Activity 3.1), one of the young men at the club, Peter, was served a highly publicised anti-social behaviour order (asbo) – reportedly served because of his 'intimidating behaviour as the leader of a gang of local youths whose actions included using people's wheelie bins as sledges and giving out verbal abuse' (Redfield Evening News). The asbo prohibited Peter from entering the neighbourhood in which he lives (with exceptions for travelling on public transport and medical appointments) and from associating there with named friends. Any breach of the order, which was to last for two years, would risk Peter being arrested and imprisoned. The asbo was reported with a photograph of Peter in the Redfield Evening News, on posters in local shops and on a leaflet circulated to every property in the neighbourhood. Peter and his friends (many of whom were also named on the asbo) felt that the

63

ACTIVITY **3.5** *continued*

order and its coverage were disproportionate and unjust, and they felt angry about it.

In your own youth work context, consider how Peter and his friends might feel about this situation and reflect on what courses of social action might be realistically possible for them to take in response.

In recent times, there has been a growing interest in mobilising collective action for social change around a 'rights-based' agenda. For instance, Ledwith and Springett cite Damian Killeen, a consultant on social justice and sustainable development, who adopted a rights-based approach to PAR through asking 'is poverty in the UK a denial of people's human rights?' given that 'poverty and discrimination contravene the Universal Declaration on Human Rights' (Ledwith and Springett, 2010, page 25). A similar rights-based approach was recently adopted by a research partnership – comprising Save the Children (NI), The Prince's Trust (NI) and Queens University, Belfast – into the well-being of some of the most marginalised young people in Northern Ireland (McAlister et al., 2009). The research highlighted how young people in Northern Ireland were experiencing a lack of respect and age discrimination in all areas of society but particularly in the sphere of participation in key decisions affecting their lives – a flagrant breach of the UN Convention on the Rights of the Child. As a consequence, they were left feeling 'undermined, unimportant, excluded and resentful' (McAlister et al., 2009, page 156) in their communities. Consequently, building safer, inclusive communities requires greater mutual respect and genuine opportunities for young people to be listened to, so that the structural, cultural and sectarian contexts shaping their life chances and well-being can be better understood. This understanding contrasts with contemporary mainstream social policies largely aimed at addressing 'youth problems' by prioritising 'changing individuals' behaviours rather than challenging and adapting the institutional processes that contextualise the lives of children and young people' (McAlister et al., 2009, page 15).

C H A P T E R   R E V I E W

There is an urgent need to embed youth participation in social policy making and practice if the decline in young people's well-being in Britain is to be reversed. Moreover, this participation needs to allow young people's voices to be genuinely expressed, heard and acted on in ways suggested throughout this chapter. Thus far, this has not happened and the growing encouragement for user participation over the last 30 years has largely been aimed at meeting the managerialist imperatives of the public sector – for example, management efficiencies and cost-effectiveness in the delivery of services; the engagement of 'troublesome communities' in the interest of 'social cohesion'. The participation tools on offer have been largely tokenistic.

This 'lack' in mainstream youth participation practices was certainly evident during the author's placement at the Octagon Youth Club, Redfield DC (described in Activity 3.1). Throughout this time, the author sought to generate spaces for radical youth work interventions that would respond to the group's critical awareness of sources of their oppression by facilitating possibilities for them to engage in collective action for positive social change. One example of this related to Peter's asbo (discussed in Activity 3.5) where the author felt that the young people's anger could be channelled into some form of such action – for example, a campaign against the local media's demonization of young people (such as organising a petition or picketing the offices of the *Redfield Evening News*). However, this was not possible due to the contemporary institutional context of the placement. Most significantly, the Lead Youth Worker's perspective of the role of Octagon Youth Club was the provision of 'strictly-managed fun activities that would engage young people' (cited in Activity 3.1). This generally excluded activities that failed to add 'value' to the context driving the imperatives of youth work in Redfield – a context shaped by managerialist ideology 'culturally enforced through the tyranny of "good practice"' (Belton, 2010, page 80). As a consequence, the author was told to concentrate on building relationships with the young people via 'fun' activities (activities that largely accorded with gendered stereotypes – table sports, basketball, badminton and football for the young men; Facebook, Wii dance routines, and arts and crafts for the young women). While developing trusting relationships through activities and 'engaging in conversation' (Smith, 2010, page 31) is at the heart of youth work, it is argued here that youth workers also have a moral imperative to respond to what is revealed through these conversations – particularly when what is revealed are young people's critical awareness of the sources of their oppression. Youth workers who fail to practice in this way are culpable of perpetuating the structural causes of young people's declining well-being through their complicity with the domestication of the dominated and, as a corollary, are guilty of symbolic violence.

FURTHER READING

The Children's Services Network (CSN) (2009) *Youth Participation: Growing Up?* London: CSN/Local Government Information Unit. Available online at **https://member.lgiu.org.uk/whatwedo/Publications/Documents/Youth%20participation.pdf** (accessed 18 March 2011). *This Local Government Information Unit pamphlet offers a useful analysis of ways local authorities have been trying to engage young people in democratic processes and in the design and delivery of services. A number of key recommendations are made which aim to ensure youth participation can become more meaningful and effective.*

Flores, KS (2008) *Youth Participatory Evaluation: Strategies for Engaging Young People*, San Francisco, CA: John Wiley & Sons. *Sabo Flores' book offers a detailed account of each stage involved in the youth-evaluation process – from designing a project through to its development, training programmes for young people in methods and finally the analysis and evaluation itself. The book offers a number of examples from participatory research Flores was engaged in.*

Matthews, H, Limb, M and Taylor, M (1999) Young people's participation and representation in society. *Geoforum*, 30(2): 135–44. Available online at ***www.sciencedirect.com/ science/article/pii/S0016718598000256*** (accessed 18 March 2011). *This paper offers a cross-national comparative perspective of children's and young people's participation and representation in the United Kingdom, mainland Europe and beyond. By making such comparisons, the authors offer important lessons for the debate on youth participation in the United Kingdom where mechanisms for involvement appear to be less well developed.*

Young, L and Barrett, H (2001) Adapting visual methods: action research with Kampala street children. *Area*, 33(2): 141–52. Available online at ***www2.warwick.ac.uk/fac/ med/study/cpd/current/pgle/modules/me937/0510/documents/10_action_research_ street_children.pdf*** (accessed 18 March 2011). *This paper assesses the value of visual 'action' methods as an innovative technique for eliciting information from street children. It concludes that visual methods allow a high level of child-led participation in research and provides a stimulus for eliciting further oral material.*

USEFUL WEBSITES

"Include Me Too" (the participation of disabled young people): www.includemetoo.org.uk

Partnership Works Partnership: www.participationworks.org.uk

Youth Work Matters resources: www.youthworkmatters.org/resources.asp

Chapter 4
Empowering others – working in an organisational context

CHAPTER OBJECTIVES

This chapter will help you meet the following National Occupational Standards:

2.3.2   Develop a culture and systems that promote equality and value diversity.

3.3.1   Develop productive working relationships with colleagues.

3.3.3   Involve, motivate and support volunteers.

5.1.1   Work as an effective and reflective practitioner.

5.2.1   Provide leadership for your team.

It will also introduce you to the following academic standards as set out in the QAA Youth and community work benchmark statement (2009).

7.1   Question and be prepared to deconstruct taken-for-granted and common-sense professional understandings.

7.2   Manage complex accountabilities, including being able to compromise and negotiate without losing integrity and professional principles.

Operate as critical and reflective practitioners.

Exhibit insight and confidence in managing themselves and draw on conscious use of self in working with others and in leading or participating in teams.

Introduction

In recent years, youth and community work organisations have become more 'professional'. Gone are the days (if they ever existed) where we are free to decide our own priorities as autonomous organisations. Now all organisations – statutory or voluntary, large or small, national or local – have strategies to work within and targets to meet. Organisations are inspected, and the results from these inspections matter. Organisations are accountable to numerous stakeholders such as funding bodies, government departments, local councils, partner organisations, community members and, of course, young people.

Developing the skills for management has become an integral part of professional qualifications in youth and community work. As students, you can expect to learn about strategic planning, performance review, recruiting and managing staff, fundraising, financial planning and managing change. You will probably study theories of motivation, of group dynamics and of leadership. The majority of reading material, however, will almost certainly come from the extensive literature about management and organisational theory, most of which has its origins in business settings. Two notable exceptions to these are Ford et al. (2005) and Tyler et al. (2009) (see 'Further reading'). The 'business' of youth work, though, is not about making profit, and it therefore follows that traditional management and organisational theories do not always fit our context.

This chapter is not a 'how to' guide to management. Instead, it will take a fresh look at key aspects of organisational theory – in particular, *leadership*, the development of *organisational structures and cultures*, models of *decision making* and *the management of staff* – and it will argue that we have to find ways to ensure that these are consistent with empowerment. We must find ways of integrating the *values* of youth and community work into our leadership and management practice. In essence, we must find ways to ensure that organisations can be effective and yet still be empowering.

Working in an organisational context

As youth workers, our practice is underpinned by the principle of empowerment. This brings with it a particular set of values about working with young people, which in turn have a knock-on effect in terms of how we work with staff. To be able to take the risks that empowerment demands, staff need to feel trusted. They need to know that if they work in empowering ways with young people, their organisations will back them up. Take, for example, a case where a staff member talks to a young woman under 16 about her pregnancy. Does the agency have a pre-set agenda about how these conversations will progress? If it is genuinely empowering, the answer is probably no. They will expect that the staff member will build a strong relationship with the young person, so that over time, she is in a position to make her own informed choice about what she wants to do and the support that she needs. The staff member needs to feel that their organisation trusts them to work within the organisation's values and to support the young people in the best possible way. Organisations that operate on a 'blame culture' do not support staff to be empowering. They encourage staff to stick to rules, to avoid taking risks or, in some cases, to take risks but keep this secret. None of these are good for staff, for young people or for the organisations themselves.

Our commitment to offering empowering environments in organisations affects all aspects of organisations – individual relationships between staff, the structure of the organisation, leadership and management functions, the decision-making processes, and arrangements for managing, supporting and supervising staff. The structures, processes and practices of our organisations must be consistent with the values of empowerment. If we try to mould our organisations into models prescribed by traditional management theory, we will find ourselves working in incongruent organisations – organisations that say one thing but do another, and organisations that do not offer the environment where staff can work in genuinely empowering ways.

Leadership

Leadership is a contested concept. The words 'leader' and 'leadership' do not mean the same thing to all people. As Jackson and Parry argue, 'Leadership is a phenomenon that everyone has an opinion on but few seem to agree exactly what it really is' (2008, page 12). For this reason, any comment on the theory of leadership must start with a discussion about what it actually means – and therefore what it might mean within youth and community work.

A dictionary definition of 'leader' is 'the person who leads, commands, or precedes a group, organization or country' (Pearsall, 1999). This particular definition mirrors conventional concepts of a leader whereby this person is the 'head' of an organisation, but rest assured – this is not the only way to see the role of 'leader'. Some youth and community workers are uncomfortable with the idea of being a 'leader' because it brings with it the thorny issue of power. There are conceptions of 'leader' (to be explored), which are more fitting with the values of youth work.

The word 'leadership' is not synonymous with the idea of one leader. 'Leadership' can be seen as a task, a function – but not necessarily a task that must reside in one individual who has the label of 'leader'. Leadership can be shared among several individuals and among groups. It can also be shared with young people. To explore further, it might be worth exploring your own ideas about leadership (see Activity 4.1).

It is worth noting that 'leaders' and 'managers' are not necessarily the same thing. Leadership is often seen as having a vision and being able to inspire others. Management is the process whereby this vision is turned into realistic plans, goals and targets. In the case of youth and community work though, our 'leaders' and our 'managers' are often synonymous, especially if we work in small organisations. Throughout this chapter, therefore, there will be no further exploration of the distinction between the two.

ACTIVITY **4.1**

Questionnaire
(Adapted from Raelin, 2003, pages 86–7)

Mark where you stand on the leadership views using a scale of 1–5. Mark 1 if you completely agree with the left viewpoint, and 5 if you completely agree with the

ACTIVITY **4.1** *continued*

right viewpoint. There is no correct answer; the questions are trying to help you to identify your values about leadership.

1	Organisations are most effective when they have one strong leader	1-2-3-4-5	The functions of leadership can be shared among many group members
2	Sharing power as a leader would be abdicating responsibility	1-2-3-4-5	Sharing power as a leader is a natural and desirable activity
3	Once you're a leader, you don't relinquish it to anyone else	1-2-3-4-5	Once you're a leader, you share it with others who may also be leading at the same time
4	One person should ultimately make the decisions on behalf of others	1-2-3-4-5	Decisions should be made by whomever has the relevant responsibility
5	A leader's duty is to control the direction of the organisation	1-2-3-4-5	The direction of an organisation should arise from the entire group
6	A leader should speak for the entire group	1-2-3-4-5	All staff should feel confident to speak for the entire group
7	The leader has responsibility for sorting out problems in organisations	1-2-3-4-5	There is no one person with responsibility for problems; this can be shared
8	Leaders should keep a professional distance from other members of the team	1-2-3-4-5	Leaders should engage in a public dialogue and be open with other group members

The inclusion of this questionnaire is not intended to suggest that there are clear-cut answers to the questions. As a general rule, however, the more answers that you scored as 1, the more you appear to concur with traditional conceptions of leadership. The more answers that scored 5, the more that your values will resonate with some of the non-traditional leadership models that are presented in this chapter.

Rather than merely looking at your scores, though, it might be more interesting to explore your *reasoning* behind your responses. You could try discussing this with a friend or a colleague and see whether you can articulate your own values and ideas.

How do these ideas of leadership fit with youth and community work? *The National Occupational Standards for Youth Work* include the following: 5.2.1 Provide leadership for your team. This includes statements that suggest that the leader should 'encourage and support others to take decisions autonomously' and 'encourage team members to take the lead when they have the knowledge and expertise and show willingness to follow this lead'. These are unambiguous statements that

Autocratic
Leader-centred
Power residing at 'the top'

Democratic
Group-centred
Shared power

Figure 4.1 Leadership continuum

indicate that youth work leaders are encouraged to incorporate concepts of shared or collective leadership into their practice.

Leadership is often represented as being on a continuum (Lewin et al., 1939); an example of the continuum representation is shown in Figure 4.1. All organisations, it is argued, can be placed at some point on this spectrum. More traditional 'command and control' organisations will be closer to the left side '**autocratic**', and less conventional '**democratic**' organisations will be towards the right. There is one further category: that of '**laissez-faire**'. Laissez-faire organisations are, in effect, leaderless. This is not because leadership is necessarily shared among others but because the leader has absented himself or herself from much of the business of the organisation. This may be because the 'leader' lacks essential leadership skills, or more positively, because they have made a conscious decision to offer high levels of autonomy to staff.

This chapter will explore three concepts of leadership, which are located at the 'democratic' end of this spectrum. These styles of leadership are more consistent with the values of youth and community work than the traditional autocratic approaches. The first relates to the development of leaderful practice. Two examples of leaderful practice will then be explored: collaborative leadership and servant-leadership.

Leaderful practice

The use of the word 'leaderful' gives a clue as to what it might mean. To suggest that an organisation is leaderful indicates that the task of leadership is shared among a number of people. It is a move away from the concept of one single leader. This is outlined by Raelin:

Leadership is being seen more as a plural phenomenon, something that the entire community does together. It does not need to be associated with the actions of a single operator. People in the community assume leadership roles where necessary, and through this collective action, leaderful practice occurs.

(2003, page 113)

In a youth and community work setting, the idea of a *community* is likely to include paid staff members, young people, volunteers, managers and possibly management committee or governing body members. Leaderful practice is based on the premise that all of these individuals have something to contribute towards the leadership of an organisation. Importantly, it does not suggest that everyone has the same role to play, or indeed that everyone has identical skills, knowledge and aptitudes. It is a *principled position* that works from a place of wanting to include (and indeed, empower) people who have an interest in the organisation.

Take, for example, a small independent youth work agency that is open during evenings and weekends and offers drop-in youth work sessions to young people living on an estate. Is there one leader here (i.e. the manager)? Or is it possible to imagine that the young people, the volunteers and the staff could share leadership? Young people might be able to play key roles in advertising the centre and in recruiting new members. Front-line staff might be best placed to develop the service in line with the needs of the members. The manager might play a key role in promoting the project to existing and potential funding bodies. Now, be careful. This organisation can only be described as *leaderful* if these individuals have a genuine role in leading their particular area of work. This is where problems can arise. Sometimes it is easier for a manager to delegate an area of work to someone else – rather than share responsibility for leadership. Young people are not leading, for example, if they are getting involved with advertising and recruitment through a strategy designed by someone else. To lead, they must be involved in discussions and decision making. This has implications for the way that organisations are structured and the way that decisions are made (more later on these areas).

Collaborative leadership

Collaborative leadership, as described by Peggy Natiello (2001, pages 59–85), makes explicit that there are power dynamics within organisations. Leaders and managers are often perceived as more powerful than front-line staff, volunteers or young people. In addition, there are personal power dynamics in that some individuals have a stronger sense of self and a higher level of self-confidence which in turn can give an impression of a powerful individual. The model of collaborative leadership starts from the position that its youth work managers or leaders must acknowledge the issues of power that are present within their organisations and within their relationships. Denying or minimising the significance of power is likely to increase its impact. Once power issues have been acknowledged, active choices can be made to address the imbalances that exist.

Collaborative leadership is an attempt to share power within organisations, to recognise that leaders do not necessarily have more expertise than the people with whom they work. 'Collaborative power represents a different paradigm of power' – a challenge to traditional, authoritarian ways of organising (Natiello, 2001, page 61). A leader who works with people collaboratively uses processes and systems that deliberately include people, where decisions are made collectively, where creativity and fluidity are encouraged. Leadership, power and influence flow from one person to another in an organic way – one individual does not have more influence over decision making purely because of their position within the organisation.

Talking about issues of power within organisations can cause anxiety. This is because power is often seen as negative. If someone has power, then this is a bad thing. Power in itself, however, is neither good nor bad; it is neutral. After all, we are committed to empowerment, and this implies that we want people to have more power. It is the way that power is used and abused that can make it appear either good or bad. In the model of autocratic leadership, power is located with individuals purely as a result of their organisational position. Collaborative leadership challenges this and instead places power in the hands of those best positioned to use it.

Take an example from a youth work setting. There is a project with six staff members and an activities budget of £25,000. This has been allocated so that a range of creative and innovative projects can be developed to meet young people's needs across the city. There are tough targets for how many young people should be engaged in activities and how many qualifications should be achieved. There is some flexibility, though, about how the budget is spent. Specialist staff might be employed, residentials could be offered and new resources and materials could be purchased. It could be spent in equal proportions throughout the year, or it could be weighted, so that more is spent in the first half of the year. Who should make the decisions about how this budget is allocated and by inference, the nature of the work that should be done?

In an autocratic model, these decisions would be made by the leader, the manager or possibly the finance worker. In a model of collaborative leadership, more people would have an input into the outcome. This would almost certainly involve the six project staff members, but it might also involve young people themselves. However, this is worth noting – this does not mean that the leader, the manager and the finance worker are not involved. Sharing power among those best placed to use it does not mean that power is taken away from people in particular organisational positions. In this case, all individuals will have their own perspectives by virtue of their organisational or personal positions, and between them, they have all of the resources in place to be able to make a good decision.

Using a model of collaborative leadership means that traditional distinctions between roles become less important. There is no reason to think that someone who has the title of 'Team Leader' is any better equipped to make a strategic decision than someone without this title. Collaborative leadership means breaking down some of the barriers between roles and building stronger relationships as individuals.

Servant-leadership

Servant-leadership is a specific model of creating leaderful practice. It was developed by Robert Greenleaf in the 1970s, and it is used in many different types of organisations including some large multinationals (most notably, Starbucks). It is important to note that organisations using servant-leadership usually do have one clear leader. This leader, however, is motivated by a set of values, which promotes the idea of creating leaderful organisations. The approach is strongly linked with values about wanting to enable others to share power.

Some might assume that the use of the word 'servant' implies an unhelpful power dynamic; one in which the 'servant' is expected to be at the beck and call of someone else. This is not the case. The use of 'servant' is intended to signal that a different type of leader can exist – one where the role of the leader is to see others – staff, customers, community – as their number one priority. They have to put the needs of others above their own ego or their own career path. The job of leader is to work to create environments where other people can thrive. It has been explained in the following way:

> *Servant-leadership is one model that can help turn traditional notions of leadership and organizational structure upside-down ... The focus of servant-leadership is on sharing information, building a common vision, self-management, high levels of interdependence, learning from mistakes, encouraging creative input from every team member, and questioning present assumptions and mental models.*

> (Spears and Lawrence, 2002, pages 142–44)

In a youth work setting, a servant-leader would see their role as helping others to thrive. It is thus closely linked to ideas of empowerment. The servant-leaders do not absent themselves from the process – far from it – but they do work from the principle that they want to enable others to fulfil their potential. They will at times stand back. An example might be of a youth work organisation that has a charismatic, popular manager. This individual has been involved in this organisation for many years and is well respected among their own staff team, young people and partner organisations. There is a danger that this person could start to be seen as the font of all knowledge, as the person with the answers to everything and as the one who knows best about the organisation. If this person was a servant-leader, they would be wary of this. They would want to be reflective about their practice and ensure that they were enabling others to share leadership wherever this was possible. This would mean listening to others, empathising and being willing to learn. It would entail making a conscious effort to build a sense of community and of ensuring that everyone was equal within the organisation.

Servant-leaders are different from autocratic leaders because of their values and their practice. They also have particular personal characteristics. They must have self-awareness and self-esteem or they will feel threatened by sharing power. They must be trustworthy. They must be willing to make mistakes and to enable others to do so. They must be prepared to learn (Bennis, 2002). Many of these characteristics overlap with essential skills for empowerment, and so if youth work leaders were servant-leaders, it is likely that they would work in ways that were consistent with youth work values.

Striving to develop leaderful practice is consistent with the values of youth work and particularly those of empowerment. It is important to realise, however, that sometimes decisive action needs to be taken. In these cases, someone (be this a leader, manager or worker) has to feel confident that they can act quickly and that they will be supported in doing so. Developing leaderful practice does not mean that everyone has to be involved with every decision. This would be unworkable and, indeed, undesirable. What it does mean, however, is that an organisation has a commitment to sharing leadership and responsibilities and to enabling people to be genuinely involved with the organisation. It is these principles that guide the practice and that are consistent with the values of youth and community work.

For alternative models of leadership to be viable, however, organisational structures and cultures must be consistent with the principle of creating leaderful practice. It is to this that we now turn.

Organisational structures and cultures

There is no one 'best way' to structure an organisation. Every organisation is unique, and the 'best structure' is entirely context specific. Is this an international organisation with a number of local projects, for example, Save the Children or OXFAM? Is it a youth work project that is run as part of a large statutory service, such as a city or county council? Is it a small independent charity that raises all of its own funds and is run entirely by volunteers? Is it a large youth work project with a series of self-contained projects? Each organisation will choose its own structure. Nonetheless, the way that an organisation is structured does communicate a great deal about its leadership style and its decision-making processes. 'Traditional' organisations are structured as pyramids with power residing with the person at the top. This person (or these people) takes control of the organisation. At the other end of scale are collectives that attempt to share power and control among all group members.

Organisational cultures might best be described as 'the way we do things round here' or 'the way we think about things round here' (Hudson, 2002, page 235). There are three levels in which organisational cultures can be expressed:

1. Through visible representations

   For example, notice the contrast between a youth project with a plush reception area and a smart receptionist – and an informal youth club with an open door policy. How do the different 'atmospheres' of these organisations affect visitors, staff and young people?

2. Through group behaviour

   New people watch and learn from those already in organisations. What do new staff members learn about watching the rest of the team interact? What do young people understand about your project from the way that you talk to them?

3. Through underlying beliefs

   What values are held by your organisations and the people within it? For this, try to look beyond standard practice such as 'we are committed to equal opportunities'. For example, what do people believe about how young people learn? Do we believe that some young people have more potential than others?

Organisational cultures can be deeply engrained. Sometimes they are so deep that people within the organisation are barely aware of them. Take an example of a youth project that recruits six new trainees. After a few weeks, it becomes apparent that four of them are doing very well, but the other two are having problems. No one can quite put their finger on it, but these two just do not seem to 'fit in' as well as the others. Why is this? The chances are that some of the answers can be found by looking at organisational culture. What assumptions have been made about how the trainees are expected to behave and are these assumptions fair? Do these two not 'fit in' because they are in some way challenging the pre-existing organisational culture?

ACTIVITY **4.2**

Draw an image to represent your own organisation (and if you wish, ask colleagues to do so as well). Try and draw the first thing that comes into your mind. There is no right and wrong way to do this. When you have finished, reflect on what you have created. If colleagues have participated, compare your images.

What does the image tell you about how you perceive your own organisation? Are the colours or shapes significant? What strikes you first about the image? Are there any feelings (e.g. anger, joy and confusion) attached to it?

If other people have created images, what are the similarities and differences between them? Some people might have drawn a diagram representing the staffing structure; others may have drawn a caricature; others a scrawl of colour. They all mean something different.

Your image(s) will tell you something significant about the structure and/or culture of your organisation.

Students undertaking this activity will often draw a diagram that represents their organisation's management structure. It will show, for example, the manager, team leaders, part-time youth workers, caretakers, administrators, management committees or governing bodies. Sometimes the chart will include volunteers, and even less often it will include young people. Frequently, though not always, the images drawn mirror 'traditional' organisational structures, where power resides at 'the top' with the manager or management committee. These representations communicate a great deal about the **structure** of an organisation, and we can make a series of assumptions about where power is located, how decisions are likely to be made and who is expected to shoulder the responsibility.

Occasionally, students will create an entirely different type of diagram for their organisation. Rather than using formal structures, images can be more representative of how an organisation might feel. In one group, for example, a student drew a picture of a high court judge wearing wig and gown. The face was scowling, and the finger was wagging (it should be stressed that this was *not* a youth centre). The student managed to communicate something powerful about the organisation – something that might best be seen as organisational **culture**. It suggested that the organisation held particular values about young people, and in particular, that young people might feel told off or punished. It sent a strong message about the power relationship between workers and young people. Incidentally, through drawing this image, the student was able to articulate her feelings about working within this organisation and to reflect upon some concerns about practice.

Other images that students have found helpful when describing their organisations have related to the following questions: what colour would your organisation be? What kind of animal best represents your organisation? If your organisation were a type of food, what would it be? Although these questions sound frivolous, an exploration of your initial responses might shed light upon your assumptions, perceptions and feelings about your own organisation. This can be helpful when we start to bring some organisational theory into the discussion.

Gareth Morgan uses metaphors to illustrate a range of ways that we 'see' organisations. These include organisations as machines, as brains, as organisms, as cultures and as political systems (Morgan, 1997). The distinctions are important as they are illustrative of the structures, processes and value systems of organisations. For now, just two metaphors will be explored: organisation as machine and as brain. These have been selected because they represent two ends of a spectrum. The first connects with the traditional autocratic leader using a command-and-control style. The second is diametrically opposed to this and shows a self-organising system with no single leader. This metaphor fits particularly well with the principle of empowerment.

Organisations that could be characterised as a 'machine' are best illustrated by F.W. Taylor (2003), an early proponent of the scientific school of management. The parts of an organisation, and the people within it, are cogs within a machine. The way to be most efficient is to have clear plans and procedures and to operate a command-and-control process. This was summarised by Morgan:

> *Set goals and objectives and go for them. Organize rationally, efficiently, and clearly. Specify every detail so that everyone will be sure of the jobs that they have to perform. Plan, organize, and control, control, control.*

> (1997, page 26)

A good example of the organisation as a machine is a production line. When making cars, every individual has a particular component to fit, a role to play. If someone is too slow, the whole production process is affected. The way to ensure efficiency is to have a smooth operation where every individual knows exactly what they are to do, how and when. Calculations can be made as to the most efficient way to complete a task. There is no room for individuality. Everything has to be done to specification. The role of the leader is to be at the top of the hierarchy and to clearly control the individuals and the organisational processes below them.

The mechanistic analogy has been challenged by those who argue that people are not machines. This argument is powerful in a youth work context. Youth work organisations are not machines. Machines do things or make things. There is an end product. This end product is uniform. Machines can be fine tuned and developed, so that the product is the best on the market. The product can be controlled. As youth workers, our primary role is to support young people to develop – whether this is called youth development, fulfilling potential, increasing self-esteem or improving skills is beyond the realms of this chapter – and therefore to refer to young people as 'end products' is problematic. Young people are not products because they cannot be controlled. Nothing that the 'machine' does can ensure that they will develop in a particular way. Young people are unique beings, and they will all develop differently. Similarly, our 'resources' are human beings too. We have paid and unpaid staff, and all the skills and expertise that they bring. That is all. These people are not parts of a machine. They will not all work in exactly the same way on every occasion. They will have good days and bad days. They will be recruited, and leave and be replaced, and the replacement will never be exactly the same as the person who left. This, therefore, is not science. It is not mechanistic. The metaphor of 'machine' does not work.

An alternative metaphor is that of organisations as brains (Morgan, 1997). This is a way of describing organisations as self-organising systems, the antithesis of the image of organisations as machines:

> *When it comes to brain functioning it seems that there is no center or point of control. The brain seems to store and process data in many parts simultaneously. Pattern and order* emerge from the process; *it is not imposed.*

> (Morgan, 1997, page 75, emphasis in original)

From this perspective, organisations are organised from within. A brain does not have a leader. It is genuinely self-organising and self-regulating. It 'engages in an incredibly diverse set of parallel activities that make complementary and competing contributions to what eventually emerges as a coherent pattern' (Morgan, 1997, page 78). The significance of this metaphor for youth work is that we have to let go of the idea that everything can be controlled. It requires a degree of trust that people (staff *and* young people) are capable of creating and developing systems that work. These systems do not need to be imposed from outside.

Dee Hock was a senior manager within Bank of America. He was given responsibility for the development of the VISA card, a project that would become a trillion dollar business. Hock was highly unusual because he was explicit in his commitment to self-organising principles. He was critical of the image of organisation as machine. For him, the most important aspects of organisations were not 'mechanical plans, detailed objectives, and predetermined outcomes' but rather 'a clear sense of direction, a compelling purpose, and powerful beliefs about conduct in pursuit of it' (Hock, 1999, page 202). Hock coined the phrase 'chaordic', by which he meant that

> *chaordic [kay-ordic] adj. from chaos and order.*
>
> *1. the behavior of any self-governing organism, organization or system which harmoniously blends characteristics of chaos and order.*
>
> *2. patterned in a way dominated by neither chaos or order.*
>
> *3. characteristic of the fundamental organizing principles of evolution and nature.*
>
> (1999, page 1)

The VISA card was issued by hundreds of different banks all over the world but did not have one controller. It was developed through a chaordic process. This meant that

> *leaders spontaneously emerged and reemerged, none in control, but all in order. Ingenuity exploded. Individuality and diversity flourished. People astonished themselves at what they could accomplish and were amazed at the suppressed talents that emerged in others … Position became meaningless. Power over others became meaningless. Excitement about doing the impossible increased, and a community based on purpose, principle, and people arose.*
>
> (Hock, 1999, pages 206–7)

An example from a youth work context might involve the way in which activities with young people are organised. Can there be a formula for what always works? If a particular project has worked well with a group of young people in one part of the city, can we assume that the same project will work elsewhere? Experience suggests that this is not the case. As all young people are different, and every group is different, and every community is different, youth workers need to be creative and innovative in the way that they work. They have to be prepared to adapt ideas, to listen to young people, to be flexible in their approach, to trust that some level of order will emerge from chaos. They have to be trusted, as professionals, to use their skills and aptitudes in the most effective way. This is not possible in a command-and-control system. They have to have the freedom to self-organise.

So what does all of this mean for the structure and culture of youth and community work organisations? It means that our structures and processes must fit with our values. Youth work organisations are value-driven organisations. We hold a set of philosophical beliefs about human beings, about learning, about growth and about empowerment – and from these our practice grows. We must make sure that our organisations are consistent with our values.

Steven Covey calls this 'alignment':

> *Once you have chosen the words that define what your vision, your mission, your values are, then you have to make sure that all of the structures and systems inside the organization reflect this … You can't come up with*

competitive compensation systems and still say you value cooperation. You can't say you value the long term when you're totally governed by short-term data. You can't say you value creativity when march-step conformity is the thing that's continually enforced. You can't say you value diversity when deep in the bowels of your recognition systems are prejudices about different kinds of groups or people.

(2002, pages 28–9)

This alignment of values, structures and cultures also influences the way that decisions are made within organisations. Let us now look at this.

Models of decision making

One common way of analysing decision making is to use a spectrum of four points:

Tells	*Manager identifies problem, makes decisions and then announces it*
Sells	*Manager makes decision and then persuades people of its worth*
Consults	*Manager identifies problem, asks for opinions, and then makes decision*
Joins	*Manager identifies problem and passes decision making to the group, with themselves as just one member*

(Tannenbaum and Schmidt, 1973, pages 162–4)

If this spectrum were to be superimposed upon Figure 4.1 (leadership continuum), it is likely that we would see that autocratic organisations have a tendency towards the 'tells' and 'sells' styles of decision making, whereas democratic organisations are more in line within the 'consults' and 'joins' approaches. What is interesting, however, is where leaders and managers appear to be adopting one style, but analysis suggests that another is in play. Have you ever been in the situation where you are asked for your views on how a particular problem might be addressed (looks like consults/joins), but then you are told what the outcome will be (i.e. tells/sells). In this case, the manager has used the method of consultation as a way of persuading you of the correct outcome. They have used a sells approach, but you think it is a consults approach. Confusion (and sometimes anger) is the result.

ACTIVITY **4.3**

Think back to a recent decision that has been made by your organisation or an organisation that you are familiar with. Try and think of a strategic one (i.e. one

---

that affects the long-term future of the whole organisation) rather than an opera-tional one (e.g. how many cups to order). It might be about applying for a new funding bid, moving premises, changing a logo, deciding to forge a new partner-ship or changing a policy.

Consider these issues:

How was this decision made?

Who was involved with the process?

Who were seen as important stakeholders?

Did you play a role?

Who made the final decision?

Did everyone agree with the final decision?

Where does this decision fit within tells-sells-consults-joins?

Youth and community work organisations need to be careful to ensure that the methods used for decision making are consistent with the values of youth and community work, the style of leadership and the organisational structures and cultures. If these are all consistent, then staff, volunteers and young people can trust their organisations. Organisations that inspire trust are much more effective (Spears and Lawrence, 2002).

It is not possible to suggest, however, that decision making should always take place in a particular way. Let us say, for example, that we wanted to use the 'joins' approach. This might work well when making decisions about what activities to run or what new policies to develop. Where it might fall down, however, is when a manager is in a large meeting with other organisations, and he or she is invited to give an organisational perspective on a particular issue. From this, a conversation ensues, which leads to an exciting multi-agency funding bid. It is important that the manager is able to engage in this conversation at the time. To suggest that they should involve everyone in their organisation would be unworkable – and it might lead the manager to ask questions in relation to their own autonomy and freedom to do their job. In this instance, the manager might have to engage in the conversations at the meeting and then return to their own organisation and use a 'sells' approach for whatever has been discussed.

As a general rule, however, it might be expected that youth and community work organisations are more comfortable with the 'consults' and 'joins' approaches than with the other two. Imagine that a decision needs to be made about whether a particular young person should be allowed to become a volunteer. There might be concerns about this individual in terms of their behaviour in the past, their volatile temperament and their complicated relationships with other young people. Staff members ask the manager what should happen. The manager has a choice. He or she could make a decision outright (tells or sells), but what is more likely is that they elicit views from others. Which staff members know this individual? Why do they want to be a volunteer? Are they the same person that they were in the past, or is there any evidence that they have changed? What are the positive outcomes that might result from enabling them to be a volunteer? Is there sufficient training and support in place? Unless the manager knows the young people personally, it is likely that they are not best placed to make a decision without consultation. They will therefore choose a 'consults' approach, or in some cases, the decision will be made collectively ('joins'). Everyone who participates in decision making will have some responsibility for the decision that has been made.

CASE STUDY

Sands School

To appreciate the uniqueness of this case study, you have to be prepared to clear your mind of assumptions of what 'schools' are like. This is a case study about a school, but it is an unusual school, and it is one that youth and community work organisations can learn from.

Sands School is a very small school (approximately 65 students and 15 staff). It is independent, which means that it has a great deal of control over what it does and how it operates. It is still subject to external inspections by Ofsted. In its last Inspection Report, it was rated as 'good' in relation to the overall quality of education and 'outstanding' with regard to the spiritual, moral, social and cultural development of students.

Sands School is a democratic school. This means that it has an explicit commitment to involve students in decision making. It wants students to have control over their own lives and the life of the school. It offers students a great deal of freedom, including the freedom to choose whether to attend lessons. In turn, it expects students to take responsibility for themselves, their own decisions and for the school. The principles, values and ethics are reminiscent of many of the values of youth and community work.

Sands School has no Head Teacher. This does not mean that someone is Head in all but name – there really is no Head Teacher. The school is structured in such a way that the School Meeting is the central decision-making body, and all decisions are made here. All students and staff attend this meeting, and decisions are made by majority vote. This means, in effect, that students have the power to control the direction of the school. There is also a School Council for which the School Meeting has delegated some tasks such as dealing with requests from visitors and dealing with interpersonal issues between students. This School Council is an elected body and at times has consisted entirely of students. These two meetings are important processes in how this school operates, but they are accompanied by many other processes, all of which are designed to ensure that the school is genuinely demo-cratic. This school is run as a community of students and teachers, and it works.

Sands School pushes the boundaries for empowerment to their extreme. For instance, the School Council suspended a student for suspected drug taking. At this point in time, the School Council was made up entirely of students and was chaired by a 14-year-old. How many youth organisations would be willing to allow one group of young people to exclude another? Take another example. The school has an admissions process, which means that all decisions about whether new students and teachers should join the school are taken by the School Meeting. In effect, there is a majority vote to decide who is allowed to join the school. Would youth workers want this process in place to decide which new young people or staff can join our youth centres? The answer to this is probably 'no', but this is not to say that the process is not effective at Sands School. In fact, it is seen by students as central to the way that the school operates. They can influence who comes and who goes.

This case study should be interesting for youth and community workers for several reasons. First, the age of the students at Sands School is 11–18 years. This suggests that young people of this age are capable of taking a high degree of responsibility. Second, the teachers at this school display many of the same values and attitudes that are engrained within youth work – respect, equality, freedom and empower-ment. Third, the leadership, organisational structures and cultures, and decision-making processes are unusual but interesting. Some if not all of them could work within a youth and community work setting.

Sands School has different aims to youth and community work. We are not try-ing to achieve the same thing. Our client group is different. Our way of working is different. Therefore, it follows that the way that we structure our organisations needs to be different too. But in the same vein, we are vastly different from cor-porate organisations and from businesses that operate to make profit. What do we have in common with these? Why would we choose to model ourselves on these organisations, any more than we would on the Sands School?

If a school can run with no Head Teacher, surely a youth and community work organisation can also use alternative models of leadership?

Management of staff

An effective staff team, whether paid or voluntary, is the lynchpin of any organisa-tion. Without skilled and motivated staff, the aims of youth and community work will not be met. We rely on staff not only to plan, deliver and evaluate work but also to build strong relationships with young people. It is this relationship building that is at the heart of youth work (Young, 2006).

It is one of the greatest challenges to youth and community work managers to deal with difficulties with staff. What happens, for example, if a volunteer does not adhere to the values of youth work in the way that they talk to young people? What should managers do if paid staff are not working effectively with colleagues? What can be done about a de-motivated team?

There is a great deal of material about 'good practice' with recruitment, selection, training, supervision, dealing with disciplinary issues and grievances. This chapter will not reproduce this material. Instead, the question of how staff issues can be addressed in ways that are consistent with the values of empowerment will be explored.

First, it is worth exploding one myth. Being empowering in organisations, and being empowering in relation to staff, is not about being nice to people. It is perfectly appropriate for staff members to be challenged if they are not working satisfactorily. What is important, however, is that we have developed the kinds of relationships where challenges can be seen as constructive, and where staff members are given the opportunity to learn and develop. We must place relationships at the heart of our work with each other and not just at the heart of our work with young people.

ACTIVITY **4.4**

Imagine that you are a manager within a small youth work organisation. Fred has recently been recruited as a full-time staff member. At interview, he impressed everyone with his previous experience, with his ideas for projects and with his apparent commitment to the attitudes and values that are essential within youth work.

When Fred started in post, you encouraged him to be creative and innovative and to come up with his own ideas. You did not want him to feel constrained by what had been done before. You felt that this was a chance for new projects to come forward. He was enthusiastic and stressed how excited he was to be able to given such freedom and trust.

After a few months, you start to worry. Other members of the team have been complaining because they never know where Fred is or what he is doing. When questioned by them, he always explains that he is off somewhere, doing something – but no one is really sure what this might be. You feel sure that Fred is doing a good job, but you arrange to meet with him anyway to get an update on exactly what he had been doing.

Things to think about:

What will you say to Fred in the meeting?

Is there anything you want to say to the other staff?

Is there anything that you wish you had done differently?

With hindsight, what have you learnt about how to manage staff?

You might like to think about whether there is anything in this example that is reminiscent of your own experience of working – either from the position of Fred or from the role of the manager.

Fred is an example of someone who wants to have autonomy and freedom. Indeed, he may well be someone who thrives in this environment. He may well be doing an extraordinary job. Nonetheless, the fact that he appears unwilling to talk to other staff members about his work is in itself worrying. Being autonomous and free (indeed, empowered) does not negate the importance of accountability. We should all expect to be accountable. Having autonomy does not mean that Fred is in complete control of what he does. No one is in complete control of their own work. He needs to be accountable to other staff and to young people. There are project aims, and targets, and monitoring procedures. Working towards goals and adhering to policies are not optional. This point is summarised by Bell and Bell (2003): 'Empowerment does not mean unlimited license … "just do whatever you need to do … " It means responsible freedom'.

The concept of 'responsible freedom' is a useful one, as it implicitly acknowledges that staff members have wider responsibilities. They are not young people, users or beneficiaries of a service – and even if they were, they still could not do whatever they wanted. Freedom is always limited.

A key issue with regard to Fred is that you, as the manager, have not yet established a strong relationship. You have only known him for a short while, and you have no experience of the way that he works. You are basing your judgments about him on trust – and trust in itself is not a strong enough basis for managing someone. You must find a way of developing a stronger relationship with him and encouraging him to develop relationships with his other colleagues. These can then be the basis through which trust can be formed.

There is another possibility to consider with regards to Fred. Despite his enthusiasm about being trusted, he might feel lost and unsure about what to do. His reluctance to engage with colleagues may be because, in fact, he has not been doing a great deal of work. If this is the case, then Fred is an example of someone who experiences the collaborative power model as a void. These individuals stand on the outside, feeling anxious or vulnerable about what is expected of them, or even resentful that no one is helping them by issuing clear instructions and telling them what to do. Should they be left to find their own way, and risk floundering, as Fred has? Or is there a more helpful way of supporting them?

Offering useful supervisory relationships is one way of helping individuals. Valentine argues that good supervisory relationships can be seen as an opportunity for the supervisor and the supervisee to work together to create a situation that best meets the interests of all parties, including the organisation as a whole. This allows 'the supervisor to engage in the relationship as an equal partner rather than solely as an understanding listener, with their own legitimate interests and concerns' (Valentine, 2004, page 125).

In the case of Fred, it would have been useful if, at an early stage, an open and honest relationship had been established between himself and the manager (who is assumed to also be the supervisor). It would have been clearer from the start what was expected from Fred, and what he could expect from the organisation. What did 'autonomy' mean, for example? How did this relate to his accountability to other staff and to young people? This may well have helped to address some of the issues that were to arise later. It means being clearer about the 'contract' that there is between him, the manager and the organisation. If this had happened, it might have helped him to step into his personal power and use it in a constructive way that would have helped him *and* the organisation. Supervision sessions would have been a concrete way of monitoring his progress and a space for him to ask for the help that he needed.

However, situations will arise in youth and community work, as in any organisation, where it is clear that a staff member is not working effectively and that no amount of support will remedy this situation. It has not yet reached this point with Fred, but in other cases, it might. At times like this, we have to look towards formal disciplinary procedures. It is important to be clear here. Disciplinary procedures should be a last resort, when all other avenues for resolving issues have been exhausted. They are, nonetheless, important procedures, and in certain cases, there is no choice but to use them. This can be an uncomfortable decision for managers; however, it is worth remembering that staff members are not the same as young people. Working with young people is the core business of our organisations. We want to be empowering. We want to help them to grow. We encourage them to make mistakes and to learn from them. Staff are different. We might still want to be empowering and to help them grow – but not at the expense of the work with young people. Staff have voluntarily chosen to apply for jobs within our organisations. As part of this, they will have made claims about their skills, knowledge and aptitudes. They have agreed to work within policies and procedures. They have a responsibility, therefore, to work in the best interests of the organisation. If there comes a point where the needs of the organisation, and in particular, the needs of young people, are at odds with the staff member, the young people must come first.

The management of staff, especially where difficulties arise, is one of the most challenging jobs for managers. It is nonetheless still vital that we manage these relationships in a way that is consistent with the values of youth and community work. Staff need to feel respected, valued, trusted and supported – and yet it is of course still appropriate that they feel challenged, constructively criticised, questioned and held to account.

Concluding comments

There are copious amounts of management and organisation theory on the shelves of bookshops and libraries. New websites seem to appear every day. Yet we must not assume that all of this theory is relevant and applicable to the context of youth and community work. We have a set of values that underpins our work with young people. We must make sure that the way that we run our organisations does not contradict these values.

We must, therefore, develop our own organisation and management theory that fits our own context. We must find ways of working within organisations that are consistent with the underlying principles of youth and community work. To do this, we need to be prepared to engage with traditional organisational theory, but we must critically analyse its usefulness in our own contexts. We must ensure that our organisations are fit for our own purpose.

CHAPTER REVIEW

This chapter has explored central issues within organisations – leadership, organisational structures and cultures, decision making, the management of staff – and has offered ways in which these can be consistent with youth and community work values, particularly empowerment.

The following points have been highlighted:

- Organisations that want to be empowering should strive to be leaderful, rather than using models where power resides in one single leader.

- The structures of our organisations communicate volumes about our values and principles. Organisations that seek to be empowering should consider the metaphor of the 'brain' that is representative of a self-organising system.

- Organisational cultures need to be developed to ensure that they are consistent with the principle of empowerment.

- An analysis of how decisions are made within organisations is useful as it highlights whether the methods used are consistent with shared leadership and with empowering structures and cultures.

- The management of staff is a key issue within organisations. The value of putting strong relationships at the heart of organisations has been highlighted, and the role of good supervision within this has been stressed.

FURTHER READING

Ford, K, Hunter, R, Merton, B and Waller, D (2005) *Leading and Managing Youth Work and Services for Young People.* Leicester: National Youth Agency.

This offers useful information on key issues in managing youth services, such as planning, performance review, managing staff and so on.

Jackson, B and Parry, K (2008) *A Very Short, Fairly Interesting and Reasonably Cheap Book About Studying Leadership.* London: SAGE Publications.

Although not specific to youth and community work, this book offers a comprehensive overview of most of the major literature on leadership theory. It is accessible and well referenced. It even includes recommendations on what films to watch with regard to leadership and many relevant websites.

Tyler, M, Hoggarth, L and Merton, B (2009) *Managing Modern Youth Work*. Exeter: Learning Matters.

This is an excellent book with chapters on many issues about management – managing resources, people and so on.

Chapter 5
Resilience

C H A P T E R   O B J E C T I V E S

This chapter will help you meet the following National Occupational Standards:

1.1   Facilitate learning and development of young people through youth work.

1.2   Plan and implement learning activities in youth work.

1.3   Promote young people's self-awareness, confidence and participation.

1.4   Promote access to information and support.

It will also introduce you to the following academic standards as set out in the QAA Youth and community work benchmark statement (2009).

4.6.1   Models and meanings of development through the life course:

–   the links between education and development holistic approaches

–   the physical, mental, emotional and spiritual aspects of resourcefulness and resilience

–   critique of normative and deficit models of development

Introduction

The practice of youth work is dependent on the theoretical approach that individual youth workers bring to their practice. Perspectives on youth are related to biology, psychology or sociology or a mixture of these disciplines. Historically, the perspective that has dominated the debates and research on young people is one based in biology and developmental psychology (Hall, 1904). This is the view that young people experience a period of adolescence as a time of storm and stress shaped by the hormonal changes that they experience. The works of Freud contributed to this view as he viewed adolescence as a period of internal struggle. He viewed the pre-adolescent period as a time when the child develops a balance between the 'ego' and the 'id'. In adolescence, the child is dealing with instinctual impulses that disrupt this balance. The ego is torn between the strong impulses of the id and the restrictions of the 'superego'. This conflict makes adolescence a time of tremendous stress and turmoil. The perspective on youth that emerges from these disciplines is that young people are transitioning from children to adulthood, and the focus in these approaches is on the problem of youth and the ways young people can be helped or supported to avoid risky or destructive behaviour patterns.

One of the perhaps most dominant themes in the sociology of youth (see Brake, 1980; Frith, 1984) is that it takes issue with the notion that you can approach the study of youth from the existence of essential characteristics in young people because of their age and the assumed link between physical growth and social identity – that is, *the concept of adolescence*. The argument is that what limits this concept is that it is ahistorical and static and that age as a defining feature gives insufficient weight to difference, process and change. The use of age as a category approach tends to rest on the assumption that the similarities within the category are more significant than the differences. It offers little grasp of the ways in which the experience of growing up is a process, negotiated by young people as well as being imposed on them. The themes in the literature on young people from sociology focus on this issue of definition: dependence and independence; changing responsibilities and social, economic and generational differences between young people as key aspects in the development of life.

ACTIVITY **5.1**

Youth describes an age group that is distinguishable from children and adults. What would sociologists suggest are the problems with this?

When you allocate young people to this group, for example, from age 11 up to 25 years; does a 25-year-old have more in common with an 11-year-old than with a 26-year-old? Does using age as a division help?

At what age do children stop being children and become 'young people', and what differences define this?

At what age do people become adult and why?

The term youth, then, describes some aspects of people's social position, which are an effect of their biological age but not completely determined by it. If, for example, the end of youth is marked by taking on adult roles – marriage and children, work and a career, our own home – then people stop being young at a great variety of ages. The picture is even more complicated if we compare similar age groups in different societies or at different historical times. Everyone makes a move from child to adult, but different societies at different times organise the move differently. The transition can take days or years. The task of sociology and anthropology is to show how particular societies organise the process of growing up. For sociology and anthropology, youth is not simply an age group, but the social organisation of an age group. Sheila Allen, in her 1968 article, 'Some theoretical problems in the study of youth', states that *it is not the relations between ages that creates change or stability in society, but change in society that explains relations between different ages* (Wyn and White, 1997, page 9).

The social construction of youth

Youth describes the movement between dependence and independence, and the concept of 'dependence' has to be related to particular institutions in society. An important aspect of the transition from childhood to adulthood concerns the idea of 'responsibility'. Young people begin to take on more responsibility for their lives in relation to homework, evening and weekend employment, studying, leisure behaviour and social relationships.

The organisation, norms and values of a family will shape how much dependence or independence a young person is allowed. The education system marks the initial move towards independence from the immediate family. Schools are the only institution which give people of the same age a common experience formally and which treat age with biological precision – we have to attend school from ages 5 to 16 years whatever the differences. Youth culture is particularly associated with leisure activities, and it is this – clothes, music, other interests and activities – that makes them appear as a distinct social group. So much of the sociology of youth is about the sociology of leisure, as it is here that young people most visibly behave independently – expressing non-adult preferences and values.

When people enter the labour market and earn a wage of their own they take on adult status. With the development of industrialisation, the duration of the transition from childhood to adulthood has lengthened. The division of labour has become more complex, the production process increasingly more technological, so economic roles in society need more preparation and more training. Young workers certainly have more independence than those at school (or the young unemployed) but their progression towards adult status continues. This is partly a matter of money – young people are paid less than adults, and it is assumed that they still live with their parents, having no 'dependants' of their own. The organisation of the workplace will also impact on this – for example, if young people enter an apprenticeship scheme, they are still dependent on adult authority. Young people are expected to 'mature', and if maturity is an even vaguer concept than youth, it nevertheless lies behind the most precise way in which society defines the youth/adult divide, with the law.

Quiz: At What Age Can a Young Person:

Leave home

Hold a tenancy

Leave school

Smoke cigarettes

Buy or drink alcohol

Drive a motor cycle

Drive a car

Marry

Consent to heterosexuality activity

Consent to homosexual activity

Vote

Receive benefits

Be charged in an adult court

Stand for parliament

Join the army

Answers to Quiz

Leave home	18 years
	A 16- or 17-year-old will need consent from a parent or guardian to leave home, but if they leave against their parents' wishes, they are very unlikely to be ordered home unless they are in some danger
Hold a tenancy	18 years
	However there are ways in which a landlord can rent accommodation to someone under 18 years
Leave school	16 years
Smoke cigarettes	It is not illegal for children and young people under the age of 18 years to smoke tobacco. It is however illegal for anyone to purchase tobacco if aged under 18 years or any person over the age of 18 years to buy tobacco for a person under 18 years
Buy or drink alcohol	Before the age of 18 years, you are not allowed to buy alcohol in pubs or shops, or drink alcohol in pubs. It is also unlawful for anyone else to buy alcohol for a person aged under 18 years to consume in a pub. If you are aged 16 or 17 years you are entitled to drink wine, cider or beer to accompany a meal in a hotel or restaurant. Any child over the age of five years can drink alcohol at home or on other private premises. It is an offence to give alcohol to a child under five years, even in her or his own home
Drive a motor cycle	16 years up to 50 cc
Drive a car	17 years
Marry	16 years, with written consent of parents or guardians
Consent to heterosexuality activity	16 years

Consent to homosexual activity	16 years
Vote	18 years
Get benefits	Young people who are 16 or 17 years can only claim benefits, such as jobseekers' allowance, in limited circumstances. Under 25 years receive a lower rate of benefit than those over 25 years, and 16- to 17-year-olds receive less again. The majority of 16- or 17-year-old care leavers are provided with financial support by social services and most cannot claim benefits
Be charged in an adult court	18 years
Stand for parliament	21 years
Join the army	16 with parental consent

One of the striking things illustrated by the quiz is the quantity of restrictions and constraints placed on young people – their lack of control and their powerlessness.

Youth and social differences

It is misleading to emphasise the qualities or otherwise of 'Youth' per se, because the young are neither a homogeneous group nor a static one (Jones, 1988, page 707).

So far the discussion has centred on what young people have in common, but while they may therefore share problems of dependency in family, school and work, and may be defined as equally responsible (or irresponsible) in legal terms, they face these problems from different institutional positions. An important difference among young people is 'gender'. Growing up male and female involve different activities, different constraints and different patterns of socialisation. This is not only a result of the sexual differences focused by puberty but also a consequence of boys' and girls' different roles in the family. As long as adult men and women are not equal (e.g. in terms of job opportunity and wages) so women will be in some respects 'dependent' on men, and this obviously has consequences for girls moving towards 'independence'.

Another difference is social class. A 16-year-old working-class male school leaver looking for a job is 'young' in different ways to a 16-year-old public school boy getting ready to do A levels and expecting to go to university to get professional qualifications. There is a structure of power and wealth in society that impacts on young people. This structure of power and wealth is shaped by history. The sociologist Karl Mannheim drew attention to the importance of the term 'generation' to explain that people grow up at particular historical moments and may therefore share crucial historical experiences with members of their age group. War is the most commonly cited experience that may bind a generation together; also technological changes and booms/slumps in the economy produce 'boom', 'cyber' and so on generations.

Statistic

Staying on in some form of post-16-year education is now the experience of nearly four in five young people in most parts of the country (Office of National Statistics, 1999).

Yet, less than half did so in the late 1980s.

Participation in further and higher education also rose from 11% in 1975 to over 30% in 1995 (cited in Coles, 2000, page 5).

Historically then, as well as sociologically, youth is the product of the shifting relationships of family, school and work. Both youth and childhood have had and continue to have different meanings depending on young people's social, cultural and political circumstances.

This means that the focus on youth is not on the inherent characteristics of young people themselves but on the construction of youth through social processes (such as schooling, families or the labour market). Young people engage with these institutions in specific ways, in relation to historical circumstances. As discussed in Wyn and White's *Rethinking Youth*,

> *European youth do not exist … young people in the different countries and regions that make up Europe negotiate very different circumstances from each other. They are shaped by both the material*, objective *aspects of the cultures and societies in which they grow up; and by the ways in which they* subjectively *interpret their circumstances.*

> (1997, page 9)

Sociology views youth as a social construction, shaped by social, economic and cultural factors. Despite the differences between the biology and psychological accounts discussed at the opening of this chapter, there are similarities. *Within the sociological perspective, youth still emerges as a problem*.

Problem youth

The theoretical approach that shaped the sociology of youth in the 1960s is one that emphasises the contradictions facing young people, particularly young men, in post-war capitalist society. Central to this approach is the Birmingham School, which produced a series of studies examining the complex relationship between class, economic structures and cultures and youth subcultures. These studies used the methodological approach of a Marxism shaped by the works of Gramsci and Althusser. The prime explanation given for the emergence of youth subcultures is that they are a form of resistance by young people to the contradictions presented by the established social order. Subcultures emerge as a way for young people to make sense of their marginality, their lack of control, in society and as a form of resistance to the dominant culture (Hall and Jefferson, 1976). *The focus is on youth as a process.*

Young people are embarking on a process involving transitions in many dimensions of life, towards becoming adult and establishing a livelihood. Yet, increasingly, the meaning of adulthood – and how it is achieved, marked, acknowledged and maintained – is ambiguous. The period of youth is significant because it is the threshold to adulthood, and it is problematic largely because adult status itself is problematic. Subcultures emerge as a way for young people to make sense of their marginality. Thus, for some sociologists, the development of subcultures is to do with how young people handle the contradictions of the social construction of youth.

What are these contradictions?

The contradictions facing young people were discussed in a series of texts dealing with masculinity and transition to adulthood (Willis), powerlessness (Cohen), alienation and the lack of a political alternative (Seabrook) and later with the influence of the women's movement, studies of femininity and young women (McRobbie). These themes are discussed alongside the idealisation of youth as a time of freedom for mobility and without responsibility, of endless opportunities for creativity and experimentation. What emerges from this approach is again the problem of youth, through unemployment resulting in continuing dependency on parents or the state – a long transition to adulthood, the alienation resulting in a drug culture or the difficulties in facing young people growing into the rights and responsibilities of citizenship.

ACTIVITY **5.2**

What issues or problems challenge you and how do you overcome them?

Do you value what young people say? How do you let them know this?

What do you do if their values are very different to yours?

Deficit model in contemporary politics and policies

Currently, the policies and analysis of young people who are not in education, employment or training are shaped by the notion of deficit and risk and as Jeffs and Smith (1999) state, these young people are demonised as 'thugs, users or victims'.

There are a number of problems with these approaches. First, categorising young people as at risk of social exclusion by listing the risk factors can have the effect of lowering expectations among the professionals whom they encounter. The professionals may have low expectations and this can result in a self-fulfilling prophecy of enhancing the young people's propensity to 'risk' and/or lowering their aspirations and ambitions. Second, these ways of framing groups of young people have not resulted in any major shifts.

Mizen's (2003) review of New Labour's youth policies also indicates that after some initial successes in relation to the targets set by the government on participation in education for 16- to 18-year-olds, these too have had a minimal impact. He states that improvements registered between the low point of 1997 (74.9% of the cohort) and 2001 (75.5%) have been slight and unevenly distributed. Staying-on rates for 16-year-olds have declined throughout this period and, for 17-year-olds, remain static, with the proportion of 16- to 18-year-olds remaining in education and training in 2001 still lower than the comparable figure for John Major's last full year in power (76.3%). In relation to undergraduate students numbers actually fell by nearly 50,000 between 1996–97 and 2000–01 (Mizen, 2003, page 465).

Mizen's article also points to the lack of change in the figures for truancy and the little, if any, variation in permanent school exclusions, while the 'proportion of young people not in employment, education or training between 2000 and 2001 [has] returned to the level of the final three years of Conservative rule' (Mizen, 2003, page 466). For writers such as MacDonald and Marsh (2001), Byrne (1999) and Levitas (1998), the policies based on the concept of social exclusion are at best flawed and contradictory. In *The Inclusive Society? Social Exclusion and New Labour* (1998), Ruth Levitas traces these contradictions to three competing discourses in the policies of New Labour. She argues that the inconsistencies generated by these discourses ultimately ensure their failure to deliver social cohesion and social inclusion. She labels these discourses as RED (redistributionist discourse), MUD (moral underclass discourse) and SID (social integrationist discourse).

The first, RED, refers to redistribution of wealth and resources, which has as a central focus the construction of an anti-poverty strategy as a mechanism for social inclusion. In other words, this perspective takes a structuralist approach to social exclusion. MUD refers to Murray's (1990) thesis of the underclass, and this discourse contains a conservative and moralising approach to the socially excluded. Here, the explanation for exclusion is constructed as individuals living on benefits, supplementing incomes with criminal activities, thus producing a culture of state dependency and deviancy. In this discourse, the socially excluded are self-excluding through their behaviour. Such behaviour is gendered and emphasises the role of 'lone mothers' as undermining the role of the family in reproducing 'socially accepted' norms and values including the work ethic and adherence to societal laws. As Murray states,

> It turns out that the clichés about role models are true. Children grow up
> making sense of the world around them in terms of their own experience.

*Little boys don't naturally grow up to be responsible fathers and husbands.
They don't naturally grow up knowing how to get up every morning at the
same time and go to work … That's why single parenthood is a problem for
communities, and that's why illegitimacy is the most worrisome aspect of
single-parenthood.*

(1990, page 31)

The third discourse, SID, refers to the strategy adopted to combat social exclusion. The emphasis here is on policies that widen access to employment, education or training to gain paid work in the labour market. Employment is seen as the mechanism for achieving social integration and social and community cohesion.

There is some overlap in these discourses and this can be illustrated with reference to the work of Frank Field (2003). Field was a former director of the Child Poverty Action Group and the Low Pay Unit up to his election to parliament in 1979. As minister for Welfare in the Department of Social Security from 1997 to 1998, he moved from an analysis based on the politics of class to one based on the politics of behaviour. In the move, he re-invigorated nineteenth-century debates on poverty by reproducing notions of the respectable, deserving poor in contrast to those who are undeserving.

Like Murray, Field (2003) outlines the impact of vandalism and anti-social behaviour on communities and the lack of police powers to combat youth delinquency. He argues that the causes lie in the rise of dysfunctional families who do not teach young people a 'set of common decencies' and moral and social responsibilities for their actions. His strategy focuses on changing the behaviour of young people by giving the police powers to act as surrogate parents if parents are unable to control their children. The Crime and Disorder Act 1998 sanctions this strategy by giving the police powers to enforce curfews and anti-social behaviour orders. Field also attempts to link the receipt of benefits to the notion of civic responsibility by contract compliance. The welfare contract would outline the rights and responsibilities of the recipient to the society and to their community.

Some of the contradictions of these approaches are highlighted by Williams (1998) when she argues, for example, that Welfare to Work programmes for women fail to acknowledge their child care responsibilities and their unpaid labour in the home. She states that the focus upon the labour market as a solution to integration obscures the very processes within the labour market, which render some groups of people at much greater risk of poverty (1998, page 17).

Similarly Levitas (1998) argues that the focus on paid work or, in the case of young people, the emphasis on education, employment and training as the chief mechanism for social inclusion in New Labour's policies, places the responsibility and remedy onto the individual and shifts attention away from the inequalities of wealth in society and the lack of stable employment prospects. In addition, there appears to be a lack of awareness of gender inequalities, homophobia, institutionalised racism and discrimination towards people with disabilities, all of which produce distortions in the labour market. The deficit model does not work, and there is a need to contest the assumptions and stereotypes which shape this approach to working with young people.

REFLECTIVE ACTIVITY

Bring to mind a young person for whom you have concerns. Divide a piece of paper into two columns.

On the left side list the problems and challenges facing this person.

On the right side, list the positive things or resources this young person has.

My expectation is that the left hand side will be easier to complete than the list on the right hand side. You might notice that these items are purely diagnostic, whereas the items on the right hand side are the potential building blocks or foundation stones.

Themes in the deficit model

The discourse on the deficit model can be easily recognised by a number of terms commonly used in policy documents, the popular press and within the general population when discussing young people. These terms are 'deviant', 'dangerous', 'delinquent', 'disordered' or 'vulnerable'. These labels are normally used to describe young people who are deemed to have risk taking and unhealthy lifestyles or who are the resource poor – 'mad', 'bad' or 'sad'.

The article by Jeffs and Smith (1999) outlines the problems of conceptualising young people through the 'deficit' model. It begins,

> *Politicians and policy makers in Britain and Northern Ireland currently tend to talk about young people in three linked ways – as thugs, users and victims. As* thugs *they steal cars, vandalize estates, attack older (and sometimes, younger) people and disrupt classrooms. As* users *they take drugs, drink and smoke to excess, get pregnant in order to jump the housing queue and, hedonistically, care only for themselves. As* victims *they can't find work, receive poor schooling and are brought up in dysfunctional families. Yet so many of the troublesome behaviours associated in this way with young people are not uniquely theirs.*

(Jeffs and Smith, 1999, page 45)

However, what is missing from this piece is an articulated alternative to this conceptualisation and one that can be utilised in youth work practice. Another term for the deficit model is the 'problem-focused' approach. The same process of identifying risks, dysfunctions, deviancy and lack of competencies are linked with this approach. Though perhaps not as derogatory as the notion of deficit, this perspective also means that workers bring a particular set of expectations of young people to their work, so that, however well meaning, the strategy will be one of prevention rather than exploration and high expectations.

A more positive set of interventions using government funding for widening participation in education has produced initiatives that are focused on finding the 'gifted' and 'talented' among the social excluded. This approach is similar to the deficit model, that is, it is based on the premise that 'talent' is a scarce resource in the population, and this approach thus reproduces a conservative and limited analysis of the capacities of young people. The literature on leadership duplicates this idea that every group needs a leader to succeed. These ideas are widely circulated through projects and activities with groups and communities considered as socially excluded. This impacts on the role of the youth worker in that they can become part of the process of reproducing rather than negotiating and challenging dominant ideas in society.

Strengths-based work versus work on resilience

More usefully, there has emerged an approach to working with groups of young people deemed 'at risk' or a 'risk to society', which is critical of the deficit-based approach to young people and seeks to promote a 'strengths-based' orientation. Some work has been done on this in the United States and Canada with particular regard to work in formal institutions, for example, schools and health care programmes. This work provides a different strategic approach for youth workers and enables them to develop types of programmes with young people based on their experiences. Both strengths-based and resilience vocabulary are interchangeable in some of these studies. We need to explore the different terminology used in this new approach, that is, what is the difference between strengths-based work and resiliency work?

There are some similarities between these two approaches in youth work, for example, the idea of capacity building and strengthening protective factors. The *difference* appears to be around the notion of overcoming and conquering challenges and directed towards young people who may not have any protective factors. From both perspectives, young people are viewed in terms of their competencies and the idea that young people can make a positive contribution to society. Strengths-based approaches would be centred on 'positive' youth development, whereas work on resilience is enabling young people to overcome particular challenges they may face whether in their family life, their schooling, their health, their ethnicity, peer groups or their sexuality. You can do strengths-based work with young people who may not face these challenges but may lack self-esteem, self-confidence or a sense of purpose. So there are similarities, but the client group would probably be different.

The following case study may help to illustrate the distinction I am trying to make (Source: Holland, Reynolds and Weller, 2007, pages 106–107).

CASE STUDY

Lauren

Lauren was academically able, always seen as bright at school and strongly attached to her family and community. She had professional ambitions and saw education, including university, as providing the pathway to realise these. Her family gave her considerable support: her father provided his 'princess' with material support and social capital through contacts for work; her mother provided emotional and practical support and advice, intervening at key moments to alter Lauren's trajectory. A critical moment occurred before Lauren's first interview in 1998 (aged 14 years), when her beloved grandmother died. Her grandmother had provided a strong value base for Lauren and was part of a rich vein of adult female culture on which she drew to construct her own identity. However, at her second interview in 1999, Lauren had been going through 'a bad patch'. She had been in a relationship with a 'bad boy' who had gone to prison and had been drawn into the criminal and drug culture of the estate. Her mother had intervened and helped her get back on track: Lauren said that she was her 'saviour' who 'sat me down and we had a chat about it all, she put me right really. Helped me see where I'd been going wrong … we sorted it out'. Lauren reasserted herself as a good pupil, did very well in her final examinations at school and went on to college to do Advanced Levels.

But after a few months at college, Lauren lost confidence and became very stressed. Her mother intervened once more, suggesting that perhaps she was not a paperwork person but a more practical person. She advised Lauren to give up college, steering her towards training and to work in 'hair and beauty'. Her interviewer commented that 'a sense of instability and chaos, linked to rapidity of change underpinned all Lauren's interviews' (Researcher Notes). Lauren had considerable personal resources to draw on, she was able, had a strong work ethic and a desire to succeed through her own efforts. She was determinedly avoiding the more usual female route through early pregnancy that her peers on the estate had followed and planned to have children 'in ten years' time'. While she had considerable resources to draw on in her family and community, these bonds pulled her back to more limited horizons. At this point, it was looking increasingly less likely that Lauren would realise her academic potential and pursue the university route.

Lauren could draw on a number of supportive factors (see Table 5.1) and had resources that are not available to young people who are in care, leaving care, have left their families of origin because of violence or abuse, or who have few educational resources.

Table 5.1 Examples of risk and protective factors

Childhood factors

• Birth injury/disability/low birth weight	• Social skills
• Insecure attachment	• Attachment to family
• Poor social skills	• School achievement

Family factors

• Poor parental supervision and discipline	• Supportive caring parents
• Parental substance abuse	• Parental employment
• Family conflict and domestic violence	• Access to support networks
• Social isolation/lack of support networks	

School factors

• School failure	• Positive school climate
• Negative peer group influences	• Sense of belonging/bonding
• Bullying	• Opportunities for some success
• Poor attachment to school and recognition of achievement	at school

Community factors

• Neighbourhood violence and crime	• Access to support services
• Lack of support services	• Community networking
• Social or cultural discrimination	• Participation in community groups

Adapted from Durlak (1998) and National Crime Prevention (1999, cited in Centre for Parenting and Research, 2007).

Risk and protective factors

The influence of any of these factors on outcomes is very complex. It may be that some risk factors are more important than others and the same reasoning for protective factors. The research on these issues is still struggling with refining the analysis to the extent that the key factors are isolated, but it is not there as yet. Another complication is that experiences will differ and the impact of risk or protective factors will be dependent on the individual and mediated by the impact of their socio-economic background, their gender and/or ethnicity and their abilities or disabilities. The important point for youth workers is how they can influence outcomes by extending or providing protective factors through their interactions with young people.

ACTIVITY **5.3**

Was there a time when you felt isolated and afraid? How did you cope?

A key research finding from British studies (Rutter et al., 1998) is that young people from very disadvantaged family backgrounds can develop resilience through forming a close relationship with a supportive adult, through a positive school experience or being given an opportunity to find a 'turning-point' or (importantly from the perspective of youth work) through an opportunity to have some autonomy and control when participating in activities.

CASE STUDY

The importance of a supportive intervention

Isabel was born into a family in which, though stability was ensured through the fact that her father was in secure employment, there was little emotional or physical security. The father drank very heavily and had violent episodes. The mother was also violent and emotionally withdrawn. Neither parent saw the value of education for their daughter. Despite this, Isabel loved school and used books as a way of escaping from the tensions of the family home.

Isabel wanted to do her French examination when she was 14 years old. Her best friend Maggie, in fact she was her only friend, had not studied for the examination, did not want to go to school and wanted Isabel to be with her.

Isabel and Maggie spent the day wandering through the local park. The next day the teacher asked Isabel what happened and she guessed from her embarrassment that she had played truant. Her response was to ask Isabel to talk about what she had seen and learnt on the previous day. The teacher's response impacted on Isabel in the following way: rather than facing the barrage of criticism or angry disapproval – the response she usually experienced from adults – Isabel felt valued and cared for by her teacher. This feeling stayed with her for years.

The role of a supportive adult is illustrated by this case study and research studies with survivors of abuse also note the importance of this factor. A study of children abused by a parent (Katz, 1997) tracked their progress and adjustment for fourteen years from the age of 5. The criteria used for evaluation is mental health, school achievement and a sense of fulfilment.

> *Among members of the survivor group, there was a generally supportive adult involved in their life who proved to be a stable resource over a long period of time. This individual didn't necessarily spend a great deal of time with the child. The important protective influence was his or her stability and availability over time. Most of the survivors mentioned a teacher in school or another person who inspired confidence and encouraged them on. Among the non-survivor group, there was generally no mention of a similarly supportive adult.*
>
> *(Katz, 1997, page 38)*

ACTIVITY 5.4

Was there a time when you felt that the young person you are working with had no sense of purpose? What did you do?

Working from this perspective means working with young people to find which resilience factors can be highlighted as part of their skill set. Thus, they are not defined by their lack of 'normality', but rather the approach is one that seeks to explore with these groups the resources that they use to empower themselves. Rather than taking the role of an examining expert, the worker here will act as a facilitator and a *rapporteur* of the key factors that have enabled these young people to find their strengths and resilience in the face of a range of social deprivations.

A different approach and strategy for youth work

Example of problem youth: the case of teenage mothers

Young women who become mothers under the age of 20 years are viewed as a social problem for a number of reasons. There is a fear of young women bringing up children without a male head of household, resulting in a 'problem' family. The lack of a male breadwinner would also mean that these parents are more likely to be dependent on state funding for support and housing. These young women, by moving away from the traditional nuclear family, threaten the stability of the society, and their children are more likely to fail at school, become delinquent and break the law. This neo-liberal approach is highly popularised through the media and policy initiatives. A more systematic approach would still view young mothers as victims and vulnerable, as the statistics support the notion that the majority of teenage mothers are not from the professional class [see Social Exclusion Unit (SEU), 1999]. What is striking about the focus on teenage pregnancy and early parenthood in policy debates is the absence of perspectives from young mothers themselves.

The study by McDermott and Graham (2005) argues that, despite the social problems faced by these young women that include poverty, lone parenting and stigmatisation, they construct a resilient account of their approach to motherhood. The following statements from young women support this perspective:

> I loved being pregnant. I thought it was brilliant … had this feeling of being worthy of something and I just felt … radiant all the time. And I was looking forward to having the baby … I couldn't wait for this little thing to look after and love.

> I was like looking at him in the cot and I was thinking: 'God, he is actually mine, you have grown up now you are a woman'.

> There are a lot of things that people say about young mothers, that we have got no ambition, that we're just young people that want to get pregnant to get flats. I will tell you now, whether I got pregnant or not, I am a determined person and I would have got my own flat anyway.

> (Cited in McDermott and Graham, 2005, page 70)

103

Motherhood enabled the young women to transition to an adult status and pro-vided them with a strong attachment and a sense of self-worth and value. These attributes are key determinants of a resilient identity.

What is resilience?

Resilience refers to a capacity to do well despite adverse experience (Gilligan, 2000, page 37).

The concept of resilience has developed concurrently within a number of academic disciplines, such as psychology, education, social work and epidemiology. The number of definitions of the term is shaped by these disciplinary areas. There is an ongoing debate and literature on both the theory and the concept. To sort through the themes of this literature, it is useful to view some of the early studies as these described the factors that make up the concept, such as perseverance, positive out-look and purposefulness, and more recent studies as focusing on *how* resilience is acquired. The main areas of focus are writings that deal with definitions followed by the debate about resilience as a personality trait or an acquired skill. The key point for youth workers is that *'based on longitudinal studies, researchers have found that for every child who comes from an at-risk background who later needs intervention, there is a higher percentage of children who come from the same background who become healthy, competent adults'* (Krovetz, 1999, page 7).

The question here is what are the key differences between these two groups? Research conducted by Benard (1991, 1993, 1995, cited in Krovetz, 1999, page 7) indicates that there are four key factors that can account for resilience from chil-dren with risky backgrounds: social competence, problem solving skills, autonomy and a sense of purpose.

ACTIVITY **5.5**

Find out and list the meanings of social competence and autonomy. What would you consider to be key problem-solving skills and how would you help to develop a sense of purpose with the young people you work with?

An influential piece of research is one conducted on a group of Romanian children who were institutionalised in the notorious orphanages under Ceausescu's regime in the 1990s. Following the fall of this regime, the children were adopted and brought to Britain. The findings from the research were that, despite the consider-able problems facing these children such as emotional and social deprivation and physical hardship, approximately one fifth of the children had caught up devel-opmentally with their British cohort. For a graphic description of the conditions endured by these children, there are two short videos on YouTube and a further documentary available online (www.der.org/films/lost-and-found.html). The key point here is that this evidence challenges the idea that one's life chances are shaped by early socialisation. For example, Bowlby's work (from a psychological perspective) on the role of mothers and juvenile delinquency – *Forty-four Juvenile Thieves* (Bowlby, 1946) – appeared to strongly support the idea that the cause of troubled youth could be traced to the separation of young people from their mother at an early age and the lack of maternal love. Bowlby's arguments imply that there is an essential need for a particular type of mother–child relationship, and if one does not receive this, then the consequences for the child are that a psychopathic personality can develop. Among other feminist writers, Ann Oakley (1972) argues strongly against this essentialist account of socialisation using socio-logical and anthropology evidence to support her claims.

This chapter will follow the usage developed by health, education and social care practitioners who employ the notion of resilience to indicate how some individuals are able to 'bounce back' and be healthy, thus producing relatively good outcomes despite adversity. This approach to working with children and young people is critical of the deficit-based approach to these groups and seeks to promote a 'strengths-based' orientation (Luthar, 1991). Some work has been done on this in the United States with particular regard to work in formal institutions, for example, schools and health care programmes. Thus, the concept of 'building' resilience among individuals is becoming increasingly popular and appealing for policy makers both nationally and internationally. Some aspects of the 'building' resilience approach, however, duplicates the deficit model, and there is a need to explore the resilience factors which children and young people are currently using to manage their lives. There is then a need to produce some robust and reliable evidence-based practice tools to move forward with this strengths-based focus.

Developing resilience

One of the most useful things to do is to begin to build up a picture of a resilient person. However, when this is attempted, for example, in the work of Frankl (1959) and represented by Thomsen (2002), the elements are divided into those that are endowed by nature and those that can be nurtured. I would argue against the notion of natural attributes, for example, the notion of a natural leader or a more easy personality. Each of these characteristics has an ideological bias and can be shown to be culturally specific and developed. Let's take, for example, the notion of an intelligence quotient (IQ). These have been shown to be culturally specific and also that one can be trained to take them. So what exactly are they measuring? However, the notion that intelligence can be reliably measured enters into every day and academic debates usually without challenge or with the view that nature can be improved on, as demonstrated by the following account of emotional intelligence and resilience building.

What factors are at play, for example, when people of high IQ flounder and those of modest IQ do surprising well? I would argue that the difference quite often lies in the abilities, called here emotional intelligence, which include self-control, zeal and persistence, and the ability to motivate oneself. These skills, as we shall see, can be taught to children, giving them a better chance to use whatever intellectual potential the genetic lottery may have given them (Goleman, 1999, cited in Thomsen, 2002, page 91).

The recent development in sociology of writings on the body and the attempt to explain the complex interrelationship of biology, society and culture while rejecting the essentialist and sexist accounts of the socio-biologists is very useful. This work alerts us to the need to hold to both an account of individual experiences and the constraints of society in the development of identities and personalities. In other words, I am trying not to dismiss the role of biology or nature, but, for youth and community workers, their job is to work in the realm of the social, the local, the community and reject the notion that some people are born leaders, or bad, or sad or good or evil. The characteristics of resilience listed below can be used as a useful guide:

Good health

Easy-going temperament

Sociability

Self-efficacy

Confidence

Optimism

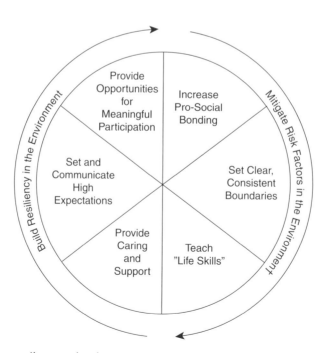

Figure 5.1 The resiliency wheel
Source: Holland et al. (2007, pages 106–107)

Hope

Social support

Problem-solving ability

Internal locus of control

Appraisal skills

Flexibility in goal setting

Ability to mobilise resources

One of the key writers on the concept of resilience is Michael Ungar (2004), a Canadian academic. In the preface to his text, he poses the idea that resilience or the lack of resilience has to do with power and experiences of powerlessness. A key writer on surplus powerlessness here is Lerner, who explains the process as follows:

> *Much of what I have been describing as Surplus Powerlessness involves conscious, though misguided, assessments of how much one can accomplish in any particular moment. The set of beliefs and feelings about ourselves leads us to feel that we will lose, that we will be isolated, that other people won't listen, and that in turn leads us to act in ways in which these very fears turn out to be true. We are so convinced others will betray us that we betray them first, and we are so sure that no one will take care of us that we act in ways that make it impossible for anybody to come close.*

(1991, page 13)

Ungar's (2004) work on resilience is rooted in his interviews with young people who engage in risk-taking activities, and this approach differs radically from accounts of resilience, which are based on young people overcoming adversity and hardship. Rather his analysis, written within a post-modernist paradigm is critical of the approach taken by professionals.

Ungar's work on resilience is unique in that he explains how young people who are living with risk and adversity interpret their actions in a way which is different from the account provided by health and social care professionals. In fact, what is viewed as risk is actually a resilient adaptation to adversity. In looking at how these young people construct their accounts of their lives and exhibit what he terms 'hidden resilience', he demonstrates how professionals working with young people who exhibit 'risky' behaviours actually hinder their development. As he explains,

> *One of the surprising things that youth tell me is that collaboration between professionals, paraprofessionals, lay service providers, families, and communities impedes the healthy development of children when caregivers participate in the construct of problem-saturated identities. High-risk youth challenge these identities by arguing, ironically, for recognition of the health-enhancing aspects of deviant behaviours such as drug and alcohol use, early*

sexual activity, time spent living on the street, self-inflicted injuries, negative peer associations, truancy, and custodial dispositions.

(Ungar, 2004, page 6)

Ungar's argument is that the young people involved with these behaviours give them a different interpretation and meaning than the one provided by professionals. His qualitative research, based on interviews with 'troubled' youth, suggests that young people give their behaviour a different meaning than a list of problems experienced by young people. The extract below, from one of his case studies, illustrates his position. His research would support the anecdotal evidence from youth and community workers who have watched the phenomenon of ASBOs becoming a badge of honour and status. As Ungar explains, the social construction of youth as a problem leads some young people to act on this construction and build their identity and a sense of power from acts that are labelled delinquent (see discussion in Ungar, 2004, pages 134–5). Using a Foucaultian notion of power, he demonstrates how these young people resist the forces of the dominant groups who marginalise and problematise them and take onto themselves a sense of their own power by constructing an identity, which they imbibe with status.

CASE STUDY

Mark

Mark described his life after being discharged from the institution as better, not so much because he was now healthy and normal but that through contact with other disturbed youth he had experienced acceptance for who he felt he really was. His explanation of his health helps to construct a link between mental health and the empowering experiences that lead to feelings of acceptance.

Mark left the hospital having authored a powerful identity as a troubled youth who was healing and who was accepted by his equally troubled peers. In the hospital everyone knows what your problems are. And you don't get the feeling of rejection because they're in the hospital too, *he explained. Acceptance as a patient ... became a catalyst for finding a place among peers and in the community that, oddly, was more powerful and health enhancing than the powerless position inhabited before being labelled clinically disordered (Ungar, 2004, page 10).*

CASE STUDY

Young woman and youth worker

Years ago I heard a story that has always stayed with me. A frontline worker in a shelter for street youth in a large city had a young woman staying there one night. This was a street-hardened child who had, as the story was told, been through a number of foster homes, some of them abusive, had experienced abuse and neglect in her own home and, finally fed up, had fled to the streets for survival. There she had found a lifestyle that involved delinquency, drugs and prostitution. The next morning, the young woman woke up and along with her friends came to breakfast. That morning, the worker on duty met an angry teen with enough attitude to survive and keep away anyone who might have considered trying to help. She had not been to the shelter before but had come in with her friends whom she was determined to impress.

Breakfast was a healthy spread of cereal, toast, some fruit and whatever else had been donated or scrounged. The room was warm and clean, although it looked more like an institution than a home. When the young woman came to the table, she complained to the worker that this was 'some lousy f-ing place', all because they did not have her favourite cereal. I am not sure quite what possessed that worker to do what he did, but there was something in the magic of such moments when we all know there is an opportunity to make a difference. The worker told me that he looked at the girl and decided that she was right and that it really was disappointing that her favourite cereal was not there. She deserved, at least once, to get what she wanted. He put on his coat and wandered the half block down to a nearby corner grocery store returning a few minutes later with the sugary product the young woman had demanded. He did not make any fuss about it. He just quietly placed it on the table in front of her with a bowl, a spoon and some milk.

Whatever happened for that young woman in that moment made a difference in her life. She began to come to the shelter regularly and attend some of the programmes that were meant to help her, first to survive on the street and then, when ready, to move permanently to a group home for youth with nowhere else to live. She even began to volunteer at the shelter. It was not therapy in the traditional sense of the word, but this 'intervention' that began with a box of cereal did privilege one young woman's understanding of what she needed. Together, she and the shelter worker had challenged the pathologising discourse that had contributed to her marginalisation. She was, after all, surviving as well as she could. Her helpers just needed to understand how she explained her behaviour (Ungar, 2004, pages 273–274).

Ungar's (2004) work provides some useful ideas for planning work on resilience. The most important lesson from his studies is that young people need a sense of empowerment, which underpins the belief that they are valued members of society. In using this concept, as with the concept of empowerment discussed in the first chapter, there is a need to look at the organisation or agency, which is delivering services for young people.

Throughout the literature on the resilience and strength approach, there is an emphasis on the problem of powerlessness and the need for workers to enable young people to come into power through interactions, interventions and activities. The need to construct a working environment, which is based on the values of empowerment, is discussed in the first chapter of this book. The starting point is the belief in the capacity of each young person to think, reflect, to accept and overcome challenges, to evaluate and learn, and to achieve a sense of purpose. It is clear from this that the worker needs this belief for themselves and their work-based colleagues.

ACTIVITY **5.6**

What work practices support resiliency among the workers and within youth work practice?

A key finding from the research on resilience is also the role of a supportive adult. The notion of support here will require the agency in the first instance to examine the literature and programmes on young people at the work place and begin to assess using interviews with young people on how they interpret their lifestyles and risk taking.

ACTIVITY **5.7**

What expectations do you hold for the young people you work with?

Workers and young people are not viewed as passive agents in this approach; rather both are engaged in joint 'sense making'. Thus, the discussions will be based on the model that both exhibit a kind of reflective intelligence as they negotiate the meaning of questions, on one hand, and the meaning of answers, on the other. This will enable the workers to join the young people in the process of analysis and interpretation.

Through the evaluation of interviews and participant observation, the aim is to explore the design, implementation and evaluation of young people's engagement to assess the factors that limit and those that support the building of resilience. There should be an opportunity for a core group of young people involved in the process to deliver peer group work in school, based on residential training weekends.

From this, the objective is the development of resources, a toolbox of methods that can be used by youth workers to engage young people in affirming their strengths, and in so doing, building resilience for a shift away from a deficits-based and toward a strengths-based approach will serve as a strong foundation for youth work practice.

Resilience is not always positive

It is necessary to mention that despite the overwhelming evidence in the literature about the positive attributes of resilience, the interpretation of resiliency may be based on ideological factors. I mean by this that fighting through adversity, over-coming obstacles, exhibiting determination and perseverance rather than weak-ness is an ideal type construct of a strong personality, and in western capitalism, strength is valued over weakness and vulnerability. Rather than resilience being viewed as a positive trait, in a study in 2007 by Solomon et al., (cited in Atkinson et al., 2009), some viewed the ability of some workers to cope in traumatic situations as based on the repression of emotions rather than on resilience. This article sug-gests that *this is an area that requires further research in terms of the relationship and interaction between these two important psychological dimensions* (Atkinson, 2009, page 141)

CHAPTER REVIEW

Nationally, the publication of *Youth Matters* [Department for Education and Skills (DfES), 2005] continues to follow the strategy adopted in *Bridging the Gap* (SEU, 1999), which individualises the problems faced by young people and discusses these problems in terms of rights and responsibilities. The structural inequalities and constraints faced by layers of young people is glossed over and the construc-tion of an umbrella policy incorporating children and youth services under the policy document *Every Child Matters* (DfES, 2003) narrows the scope of the statu-tory youth services, all of which makes for a depressing read. There is, however, a section from these policies, which could be classed as encouraging and this makes reference to youth participation in local decision making. Interestingly, the reference to participation clearly stated in *Every Child Matters* (DfES, 2003, pages 78–9) changes in *Youth Matters* (DfES, 2005). *Every Child Matters* (2003) opens up a space that stresses the participation of children and young people in decision-making processes, while *Youth Matters* conceptualises young people as consumers without any reference to empowerment and perceives participation in decision making filtered through their parents – see points 88 and 249 in *Youth Matters* (DfES, 2005, pages 22 and 66). Workers can either view the possibilities cynically or respond creatively to *Every Child Matters* to use this as a platform from which to develop models of citizenship, which can empower young people to make their own responses to local and governmental policies. The structural constraints fac-ing young people obviously need to be understood and challenged, and the social exclusion agenda can open up a space to talk about a wide range of issues and initiative activities, which can contest assumptions and stereotypes. An example from Hull is a project of young lesbians and gays in collaboration with the police on homophobia. These activities help to shift the debate from fighting to have homophobia recognised as an issue to one that centres on the best way to fight it. A similar process has happened with the anti-racist struggle in the city. I have no doubt that examples of these types of activities are duplicated across the country. They illustrate the inventiveness of workers in the context of a Conservative-led Coalition government, which is reluctant to pursue policies that could address the structural constraints faced by young people. The lack of clarity about the meaning of the concept of social exclusion is usually viewed as a negative. However, if it is accepted that the last and recent governmental approach is contradictory, this may actually open up a positive space for practitioners who are charged with implementing government strategies. Understanding and using these spaces can counter the despair experienced by workers faced with a government which continues to demonise young people. The lack of a constructive progressive political alternative means that it is only in the spaces presented by the contradictions, ambiguities and omissions of government policies that empowering youth work can presently flourish.

The purpose of this section is to adapt the concept of resilience – defined as the capacity to bounce back or resist adversity (see Newman and Blackburn, 2002) – into an application that can be used by youth workers to enable young people either to acquire or enhance the factors that foster resilience. This is based on Rutter's (2007) argument that resilience is not simply a personality trait, which is, fixed by nature. By contrast, resilience is viewed as a process that emerged from a struggle with factors such as poverty, disability, poor and inadequate schooling and teaching, dysfunctional family relationships or unsupportive family structures. The view from Rutter (2007) is that the ability to overcome these hardships is a skill that can be acquired and learned, and it is this perspective that makes this concept useful for practitioners.

FURTHER READING

Lerner, M (1991) *Surplus Powerlessness: The Psychodynamics of Everyday Life and the Psychology of Individual and Social Transformation*. New York: Humanity Books.

A very powerful and unique explanation of power and powerlessness.

Thomsen, K (2002) *Building Resilient Students*. California: Corwin Press.

This book gives a clear and useful account of using the concept of resilience.

Ungar, M (2004) *Nurturing Hidden Resilience in Troubled Youth*. Toronto: University of Toronto Press.

A very distinctive approach to the topic.

Chapter 6
Reflective practice

This chapter will help you meet the following National Occupational Standards:

1.1.1   Enable young people to use their learning to enhance their future development.

1.2.1   Plan, prepare and facilitate group work with young people.

1.3.1   Facilitate young people's exploration of their values and beliefs.

2.3.3   Challenge oppressive behaviour in young people.

5.1.1   Work as an effective and reflective practitioner.

It will also introduce you to the following academic standards as set out in the QAA youth and community work benchmark statement (2009).

7.1   Question and be prepared to deconstruct taken-for-granted and common-sense professional understandings.

Recognise and compare multiple, competing perspectives and challenge the status quo and dominant ideas.

7.2   Operate as critical and reflective practitioners.

Promote experiential learning and reflection in self and others.

Exhibit insight and confidence in managing themselves and draw on conscious use of self in working with others and in leading or participating in teams.

Introduction

Empowerment does not happen by chance – regardless of how committed we are to it. If youth and community workers want to be empowering in our work with young people, we have to have the ability to think about and reflect upon our practice. It is only through this reflection that we have any hope of becoming empowering practitioners.

Similarly, young people cannot even start to feel empowered (such as taking control of their own decisions and their own lives) unless they have started to engage in a process of critical thinking and reflection. As youth and community workers, we have to pay attention to how we might support young people in developing these skills and abilities. They are not necessarily an automatic outcome of being involved with exciting activities and opportunities.

This chapter explores the connections between empowerment and reflection. It starts with a definition of reflection, and then builds on this by looking at a range of perspectives and models. By the end of the chapter, we will have considered ways in which youth workers might develop our own reflective thinking, as well as ideas for how to build processes for reflection into our work with young people.

What is reflection?

ACTIVITY **6.1**

Imagine you are walking in an unfamiliar area and come to a branching of the roads. You have no knowledge to fall back on, no idea which way is correct. It is starting to get dark.

What do you do?

When presented with the scenario in Activity 6.1, students offer any number of answers. Some people will look around and find any information which might help them to know which way is correct. Some will take the well-trodden path. Others will sit and wait for a passer-by. Some will have been well prepared and be able to consult their GPS or map. Others will be paralysed by anxiety and not know what to do. Rarely does anyone suggest that they would toss a coin and let fate decide.

John Dewey writes about this situation in his groundbreaking text, *How We Think*. He uses it to illustrate what he means by 'reflection', explaining that

> *in the suspense of uncertainty, we metaphorically climb a tree; we try to find some standpoint from which we may survey additional facts and, getting a more commanding view of the situation, may decide how the facts stand related to one another.*

(Dewey, 1910, page 11)

This metaphorical climbing of the tree can be seen as reflection. Youth workers make decisions based on reasons. Our actions are underpinned by thought. We might be guided by gut reactions and intuition. All of these are tied up in the concept of 'reflection'. When we reach a fork in the road, we do not usually toss a coin and hope for the best. We consider our options and make informed decisions as to which path to take. Reflection is a crucial part of the thinking and decision-making process for youth workers. The process of reflection has been defined as this: 'Reflection is an important human activity in which people recapture their experience, think about it, mull it over and evaluate it' (Boud et al., 1985, page 19).

Some youth workers appear to be more reflective than others. Does this mean that reflectivity is an innate characteristic? Or is it a skill that can be learned? Given that so many professionals are required to be reflective – youth workers, teachers, doctors, police officers, therapists, social workers, to name but a few – it seems reasonable to argue that it is a skill that can be learned. And in the context of the work that we do, where we want to enable young people to reflect on their lives and take control of their futures, it is imperative that we believe that this is a skill that can be learned. A key part of our roles is to support young people to develop their reflective abilities. Nonetheless, we have a difficult challenge. As Mezirow and Associates argue,

> It is not that some adults are inherently incapable of thinking abstractly, becoming critically reflective, or making reflective judgments. It is only that they have not learned how to think in these ways. Many are socialized in subcultures – including those of schools – that place little or no value on such ways of knowing.

> (1990, page 395)

As youth and community workers, we may find that what we are trying to do is challenging for young people. They are used to being told what to do, what to think and how to behave. We are trying to do something different. We want young people to think for themselves and to make their own decisions about what to do and how to behave. This is counter-cultural and may take a great deal of 'unlearning' on the part of young people. Nonetheless, it is the cornerstone of the work that we do and is thus worth exploring in some depth.

Kolb (1984) – the learning cycle

An example of using this in practice might be a 'debriefing' discussion that takes place at the end of a youth work session. Imagine that the session has been busy, with several challenging incidents. One young person was asked to leave the building due to threatening behaviour. Another young person had an accident while playing football. Two young people complained because they wanted to do an arts session, but this had not been organised. With regard to the learning cycle, the session itself can be seen as the Concrete Experience [1]. The discussion that takes place between the staff is the Reflective Observation [2]. What happened during the football game to cause the accident? Why was the young person threatening? What explanation is there for the disgruntlement about the art workshop? Had staff indicated that this would be run this evening? The Abstract Conceptualisation [3] takes place where experiences from other sessions are brought into the discussion to find patterns or where the team tries to work out why particular incidents have occurred in the way that they have. Is there an issue with staff ratios, so that accidents keep happening? Is there an inconsistency between the behaviour of staff, so that some young people are unclear about how they are expected to behave? Finally, decisions are made about how to improve for the next session, and these ideas are implemented (Active Experimentation [4]). The arts workshop might be offered. The banned young person might be invited to have a conversation about their behaviour. New guidelines for football matches might be implemented. This next session is then another Concrete Experience [1], and staff will debrief after this [2] and so on.

Although Kolb's learning cycle can be a useful way to illustrate the process of turning experience into learning, it runs the risk of over-simplifying the process of reflection. First, it implies that the process of reflection is largely cognitive (a thinking process), and it makes no specific mention of emotional aspects. Boud et al. (1985) are critical of this, arguing that unprocessed feelings such as anger, anxiety, excitement or fear can be obstacles to reflection. For them, acknowledging and processing these feelings is an integral part of the learning cycle. In the situation above, for example, the staff member who banned the young person from the building might be feeling angry, hurt, upset, guilty or even personally threatened. If these are not acknowledged – and to some extent, processed – it will be very difficult for him or her to fully engage in the rest of the conversation. In situations like these, finding ways of talking about feelings is of paramount importance.

The learning cycle also implies that reflection is part of a *staged* process, where one step neatly starts where the other finishes. This is not always the case. Take the debriefing session described previously. Does the process of reflection really start once the youth work session has finished? Imagine that the youth project had been open for three hours. Were staff members not engaging in reflection *throughout* the session rather than just at the end? What happened, for example, when the young person was banned from the building? When was this decision made and by whom? What did they take into account when they made their judgement? Could they have employed an alternative course of action, such as giving the young person a warning, or did they have no choice? The likelihood is that the worker(s) in question engaged in a complex process of reflection that took place in virtually the same instance that they were acting. This process is described by Schön as 'reflection-in-action'. In effect, it enables the learning cycle to be concertinaed together, so that the four stages can happen at more or less the same time as one another.

Schön – reflection-in-action

The context in which youth workers operate mean that we have to be creative and spontaneous. It is impossible to plan for every eventuality. Centre-based workers do not usually know how many young people will come through the door, or what interpersonal conflicts they may bring, or whether our best-laid plans will meet their needs and interests. Detached youth workers operate with an even greater level of uncertainty. An essential skill of a youth worker, therefore, is being able to be responsive to a situation that presents itself at the time. This might be described as 'thinking on your feet'. Donald Schön, author of *The Reflective Practitioner*, calls it 'reflection-in-action', by which he means

> when someone reflects-in-action, he becomes a researcher in the practice context. He is not dependent on the categories of established theory and technique, but constructs a new theory of the unique case.

(1983, page 68)

There is a word of warning here. 'Thinking on your feet' is not the same as 'making it up as you go along'. Although they sound similar, the latter implies that a youth worker can be ill prepared and use 'spontaneity' as a cover up for this. This is not the same as reflection-in-action.

Schön describes reflection-in-action as being a 'conversation with the situation'. Given that conversation is integral within youth and community work, this definition seems fitting. Just as we use conversation with young people as a way of helping them 'make sense of themselves, their experiences and their world' (Young, 2006, page 87), we can use conversation with a situation to make sense of the contexts in which we operate. Youth workers need to pay attention to the environments we are in and the young people we are working with. As we work with human beings, and no two humans are the same, this makes all our situations unique. An activity that works brilliantly with a group of young people in one setting will fail miserably in another – yet on the surface, the situations seem virtually identical. Why is this? What can be tried instead? What is specific about each situation that makes a difference to what works?

ACTIVITY **6.2**

Spend some time thinking about the context in which you work. Imagine you had invited a youth worker from a different organisation to come and work alongside you for a few sessions.

What information do you need to give them in advance? Try thinking more broadly than the 'facts' of times and dates – what else do they need to know, so that they can mentally prepare for this work?

A 'conversation with the situation' means spending time knowing and understanding your own context. When working as a youth and community worker, it is useful to have a 'conversation with the situation' to not only try and understand your audience (i.e. young people) but also understand the organisational context in which you operate. This can make a tremendous difference to the type of work which you feel able to do, especially the risks that you feel able to take (see

Chapter 4 for more on empowerment in organisational settings). In response to Activity 6.2, you might have considered exploring issues such as the following:

- the numbers and ages of young people who attend session;

- any feedback that has been given from young people in terms of what they want from sessions or how they have responded to previous sessions;

- the 'atmosphere' in which sessions usually take place – it could be, for example, calm, volatile, excited, enthusiastic, tense, conflictual, boring, scary;

- the interpersonal issues between young people that workers might need to consider;

- the organisational culture in terms of staff support, responsiveness to new ideas.

Having a conversation with the situation can take place as part of the preparation and planning of youth work (i.e. in advance). Reflection-in-action also occurs as youth and community work is happening. If a youth worker is working on their own, this might be an internal conversation, but when youth workers operate as part of a pair or a team, it involves conversation with others. The depth and quality of relationships between colleagues will make a tremendous difference to the ease in which this can happen.

Schön also pays attention to 'reflection-on-action'. This is more closely allied to the debriefing session (outlined earlier) through which people can think back on what has happened and develop their practice accordingly. In some ways, reflection-on-action could be seen as an opportunity for people to reflect upon their reflection-in-action, to try and unpick what happened at the time and why. Reflection-on-action will almost certainly still involve conversations.

Supervision is an ideal opportunity to engage in reflection-on-action. Organisations use supervision differently, and it is widely recognised as having a range of different functions. Kadushin (1992), for example, identifies three purposes as administrative, educative and supportive. If supervisors stick closely to an administrative or managerial agenda – such as seeking information on whether targets have been met or setting future goals – they might restrict the nature of the space in terms of reflection-on-action. For a supervisee to feel safe to engage in genuine reflection-on-action, they need to feel that they are able to talk openly in a supportive and non-judgemental environment. They need to have a sense of freedom to explore their thoughts, ideas and feelings.

A C T I V I T Y **6.3**

Think about reflection in and on action.

Think back to your last few weeks at work.

Can you think of examples of reflection-in-action – where you have engaged in 'thinking on your feet'? What were these examples, and what precisely happened?

ACTIVITY **6.3** *continued*

Have you engaged in reflection-on-action? How did this happen? Were other people involved or did you do it on your own? What came out of your reflection-on-action?

Depending on the context in which you work, you might have found it easier to find examples of reflection-in-action rather than reflection-on-action (or vice versa). This is not necessarily a problem – there is no rule to suggest that youth and community must have a 50:50 balance on these two processes. However, if you find that your examples are significantly skewed in one direction rather than the other, it might highlight something important about your organisation, such as a lack of time to engage in reflection-on-action with your colleagues or a rigidity that constricts reflection-in-action during sessions.

If you struggled to think of examples of where you engaged in reflection at all, then this is worth thinking about. It is possible that your reflection on your practice is so instinctive that it is hard to identify precise occasions where it has occurred. However, what is also possible (and more likely) is that you have not been engaging in enough reflection. If this is the case, then you are on 'automatic pilot', and there is a danger that this will dramatically undermine the quality of your work.

Now look again at your responses to the questions asked in Activity 6.3. It might be interesting to consider the nature of your reflection. Given that the concepts both reflection-in-action and reflection-on-action include the word 'action', it might be reasonable to assume that some (or indeed all) of your reflection has been about your practice, your action and *what* you have done. This is of course essential in terms of reflection, but it is not the end of the story. Mezirow argues that critical reflection involves engagement with values and with taken-for-granted assumptions – and these may not have been included as part of your reflection in and on action. It is to this that we now turn.

Mezirow – critical reflection

Jack Mezirow is an advocate of transformative learning. He wants to find ways of enabling people to learn at the very deepest level. For him, this means that reflection is not just about *what* we do and finding ways to do it better – it is about unpicking the underpinning assumptions upon which we base our beliefs. It is about looking at *why* rather than how. To do this, we have to be willing to delve into our deeply engrained values and ideas, some of which may be so hidden as to be out of our own awareness. As he explains, 'Critical reflection involves a critique of the presuppositions on which our beliefs have been based' (Mezirow and Associates, 1990, page 1).

Transformative learning is the type of learning that challenges us in a profound way. It is strongly linked to learning which enables us to *make meaning*. A young person does not experience transformative learning when they are in a class that recites a list of facts and figures which they have learned by rote. They might, however, experience transformative learning if they are in a class in which they are encouraged to grapple with their own ideas and where they leave the session having questioned their own values and views about the world.

The film *'Freedom Writers'* tells the unlikely true story of an inexperienced schoolteacher's interactions with a group of students in her class at school, most of whom were described by others as 'unteachable'. The students were low achievers. Some were members of gangs. Many had personal experiences of being shot, and many had lost close friends or family members to gang violence. The majority did not want to be at school. Initially, the students were antagonistic towards the teacher (and indeed, towards each other), but through using a range of unorthodox teaching methods, relationships of trust and mutual respect began to build. One method was to encourage students to write journals. Through doing this, students began to reflect upon their own experiences. They shared some of their stories with one another. They saw the connections between their own experiences and those of others around the world. They reflected upon what they wanted out of their lives, and many made life-changing decisions about how they wanted to live. The teacher read the journals and questioned many of her own assumptions about the students and, indeed, about the value of teaching. Her life choices changed. Most of the students – and the teacher – experienced transformative learning. The lives of all of them changed as a result of being in this classroom.

Now, *Freedom Writers* is of course a film, albeit one based on a true story. As youth and community workers, we cannot expect that our experiences will make it to the big screen. However, we can at least hope that some of what we do with young people constitutes 'transformative learning'. After all, a key purpose of youth work is to enable young people to reflect upon themselves and their values. This is not something that we can do for them – they have to do it for themselves. We can, however, actively help them to do this.

Before we can support young people to engage in transformative learning, we have to be critically reflective practitioners ourselves. This is not easy, but it is something that can be learned. Stephen Brookfield offers a technique to help people to do this within organisational settings. This involves the use of 'critical incidents' (Brookfield, 1990). These are a way of encouraging people to reflect on their practice in a way that specifically addresses the underlying assumptions and values. First, a brief description of a 'critical incident' needs to be written. This is a one-page summary of a key event and includes details about what happened, who was involved, whether the event was successful and what made it good or poor. Next, a small group of colleagues look at the description and try and identify the assumptions about, for example, 'empowerment' that are embedded in the description. The analysis of the discussion will in itself highlight more assumptions – what questions are asked by colleagues, what areas of practice have heralded most interest? It is interesting to notice, of course, whether everyone's assumptions about 'empowerment' are the same, and this in itself may trigger further reflection.

The 'Big Brother' experience case study has been written as a Critical Incident. If you were to use this in practice, it would be worth considering the following questions:

- What assumptions about 'empowerment' are tied up within this example?

- What has been taken for granted in terms of youth work values?

- Which aspects of this case study are you most drawn to, and what can you learn from yourself about reflecting upon this?

Big Brother

'Big Brother' is a reality TV show, loosely based on George Orwell's notion of Big Brother watching over us. Millions of young people have seen the show and they like it. The 'Big Brother' concept has been adapted as a tool of engagement by one youth work project in Hull. They run a three-day learning experience called 'This is not Big Brother ... but it's a bit like it'. Ten young people are taken away to a remote house in the countryside. No one has the title of 'leader'; it is up to everyone to live as a community and to make decisions. During their stay, they are set 'tasks' by the character of 'Big Brother', played by the youth workers, who are not part of the young people's community. Rewards are given when the housemates successfully complete the tasks, such as access to cameras, a football, cakes, games or a stereo.

While the young people are in the house, youth workers are always nearby. They do not interact with housemates, but they observe. They try and work out how well people are getting on, who is taking a leadership role and who is struggling. Initially, housemates try and engage them in conversation, but they soon lose interest and appear to forget that they are there. The youth workers appear passive – but they are active. They are in constant dialogue with one another. They engage in an ongoing process of reflection-in-action. They compare their observations. They make decisions about when to leave the group alone and when to intervene with a task. Their choice of tasks, and of rewards, might depend on what is happening in the group. For example, a group that is struggling to gel might be rewarded with an activity that they can all do together.

Every evening, there is a one-hour group reflection session, the only structured hour in the day. The session is facilitated by the youth workers, who now leave their 'Big Brother' role. The group are encouraged to think about how they are, what they are managing well as a group and whether they would like to ask anything of the group for the following day. This helps housemates engage in reflection-on-action. There are also regular 'diary room' slots where young people can talk to 'Big Brother' on their own. This is an opportunity for them to talk openly about how they are and to get support, if necessary, to reflect-in-action. Sometimes young people have personal struggles as part of the 'Big Brother' experience as they have an opportunity to see themselves through other people's eyes. Someone might emerge as a leader, for example, who would not see themselves in this way.

By the end of three days, the group is likely to have experienced teamwork, confidence building, fun, laughter – and conflict. Through dealing with everything that they have faced, young people have almost always had a positive experience, but they have also had the chance to reflect and to learn. The final activity set by Big Brother always involves reflection on the whole experience.

There are several barriers to critical reflection within organisational settings. One issue is that asking people to reflect upon their deeply held values, and taken-for-granted assumptions, is highly challenging. It is worth remembering, however, that if we are doing our jobs as youth workers, we will at times ask young people to engage in this level of self-reflection. We ask them to be reflective with regard to their own identities, their relationships with others, their attitudes to 'race', gender, sexuality, religion and so on. As workers, it is not unreasonable to expect the same from one another. Nonetheless, it is important to ensure that we offer a safe and supportive environment to one another so as to provide the best chance for this to happen (see Chapter 4 on empowering organisations).

Another major barrier to critical reflection is 'groupthink'. This 'represents the cozy illusion that all right-thinking people agree' (Brookfield, 1990, page 185). According to Goleman (1985, page 183), 'the first victim of groupthink is critical thought'. In a youth and community work organisation, for instance, groupthink might happen at a staff meeting. Imagine that there are seven staff members, all of whom get on very well inside as well as outside of work. Someone suggests that the team should organise a big event to take place in three months time. It will cost £5,000, but this money is 'sitting in the reserves anyway'. The event might attract hundreds of young people to the local area, some of which will start to use the youth project. If this proposal is passed by the meeting after a long and in-depth discussion, which looks at all the key issues and makes an informed decision, then this is a sign of critical reflection. If it is passed after a short or non-existent discussion, it is an indication of groupthink. Groupthink is a dangerous phenomenon within organisations as it means that the desire to maintain group harmony and cohesion has overtaken the need for informed decision making and critical analysis.

The film Twelve Angry Men *is the story of a jury process. The film starts with the jury retiring to their jury room to discuss what one juror calls 'an open and shut' murder case. They have been told that their vote must be unanimous, and it is oppressively hot, which adds to a sense of urgency. The groups have an initial vote and learn that they are 11–1 in favour of conviction. The lone juror who voted against conviction is played by Henry Fonda, who initially argues that he does not know whether the man is guilty or innocent but feels that he deserves a jury who at least discusses it. He is scorned by his peers and urged to back down, but as time progresses, he challenges his fellow other jurors who present 'facts' and argue that 'they proved it in court'. His argument is simple: 'they could be wrong … it's just possible'. After a short while, they take another vote, and through this, learn that another juror has changed his vote to 'not guilty'. This man does so not because he is yet convinced by the arguments but because he feels the discussion deserves more time. He supports Fonda, explaining that 'it's not easy to stand alone against the ridicule of others'. As time progresses, Fonda continues to ask questions and be open minded, and through unpicking the 'facts', he convinces one and then another jury member that there is 'reasonable doubt'. By the end of the film, the jury returns a unanimous verdict in favour of acquittal.*

This jury might have been a perfect example of 'groupthink'. The group of 12 men has heard arguments from lawyers, which they took to be 'facts'. They listened to witnesses and assumed that they were speaking 'the truth'. They were not engaging in critical thinking. If the character played by Fonda has not challenged them to think through their assumptions, the defendant would have been found guilty within minutes of the jury entering the jury room. In the event, Fonda took the risk of being ridiculed by others, and he asked questions. He was not even sure whether he was right, but he was open minded and wanted to make sure that he was making the right decision.

Does 'groupthink' happen within your team or organisation?

If you felt like a decision was being rushed through, would you be willing to stand against your colleagues and say 'let's just talk about this'? If not, why not?

Encouraging young people to reflect

So far in this chapter, we have looked at theories about reflection and applied them to the role of the youth worker. This is important because youth workers cannot expect to be empowering if they are unable to reflect upon their practice, their underlying values and their feelings. Now we will turn to the matter of how we might encourage young people to develop their reflective abilities.

The **learning cycle** offers an obvious place to start. When we work with young people, we often offer them experiences (an activity, a workshop, a residential, an opportunity to be involved with a campaign, a one-to-one support session and even a conversation in a local park). **Experiential learning** is central to youth and community work. We give young people experiences, and we want them to learn from being part of them. However, although learning can take place as part of any experience, just offering the experience is not enough. The pivotal factor is not the experience itself, but the level of reflection that goes with it. As Boud et al. (1993, page 9) argue, 'While experience may be the foundation of learning, it does not necessarily lead to it: there needs to be active engagement with it.' This presents a challenge to youth workers. How can we ensure that young people have the fullest opportunity to *learn* from the experiences we offer them? We must find ways of building reflection into the learning process.

This takes us onto the relative merits of **reflection-in-action** and **reflection-on-action**. Both of these processes can be built into youth work. Imagine you are delivering a cookery workshop. Getting young people to reflect-in-action can take place as you go along by, for example, asking them to consider why they have chosen to use one technique rather than another or inquiring as to what they think they should do next. Reflection-on-action might take place at the end of the session. For this, all participants could be invited to have a coffee and sample what they have cooked, and the youth worker could facilitate an informal discussion about the workshop, inviting people to say what they have learnt and whether they would do anything differently if they were to cook this dish again. These discussions could be used to help the group make decisions about future sessions, even by setting their own goals about what they would like to learn. It is worth noting that this reflection-in-action is *not* the same as an evaluation session. The purpose is not to find out whether the young people enjoyed the session or to ask how they rated the skills of the facilitator. It is about *personal reflection* and not about organisational evaluation.

The cookery example is a simple way of seeing how reflection can be built into the learning cycle – but some situations are harder. This is particularly the case where *difficult feelings* are involved (an assumption has been made that the cookery workshop will not inspire difficult feelings – this could of course be wrong). Imagine you are a detached youth worker talking to a young person in a local park. This young person is someone you know well. They are telling you about a problem they are having with their mother. They keep arguing, and the young person has been kicked out of the house. They want to go back, but they are anxious about seeing their mother in case she is still angry. Now, you want to encourage this young person to be reflective about the situation, to think about the role that they have played in it and to consider the best course of action – but the feelings for the young person are overwhelming. They cannot in any way think about things 'rationally' or 'logically' until they have had the chance to process their emotions. This is where Boud et al. (1985) come in, as they recognise that **unprocessed emotions** are a barrier to reflection. As a youth worker, you will need to spend time acknowledging that the young person is hurt, angry, upset, ashamed and confused. This will have to happen before, or at least at the same time as, any constructive discussion on the best course of action. This is part of the process of reflection-in-action. Of course, at some point this conversation will end and you will move on – but when you see this young person again, you might be able to engage in **reflection-on-action**, simply by asking them how they are and how things worked out. If they seem willing to talk, you can try and get them to think back on the situation and to think about whether there is anything more to learn.

Encouraging **critical reflection** is another important way in which youth workers might support young people in self-reflection. Now, remember that this involves questioning underlying assumptions and values, and as such, might be very challenging for young people. Brookfield (1990, page 178) argues that 'questioning the assumptions upon which we act and explore alternative ideas are not only difficult but also psychologically explosive'. In fact, he uses the metaphor of educators (youth workers) as explosives experts who lay dynamite at the base of young people's psychological worlds. He points out that this must be done very carefully. Demolition experts are highly trained and do not engage in random, wilful destruction. In a similar way, youth workers must be sensitive in the way that they tackle issues that require young people to engage in this level of self-challenge.

Take an example of young people's attitudes towards sex and relationships. Young men might, for example, have highly gendered views on what it means to be 'a man' and of how to behave in relationships. Young women might have their own views on how men should behave, and in addition, their own perceptions on what being 'a woman' or 'a girlfriend' involves. Youth workers try and challenge these assumptions. They ask young people to question themselves. They pose alternative perspectives of relationships based on equality and mutual respect. They act as role models in terms of the way that they interact with male and female colleagues at work. Young people may not find this easy. In fact, a common response might be to feel threatened or defensive. They might claim that the youth worker 'doesn't live in the real world' or that 'they are just an old hippy'. These are ways of dismissing the challenge.

Nonetheless, it is essential that youth workers find ways of encouraging young people to be self-reflective at a deeper level. It is only through doing this that we have any hope of being genuinely empowering, of enabling young people to seize their personal power, to support them to make their own choices. One way of doing this might be to adapt the **critical incident** technique for use with young people. This involves offering young people an opportunity to reflect upon their deeply held values and assumptions.

ACTIVITY **6.5**

In 2009, NSPCC published a research report about teenage relationships that showed that 25% of young women experienced violence from their boyfriends (including pushing, slapping, hitting and being held down)*. Furthermore, 11% experienced severe violence (including punching, strangling and being beaten up or hit with an object). These high incidences of violence indicated that there was a level of cultural acceptability about violence in relationships. To tackle this, the government commissioned a series of advertisements to go on TV, billboards and magazines (entitled 'This Is Abuse'). The TV adverts showed a short clip of *a teenage couple in a bedroom. The young man was encouraging his girlfriend to have sex, but she refused. This escalated into an argument, where the boy smashed her phone and raised his fist over her cowering body. At the same time, the camera panned to a picture of the same young man outside the room, banging on a glass wall, shouting at his alter-ego to stop. The caption was 'If you could see yourself, would you stop yourself?' Another virtually identical advert ran, but this time, the person banging on the glass was the young woman, with the caption, 'If you could see yourself, would you see abuse'?*

These adverts have been designed to challenge young men and young women at a deep level. They are trying to challenge assumptions about what is acceptable within relationships, about what constitutes 'violence' and, in turn, to encourage young people to change their behaviour. They relate to the concept of the 'critical incident' by encouraging young people to question their underlying values and assumptions. The use of the young person behind the glass wall is an interesting way of representing this process visually – but could we find other ways of enabling young people to do this?

How might the 'This Is Abuse' advert be used within youth work settings?

How else could we develop the idea of 'critical incidents' for use in youth work settings?

*Note: the levels of violence reported by young men were also contained within the report.

The danger of **groupthink** has been identified as a threat to critical reflection. Given that young people are at a time in their lives where the opinions of other people matter intensely, it might reasonably be assumed that the risk of group-think is stronger. It could be linked to 'peer pressure' – to young people's desires to fit in and belong to a crowd. If we want young people to engage in critical reflection, then we want them to be open to asking questions, to challenging themselves and to trying out new ideas. This is impossible if they feel anxious about being teased, ridiculed or even excluded. We must pay attention to the environments in which we work, so that as far as possible, we offer a safe and supportive space for all young people. We must also accept that at times, a deep level of critical reflection might be more likely in one-to-one settings than in group contexts.

Concluding comments

Empowerment does not just happen. Youth workers cannot expect to be empowering towards others unless we are reflective about our practice. We have to be willing to think about ourselves and the work that we do, to have a 'conversation with the situation'. We have to reflect in action and to look back and reflect on action. It is through these processes that we develop our practice and become better practitioners.

We also have to be open to self-reflection and self-challenge. We have to be prepared to engage in critical thinking, to explore our deeper values and assumptions and to be willing to accept challenge from others. We have to do this because it makes us reflective practitioners – but also because we ask young people to do this. Why should they do it if we cannot?

Finally, we must find ways – safe and supportive ways – of enabling young people to develop their reflective abilities. A central tenet of empowerment is to enable young people to develop their sense of agency, to take control of their lives and their situations. They cannot do this if they are not able to be reflective about their lives, their values, their assumptions, their identities and their hopes for the future. As youth workers, we offer experiences, but to turn these experiences into learning, we must build in processes for reflection. Through doing this effectively, we can support young people to engage in transformative learning.

C H A P T E R   R E V I E W

This chapter has explored the connections between empowerment and reflection. The following points have been highlighted:

- To be empowering, it is essential that youth workers are reflective about their practice, their values and assumptions, and their feelings,

- Youth workers can reflect-in-action as well as reflect-on-action.

- The use of critical incidents is a good way of developing critical reflection, where underlying assumptions and values can be questioned.

- Groupthink is a danger within any organisation, and therefore, youth workers must be careful to ensure that they do not prioritise harmony over critical reflection.

- Youth workers must find ways of encouraging young people to be self-reflective and self-challenging, even though this could be potentially explosive.

- Offering experiences is an essential part of learning, but in itself, it is not enough. Processes of reflection must be built in to youth work processes to turn experience into learning.

- Young people are in danger of groupthink (and peer pressure), and therefore it might sometimes be more realistic to encourage deeper levels of reflection on a one-to-one rather than group basis.

FURTHER READING

Boud, D, Cohen, R and Walker, D (1993) *Using Experience for Learning*. Maidenhead: Open University Press.

This book focuses on experiential learning and includes chapters on barriers to reflection and unlearning. The writing style is accessible.

Mezirow, J and Associates (1990) *Fostering Critical Reflection in Adulthood: A Guide to Transformative and Emancipatory Learning*. San Francisco: Jossey-Bass Inc.

Although not specific to youth and community work, this book offers an interesting perspective on the nature of learning and is useful in terms of thinking about reflection in youth workers and in young people. It contains Stephen Brookfield's chapter on critical incidents.

Chapter 7

'Citizenship', globalisation and emancipation

CHAPTER OBJECTIVES

- To interrogate the contestability of 'citizenship' as a concept.
- To examine the inclusionary and exclusionary effects on young people of mainstream determinations of 'citizenship'.
- To explore the effects of neo-liberal globalisation on young people's citizenship rights.
- To investigate possibilities for forging an emancipatory model of citizenship capable of advancing the social well-being of young people.

The chapter will help you meet the following National Occupational Standards:

1.1.3   Encourage young people to broaden their horizons to be active citizens.

1.3.3   Enable young people to represent themselves and their peer group.

2.1.1   Ensure that the rights of young people are promoted and upheld.

2.2.2   Work with young people in safeguarding their own welfare.

3.1.2   Assist young people to express and to realise their goals.

It will also introduce you to the following academic standards as set out in the QAA youth and community work benchmark statement (2009).

4.5.2   Communities, networks and coalitions:

   – Campaigning and the links to social movements.

   – Debates about citizenship and democracy which may underpin practice.

Introduction

'Citizenship' is a contested concept with different meanings according to different ideological perspectives and times. How it is defined in mainstream policy discourse (i.e. by the powerful), however, is extremely important for determining who is to be 'included' as 'citizens' (together with the benefits of that inclusion) and who is to be 'excluded' as 'non-citizens' (together with the disbenefits of not belonging). As Mullard argues,

> Citizenship is of direct relevance to people's lives because it represents the benchmark of personal freedom, dignity, hope, freedom from fear and personal autonomy ... Citizenship involves the dual process of inclusion and exclusion, where some might gain rights and become the 'in group' and others may become the disadvantaged 'out group' ... The commitment to universal human rights is a pillar in the definition of citizen ... The recognition of the constituted individual able to make choices also means having access to political, economic and social resources. Commitment to citizenship also means commitment to resources.

> (2002, page 2)

In the next section, we explore how the meaning of citizenship in mainstream policy discourse in Britain has changed from an emphasis on notions of human rights (albeit flawed notions) to one emphasising a citizenship conditional on people taking greater responsibility for their behaviour, attitudes and duties.

Changing meanings of 'citizenship' in mainstream social policy

A seminal thesis on the subject of citizenship was written in 1950 by T. H. Marshall, a sociologist, charting the historical development of citizenship in Britain. Marshall saw this development as the advance of the population's legal status made up of three kinds of rights: civil, social and political. Civil rights (e.g. to own property, enter into legal contracts and freedom of speech) had been gained in the eighteenth century; political rights (e.g. the right to vote or join a political party) had been gained in the nineteenth century; and social rights (e.g. to a guaranteed standard of economic well-being) had been gained in the twentieth century (Marshall, 1950). Mullard (2002) describes this as the evolution of the 'entitled citizen' – that is, where universal access to social welfare ensures that lack of income is not a barrier to entry to citizenship.

ACTIVITY **7.1**

In your own youth work/training context, discuss with your group what resources and rights they/young people would need to attain personal well-being.

The main flaw in Marshall's thesis is that it fails to acknowledge that the advancement of citizenship in Britain had not benefitted everyone in the same way. As citizenship developed, it primarily favoured more affluent, heterosexual, able-bodied, adult white males. It had not applied equally to other social categories. For instance, political rights in the nineteenth century were confined to males (with British nationality) who owned property. Meanwhile, women, aliens and recipients of poor relief were denied the vote (Burden, 1998). Furthermore, citizenship-based social rights, as they developed under the Beveridge Plan for social welfare in the post-war period, have not been enjoyed universally. In particular, the same rights did not apply equally to women, ethnic minorities, the disabled, gays and lesbians, and children and young people. For example,

> *Black immigrant women, recruited to fill some of the least desirable posts in the health service in the postwar period, were not at the same time constructed as social citizens with health needs of their own and remain concentrated in lower grade jobs.*

> (Lister, 1997, page 171)

Research into council housing allocation procedures in the 1980s and 1990s unearthed similar denials of social rights. 'They mostly document institutional processes whereby black applicants for council housing waited longer than white people, and once rehoused received inferior accommodation to white people' (Ginsburg, 1992, page 112). The rights of Commonwealth citizens to 'citizenship' in Britain – confirmed by the 1948 British Nationality Act – had already started to be eroded by the 1960s as a consequence of immigration legislation limiting rights of entry (Shukra, 2010; Solomos, 2003). Overall, the post-war welfare state was largely constructed in the interest of the white, fit and healthy, adult male. The welfare state that emerged was one

> *... in which (i) individualised, labour-market related insurance programmes position primarily male recipients as rights-bearers and (ii) family-based means-tested assistance schemes clientise their primarily female recipients.*

> (Lister, 1997, page 172)

As Lister argues, men's employment trends continue to be privileged by social protection and pension schemes that continue to disadvantage women who have interrupted employment histories or who have depended on low-paid, part-time jobs. The failure to treat women as equal citizens to men – and consequently their children – was a fundamental flaw in the Beveridge Plan (Lister, 1997).

ACTIVITY 7.2

Again, in your own youth work/training context, discuss with your group what 'citizenship' means to them and what ways they have experienced it in their own lives. Do people feel that they have attained the necessary resources identified in Activity 7.1 and that they have achieved the same degree of personal autonomy as others? If not, why not?

The failings in the post-war welfare system did much to generate a range of social movements from the 1960s onwards who appealed to the values of citizenship rights in their campaigns for social justice – in particular, women's groups, the disability movement, and lesbian and gays (Lister, 1997). This reflects what Mullard (2002, page 3) sees as a more fruitful definition of citizenship representing 'a discourse which was emancipatory'. This means that citizenship has also to be 'about dialogue, involvement, and participation rather than a series of ascribed static rights' (Mullard, 2002, page 4). Citizenship here is seen as a dynamic process and open to change in response to changing priorities and campaigns for social rights. Allowing citizens to express their priorities requires opportunities for active collective engagement in democratic processes (see Chapter 3 for practical examples of such engagement). However, as it developed in Britain, citizenship emphasised 'rights possessed by individuals rather than as something that is collective' (Byrne, 2006, page 26). As Lister points out, this differs from the Scandinavian model of citizenship with its emphasis on

> ... *relations between citizens as a collectivity. This difference reflects the respective strength of, on the one hand, individualistic liberal and, on the other, solidaristic social democratic traditions of political thinking.*

> (Lister, 2010, pages 195–6)

Notwithstanding the differential experiences shaped by ethnicity, sexuality, disability and gender, the post-war Keynesian welfare system in Britain did represent a stronger sense of solidaristic tradition than that manifested in mainstream political thinking after the late 1970s. As Byrne observes, the combination of full employment, strong trade unions, growth in household earnings and improved social welfare meant that 'most people saw a prospect of upward mobility for themselves or their children' (Byrne, 2006, page 171). However, over the last three decades, the mainstream discourse on citizenship has shifted away from one stressing social rights to one stressing individual responsibilities.

Marshall's own concept of citizenship referred to both rights and 'corresponding duties' (Marshall, 1950, page 70), although in the case of the latter his ideas – beyond the duty to work, pay taxes and national insurance contributions, attend school and do military service – were not fully developed (Roche, 1992).

ACTIVITY 7.3

Again, in your own youth work/training context, discuss with your group what duties of 'citizenship' might mean. (You could relate these, say, to the rights and duties associated with being a member of a youth club.) In addition, what sanctions do you think there should be for people who fail to carry out these duties?

Since the 1980s, governments have abandoned Keynesian welfare strategies in favour of policies shaped by neo-liberalism. Neo-liberalism reformulates classical *laissez-faire* political economy – that is, an ideology that supports private provision and the market and is hostile to state intervention. Today, the political consensus in Britain follows this ideology as governments continue to remodel the welfare system in line with individualism and market incentives; economy, efficiency and effectiveness and the desire to cut public spending (Burden, 1998). In parallel with this development, citizenship has increasingly been redefined in terms of greater self-reliance. Under the Conservative New Right, this translated into an 'independent citizen discourse … about less government, less intervention and more reliance on individual self-help, markets and competition' (Mullard, 2002, page 7). Under New Labour's 'third way' governance, this was refined as 'no rights without responsibilities' (Giddens, 1998, page 65) – a reflection of Etzioni's (1993) notion of communitarianism and his belief that we need to correct the 'current imbalance between rights and responsibilities' (cited in Cooper, 2008, page 95).

> *For Etzioni, democracy and greater equality is achieved through individuals participating more in civil society as 'active citizens' … [His] concept of 'active citizenship' [was] taken up by New Labour and applied to its modernisation agenda for public services. In particular, New Labour's reforms aimed to improve the standard of public services by making them more accountable to 'citizens'.*
>
> (Cooper, 2008, pages 95–6)

The attractiveness of the communitarian discourse on 'active citizenship' for government,

> *… particularly with its notions of voluntarism and self-help, is clear given the emerging consensus in British social policy around neo-liberal orthodoxy and the decline in welfarist solutions to social problems … [C]ivil society … provides a 'third space' between state/market and individuals – acting as a new site of governance made necessary by the decline of the social state.*
>
> (Cooper, 2008, page 96)

This emphasis on 'responsibilisation' had been evident under the New Labour government's policy agenda on young people – particularly in relation to their behaviour, attitudes and duties. The 1998 Crime and Disorder Act, for instance, aimed to responsibilise young people to desist from engaging in 'anti-social behaviour' (however ill defined) through the threat of punitive sanctions (i.e. anti-social behaviour orders and 'naming and shaming') that lacked due process. In terms of dealing with youth unemployment, New Labour continued to pursue the previous Conservative government's emphasis on encouraging behaviour geared to 'employability' and being 'something individuals must actively achieve … Inclusion becomes a duty rather than a right' (Levitas, 2005, page 128). There has been an increasing policy focus on activating young people to get into paid work with an increasing emphasis on individualised 'casework' with young people – particularly through Connexions – to enable them to make more 'responsible' choices; this, despite today's flexible labour market where it is becoming increasingly difficult to obtain an adequate, regular income from paid work (Burden et al., 2000).

The 'responsibilisation' agenda also focused on young people's 'democratic' responsibilities. The 1997 Crick Report on *Education for Citizenship and the Teaching of*

Democracy in Schools, while radical in tone, ultimately projected a 'statist view of politics, an assimilationist view of minorities, a lack of concern about structural disadvantages and a tendency to downplay the democratic potential of multi-culturalism' (Hoffman, 2004, page 168). The Crick Report effectively

- Confined democracy 'within the framework of the *state*' (Hoffman, 2004, page 166, emphasis in original) where the responsibility to vote in government is privileged over direct civil action as a political process.

- Connected 'citizenship' to nationality where it was assumed 'that it is the ethnic minorities who must change in order to realize a common citizenship' (Hoffman, 2004, page 167).

- Sidestepped 'the impact of "race", ethnicity, gender, social class or religion' (Hoffman, 2004, page 168) in relation to access to citizenship rights.

Given this emphasis, there is little wonder that the citizenship curriculum eventually introduced in schools in 2002 proved to be more 'about the assimilation of law abiding, dutiful and productive citizens' (Packham, 2008, page 95) rather than an extension of civil rights to young people – a functionalist approach to citizenship with schools having a central role in the process.

The focus on assimilation intensified after the so-called riots in Burnley, Oldham and Bradford in 2001. Following the disturbances, New Labour's social policy agenda shifted towards greater emphasis on 'community cohesion'. The 'commonsense understanding' of the cause of the disturbances was forged by the Cantle Report (2001), commissioned by the government in the aftermath of the disturbances, which argued that the 'troubles' were largely due to the lack of inter-action between people of different cultural, religious and racial backgrounds, and that the solution lay in promoting

> … *community cohesion, based upon a greater knowledge of, contact between, and respect for, the various cultures that now make Great Britain such a rich and diverse nation. It is also essential to establish a greater sense of citizenship, based on (a few) common principles which are shared and observed by all sections of the community.*

> (Cantle Report, 2001, cited in Cooper, 2008, page 152)

David Blunkett, then Home Secretary, described the 'rioters' in Bradford as 'maniacs' and those who questioned Judge Gullick's sentencing, which had been harsher than verdicts imposed on those involved in disturbances at Burnley and Oldham, as 'bleeding heart liberals' (cited in McGhee, 2005, page 59). As was the case in the 1980s, when trouble erupted in areas of significant Afro-Caribbean settlement, the unrest was reduced by the media, the political establishment and the criminal justice system to '"simple criminality" – as deviant and anti-social behaviour rather than legitimate protest' (McGhee, 2005, page 60) by a 'group of people who had had enough, who could not depend on the police or the government to do anything about their situation' (McGhee, 2005, page 62). This reductionist stance mirrored that taken by the Scarman Report on the 1981 Brixton 'riot' when processes of subjective and institutionalised racism were dismissed as a contributory factor (Cooper, 2008).

ACTIVITY **7.4**

Read through the following summary findings from the Policy Studies Institute 4th Study (Modood et al., 1997) into 'race' in Britain and consider whether or not these factors might have had an influence on the events in Burnley, Oldham and Bradford in 2001:

- *Pakistani/Bangladeshi households amongst poorest groups in Britain; those of Indian and Caribbean origin have mixed experiences; African-Asians and Chinese doing as well as white people.*

- *Eighty per cent Pakistani and Bangladeshi people live in households with incomes below half national average; they also face widespread housing problems, especially over-crowding; African-Asians and Chinese more likely than white people to earn more than £500 pw and low unemployment rates.*

- *Ethnic minorities more likely to continue education post-16 – however, many end up in worse jobs than white people despite similar qualifications; education system failing Bangladeshi and Pakistani youth who are disproportionately without qualifications.*

As Hasan (2000, page 181) argues, urban unrest in Britain can be seen as synonymous with political action by 'communities of resistance' – defending themselves 'against an oppressive and all-too-frequent, repressive, system'. And as Paul Gilroy suggests, 'Localised struggles over education, racist violence and police practices continually reveal how black people have made use of notions of community to provide the axis along which to organise themselves' (Gilroy, cited in Hasan, 2000, page 181). Such direct social action can therefore be conceived as a form of collective struggle in pursuit of citizenship rights. However, the British government does not accept direct civil action in pursuit of social justice as a legitimate act of citizenship. In relation to young people, this was particularly evident when school pupils protested against the British government's invasion of Iraq in March 2003, and where

> *... coverage of the protests was largely negative ... with precious little support for the principle of a pupil's right to strike. In the political sphere, the generic right to participation enshrined in the UN Convention on the Rights of the Child is made conditional on adult approval of the cause espoused and of the form of participation.*

> (Such et al., 2005, page 315)

Similarly, in December 2010, David Cameron focused attention on a section of young people protesting against the coalition government's hike in student fees by describing them as 'a "mob" who had behaved in an "absolutely feral way"' (cited in Addley, 2010, page 6). Meanwhile, Cameron failed to mention the heavy-handedness of the police, and the disproportionate use of horse charges and 'ket-tling for hours thousands of people within a freezing Parliament Square' (Addley, 2010, page 6). As Noakes et al. (2010) comment,

> *The Commissioner of the London Metropolitan Police, Sir Paul Stephenson, claims that all 'right-minded' protestors will want to condemn the violence that erupted last Thursday during protests against the House of Commons vote of raising university tuition fees. As university lecturers who were present in Parliament Square during the police's 'containment' of the demonstration, we would join in condemning this violence. However, the violence we wish to condemn is not that of young people being held captive outside the Palace of Westminster, but that of the Metropolitan police themselves, whose aggressive and intimidatory tactics inflamed the situation. We witnessed police on horseback charging into groups of young people, and teenagers being batoned and beaten. When young people asked politely to be allowed to leave Parliament Square, they were ignored and detained against their will for hours without access to food, water and toilet facilities.*

> (Noakes et al., 2010, page 36)

Alfie Meadows, a 20-year-old student from Middlesex University, had to undergo a three-hour operation to treat bleeding on the brain after such an attack. Meadows' life had been further threatened by the police themselves who had, according to Meadows' mother, attempted to stop him being treated at the Chelsea and Westminster hospital where injured police officers were also being treated (Malik and Townsend, 2010). Another person was twice pulled from his wheelchair by police officers and was dragged across the ground by officers who said he was 'too close to their horses' (Addley et al., 2010, page 6). The day after the December protests, Nicky Wishart, a 12-year-old school pupil concerned about the plight of his local youth centre that was due to be closed down in March 2011, was taken out of lessons by the police under anti-terrorism legislation and subjected to inter-rogation by Thames Valley police, without the presence of a parent, 'because he was planning to picket David Cameron's constituency office' (Malik, 2010, page 7). These cases reveal how adults continue to 'frame the political debate and contain youth protest' (Such et al., 2005, page 321).

Subsequent to the debate on community cohesion, the policy agenda has moved on to address the broader notion of national cohesion around 'com-mon principles' of 'Britishness' where difference and diversity ('multicultural-ism') can be more easily managed. According to Arun Kundnani, the Institute of Race Relations, these principles effectively place limits on multiculturalism and black people are now required to develop 'a greater acceptance of the prin-cipal national institutions' (Kundnani, 2002, cited in Cooper, 2008, page 155) and integrate better into the 'British way of life'. On 8 December 2006, Tony Blair, then prime minister, warned immigrants that they must accept Britain's 'core values of democracy, tolerance and respect for the law … Our tolerance is part of what makes Britain, Britain. Conform to it; or don't come here' (cited in Woodward, 2006, page 1). As Kundnani observes, instead of asking 'how society excludes Muslims/migrants … the questions asked are about Muslims refusing to integrate … Muslims having to become more British. It is thus their "alien" values that are the problem rather than our racist values' (Kundnani, 2005, cited in Worley, 2005, page 490).

ACTIVITY 7.5

In your youth group/training session, come up with a shared definition of the 'British way of life'. You may find this difficult!

We can see here how the increasing focus under New Labour on responsibilities of citizenship was played out among young people in relation to their social behaviour, their capacity to engage in paid work and their loyalty to the British state. It is a development that continues to be prioritised by the Con-Lib coalition government. As Lister observes, shortly after entering Downing Street as prime minister in May 2010, David Cameron (2010, cited in Lister, forthcoming) announced 'I want to help try and build a more responsible society here in Britain. One where we don't just ask what are my entitlements, but what are my responsibilities'. Cameron also demonstrated his intention to continue the assault started under New Labour on multiculturalism. In a speech to a security conference in Munich on 5 February 2011, Cameron argued that multiculturalism in Britain had failed and that it was 'fostering extremist ideology and directly contributing to home-grown Islamic terrorism' (Wright and Taylor, 2011, page 1). To counter this, he argued that 'Britain must adopt a policy of "muscular liberalism" to enforce the values of equality, law and freedom of speech across all parts of society' (Wright and Taylor, 2011, page 1).

> We have failed to provide a vision of society [to young Muslims] to which they can feel they want to belong. We have even tolerated segregated communities behaving in ways that run counter to our values. All this leaves some young Muslims feeling rootless. And the search for something to belong to and believe in can lead to extremist ideology.
>
> (Cameron, cited in Wright and Taylor, 2011, page 1)

Again, the onus here is on Muslim communities doing more to integrate and curb their 'extremist' ways.

Lister notes (forthcoming), 'One difference between the Conservatives and New Labour, however, is that in the "citizenship equation" there is little or no talk now about rights to balance the emphasis on responsibilities'. What Lister also foresees under the Con-Lib coalition is

... a big role for the active citizen in the Big Society ... One of the coalition government's first statements heralds the building of the Big Society as 'the responsibility of every citizen'. It promises a voluntary National Citizen Service for 16 year olds 'to give them a chance to develop the skills needed to be active and responsible citizens' (Cabinet Office, 2010b, page 2). Moreover, Cameron and Clegg explain that the fusion of their plans and philosophies around social responsibility and the role of the state will 'create a Big Society matched by big citizens' (Cameron and Clegg, 2010, page 8).

(Lister, forthcoming)

There is an underlying assumption behind the notion of 'active citizen' presented here that, in previous times, citizens had been made to be inactive and dependent on state welfare entitlement – a perspective rooted in Charles Murray's (1990) 'underclass thesis'. As a consequence, it is a notion that adopts an increasingly hostile stance to the state, 'reflected in the absence of any talk of social rights to balance responsibilities and points to an acceleration in the shift towards greater conditionality, exclusivity and selectivity in these rights' (Lister, forthcoming).

The weakening of social rights of citizenship in Britain is often explained in relation to 'globalisation' – itself a contested concept – and citizenship beyond the nation-state.

While the term globalisation is generally used to signify a worldwide scale of commonality and interconnectedness (Hutchings, 2010), the idea of globalisation cannot be conceptualised as something distinct but rather needs to be understood as something constituted through discursive practice – that is, the way subjectivity (claims to 'truth') is produced through discourse – with significant implications for human well-being.

'Globalisation' and citizenship beyond the nation-state

The notion of 'globalisation' has provoked heated debate between 'globaphiles' (those who believe that 'globalisation' is having positive effects on human well-being) and 'globaphobes' (those who are sceptical about the benefits of 'globalisation'). Whatever one's position, there can be little doubt that the process of 'globalisation' under 'capitalist hegemony' – that is, via the way cultural norms (ideas, beliefs, institutions and practices) of one dominating class become universal and all pervasive, serving to oppress other classes without those other classes fully perceiving their oppression – is having profound effects worldwide on five key aspects of contemporary social life: the economic, the environmental, the cultural, the technological and the political. This hegemonic domination has allowed, since the late 1970s, intensified support for the neo-liberal ideological imperative – one that advocates economic liberalisation and deregulation as a means of promoting economic growth, political freedom and social well-being – a reflection of global power relations. Moreover, this domination has had profoundly detrimental consequences for human well-being in both the 'developing' and 'developed' world.

Specifically in relation to citizenship, citizenship rights in Britain and the developing world are being eroded by neo-liberal globalisation. Helped by the advance of liberalisation – that is, a relaxation of previous government fiscal and economic policies, often accompanied by the deregulation of rules that constrain the operation of free market forces – transnational corporations (TNCs) are able to seek out the most favourable deregulated global labour markets to exploit cheap labour and enhance profitability (Steger, 2009). Under these conditions, the ability of nation-states to exercise control over economic activities – as envisaged under Keynesianism (the economic theory of John Maynard Keynes who advocated government monetary and fiscal programmes to stimulate growth in times of economic slumps) – is perceived to have been eroded (Held and McGrew, 2007). As a consequence, nation-states no longer appear capable of guaranteeing standards of economic and social well-being.

What emerged in the developing world is the intensification of the 'systematic exploitation of dirt-cheap labour' (Bello, 2002, page 7) under extremely harsh working conditions (Pilger, 2002). In parallel, many of these locations have remained highly underdeveloped due to the mandates of structural adjustment programmes (SAPs) imposed by the International Monetary Fund (IMF) and World Bank – enforcing the liberalisation of local economies and lower wages. By the early 1990s, SAPs had been imposed on over 90 developing and transitional economies (Bello, 2002). Research shows that such programmes have failed both economically and socially.

> A study by the Center for Economic and Policy Research shows that 77 per cent of countries for which data are available saw their per capita rate of growth fall significantly from the period 1960–80 to the period 1980–2000, the structural adjustment period.

> (Bello, 2002, page 68)

In parallel, SAPs have led to cuts in public spending, which have translated into 'fewer social programmes, reduced educational opportunities, more environmental pollution, and greater poverty for the vast majority of people' (Steger, 2009, page 55) including young people. While these interventions were ostensibly about enabling developing nations to repay their debts to Northern banks, they permitted the enforcement of the neo-liberal political agenda by removing direct state intervention in social and economic affairs. At the same time, the World Trade Organisation (WTO) imposed agreements on trade (i.e. the elimination of quotas), intellectual property rights (i.e. permitting TNCs to monopolise knowledge-based industries and biotechnological developments) and agricultural production (i.e. opening up developing countries' markets to agricultural superpowers), inhibiting possibilities for developing nations to become economically self-contained (Bello, 2002). As a consequence, global inequality between North and South has endured (Milanovic, 2006). Essentially, 'globalisation' exacerbates poverty and inequality – making a mockery of the World Bank's claims on prioritising 'poverty reduction' (Bello, 2002).

ACTIVITY 7.6

Group exercise – linking the local to the global – suitable to a youth work or training setting – aimed at encouraging reflection on how our personal lives are already affected by globalisation. This activity is based on an idea introduced to me by Momodou Sallah from De Montfort University – for which I am extremely grateful.

Task: Look at the labels on your clothes to see in what country they were made and write the name of the item of clothing on to a 'post-it' and stick this on to the appropriate country on an atlas of the world. Reflect on what this exercise tells you about contemporary sources of production.

View John Pilger's film 'The New Rulers of the World' – available at **video.google .com/videoplay?docid=5488926059460319590#** *– and reflect on what this tells us about the effects of processes of global capitalism on developing nations. Do we in the West have a role to play in these processes? Can we, as global citizens, have a role in challenging these processes?*

While collective political identities may continue to correspond to particular places and nations – strongly based on 'psychological foundations and cultural assumptions that convey a sense of existential security and historical continuity' (Steger, 2009. page 58) – since the 1970s, the political sovereignty of the nation-state has been eroded. This has led some commentators to argue that 'politics has been rendered almost powerless by an unstoppable techno-economic juggernaut that will crush all governmental attempts to reintroduce restrictive policies and regulations' (Steger, 2009, page 63). According to such positions, the main role of future governments is to serve 'as a superconductor for global capitalism' (Steger, 2009, page 63) where states prioritise policies aimed at making their economies favourable to the needs of global investors rather than populations as a whole. In such a climate, the traditional social policy functions of western liberal democracies – protecting the social welfare of citizens – are displaced by measures prioritising the control of immigration, 'incivility' and 'crime' (Cooper, 2008). In such a context, social inequalities between citizens widen (Byrne, 2006).

> *The local and global have become increasingly entangled, with social well-being at the local level increasingly dependent on decisions made by supranational institutions … and powerful international leaders (especially the US leadership) at the global level. In such a context, it seems unlikely that the challenge of community wellbeing for the disadvantaged – that is, the need for political voice, civil and human rights, and adequate social protection and opportunity – can be truly addressed without, at the same time, democratising*

decision-making processes at the global level. Political strategies at the local level, therefore, need to engage with social movements that challenge the legitimacy of these supranational organisations who, in imposing their ideological agenda, reap destruction worldwide.

(Cooper, 2008, page 231)

Possibilities do exist for a counter-hegemonic project to emerge – one that can expose contradictions within neo-liberal discourse and offer directions for developing an alternative manifesto for global relations (one built on globalisation from below rather than above). Despite globalisation's increasingly disciplinary qualities it retains, like 'citizenship … emancipatory potential' (Lister, forthcoming). As such, like citizenship too, it is a concept that can be deployed 'by marginalised groups and social movements to stake their claims, sometimes using the language of human rights' (Lister, forthcoming). In the next section, we consider citizenship as social action for positive change.

Citizenship as social action for positive change

As Bourdieu (2002, page 1) argues, 'Globalisation is not a fate, but a politics. For this reason, a politics of opposition to its concentration of power is possible'. This possibility can be realised, argues Bourdieu, by drawing on the experience of the newer social movements. As Bourdieu explains,

The term 'globalisation' suggests the inevitability of economic laws. This masks the political reality. It is an altogether paradoxical reality which relies upon a politics of depoliticisation. It is a politics which threatens to confer a lethal status on economic forces unleashed from all control or constraint. It is a politics which secures the submission of governments and peoples to those very economic and social forces it says must be 'liberated'.

(2002, page 1)

Bourdieu (2002, page 1) argues for a different kind of politics that counters that of 'depoliticisation and disempowerment'. To achieve this, a unified Social Europe of social movements is required 'capable of bringing together the different forces [of resistance] in all their divisions' (Bourdieu, 2002, page 2).

According to Bourdieu, social movements are ideally placed to form resistance campaigns against the dominant forces of our time. This is because, first, they 'reject any kind of monopolisation of their organisation by a minority' (Bourdieu, 2002, page 2), they allow 'the direct participation of … various stakeholders' (Bourdieu, 2002, page 2) and are therefore inclusive and promote a sense of solidarity. Second, they usually organise around specific issues and are generally prepared to engage in direct action (Bourdieu, 2002). In respect of the anti-neoliberal globalisation movement, the infrastructure for such a challenge is already emerging. As Hardt and Negri (2005) observe, by colonising and interconnecting more and more areas of people's lives ever more deeply, neo-liberal globalisation is unwittingly generating the sites from which democratic alternatives to the present world order might be created.

> *You might say, simplifying a great deal, that there are two faces to globalization. On one face, Empire spreads globally its network of hierarchies and divisions that maintain order through new mechanisms of control and constant conflict. Globalization, however, is also the creation of new circuits of cooperation that stretch across nations and continents and allow an unlimited number of encounters. This second face of globalisation is not a matter of everyone in the world becoming the same; rather it provides the possibility that, while remaining different, we discover the commonality that enables us to communicate and act together.*

> (Hardt and Negri, 2005, page xiii)

Monbiot identifies similar contradictions within the neo-liberal globalisation discourse. As he suggests,

> *Corporate and financial globalization, designed and executed by a minority seeking to enhance its wealth and power, is compelling the people it oppresses to acknowledge their commonality. Globalization is establishing a single, planetary class interest, as the same forces and the same institutions threaten the welfare of the people of all nations ... Simultaneously, it has placed within our hands the weapons we require to overthrow the people who have engineered it and assert our common interest. By crushing the grand ideologies which divided the world, it has evacuated the political space in which a new, global politics can grow ... The global dictatorship of vested interests has created the means of its own destruction.*

> (Monbiot, 2003, pages 8–9)

Neo-liberal globalisation is not an inevitability nor inescapable, and organising resistance against its incursions is a possibility. As Steger (2009, page 69) reminds us, a '"global civil society" ... populated by thousands of voluntary, non-governmental associations of worldwide reach ... [who] represent millions of ordinary citizens who are prepared to challenge political and economic decisions made by nation-states and intergovernmental organizations' already exists. The task is to bring these social movements together under a broad coalition with a manifesto for an alternative world order – one offering prospects for greater social justice and human well-being for the many (Cooper, 2008). Hardt and Negri propose organising such a coalition around a contemporary version of the *cahiers de doléances* – the 'lists of grievances' that were compiled in France on the invitation of Louis XVI in return for the right to impose new taxes. By the time of the meeting of the Estates General at Versailles in May 1789, more than 40,000 lists had been compiled from all over the country addressing such issues as personal liberties relating to fair trials, freedom of expression, limits to abusive police powers and social well-being (Cooper, 2008). Hardt and Negri (2005, pages 269–70) suggest a contemporary version of this list might address three themes: 'the critique of existing forms of representation, the protest against poverty, and the opposition to war'.

ACTIVITY **7.7**

Consider a contemporary list of grievances. In your youth work or training set-ting, invite the group to come up with their list of grievances about the effects of globalisation.

The main function, therefore, of a social movement is to prevent campaigns from becoming fragmented and to organise resistance around shared objectives recognisable to each group.

> *Such similarities in the objectives of disparate political struggles highlight the usefulness, if not the complete unification of the disparate movements that young militant groups often urge, at the very least of some consideration of their action and demands. Such coordination might take the form of a network able to bring together groups and individuals in such a way that no one group dominates another; a network able to conserve all of the advantages of the diversity of experiences, perspectives and programmes of each group.*

> (Bourdieu, 2002, page 2)

In the next section, we explore possibilities for generating the kind of shared objectives around which disparate political struggles might coalesce in a single campaign for an emancipatory version of citizenship. These objectives draw largely on Nancy Fraser's (2009) assessment of second-wave feminism that offers basic principles upon which an empowering model of citizenship, consistent with the key values described by the Federation for Community Development Learning (FCDL, undated) for community development work, might be forged.

Citizenship as empowerment

'Second-wave' feminism refers to a second phase in the evolution of feminism that emerged in the 1960s – influenced largely by Simone de Beauvoir's (1949) book *The Second Sex*, which identified gender injustice under patriarchal capitalism. The 'first-wave' refers to the political campaigns that evolved from the nineteenth century for universal suffrage (women's right to vote).

Second-wave feminism offers a critique of the social rights attached to citizenship under the post-war welfare settlement. Fraser (2009, page 97) locates this critique in the context of what she describes as 'state-organized capitalism' and its four defining features:

- First, *Economism* – i.e. the use of social policy to regulate the economy; effectively, 'crisis management in the interest of capital' (Fraser, 2009, page

101) whilst deriving political legitimacy for states 'from their claims to promote inclusion, social equality and cross-class solidarity' (Fraser, 2009, page 101); the 'effect of this class-centric, economistic imaginary was to marginalize, if not wholly to obscure, other dimensions, sites and axes of injustice' (Fraser, 2009, page 101).

- Second, *Androcentrism* – i.e. the development of social policies based on the notion of the 'ideal-typical citizen as an ethnic-majority male worker – a breadwinner and a family man' (Fraser, 2009, page 101); it was also assumed that the man's wage would be the principal or sole income of the family, reinforcing his superiority in the household whilst obscuring 'the social importance of unwaged care work and reproductive labour' (Fraser, 2009, page 102).

- Third, *Étatism* – i.e. a reliance on technocratic, managerial, bureaucratic-professional processes imposed on clients rather than 'active citizens' (Fraser, 2009, page 102); this resulted in a depoliticized culture where 'Far from being empowered to interpret their needs democratically, via political deliberation and contestation, ordinary citizens were positioned (at best) as passive recipients of satisfactions defined and dispensed from on high' (Fraser, 2009, page 102).

- Fourth, *Westphalianism* – i.e. social policies aimed to 'support national economic development in the name – if not always in the interest – of the national citizenry … [T]his formation rested on a division of political space into territorially bounded politics … [T]his view channelled claims for justice into the domestic political arenas of territorial states. The effect … was to truncate the scope of justice, marginalizing, if not wholly obscuring, cross-border injustices' (Fraser, 2009, page 102).

These characteristics of state-organised welfare capitalism came under attack from second-wave feminists and other emancipatory movements from the late 1960s. In particular, by politicising 'the personal' and revealing injustices located elsewhere in everyday life, 'second-wave feminists extended the purview of justice to take in such previously private matters as sexuality, housework, reproduction and violence against women' (Fraser, 2009, page 103). Moreover, 'what connected the plethora of newly discovered injustices was the notion that women's subordination was systemic, grounded in the deep structures of society' (page 103). Overcoming this would require, therefore, a 'radical transformation' (page 104) of these deep structures. Back in the late 1960s, second-wave feminists focused in particular on challenging 'women's responsibility for the lion's share of unpaid caregiving, their subordination in marriage and personal life, the gender segmentation of labour markets, men's domination of the political system, and the androcentrism of welfare provision, industrial policy and development schemes' (page 104). They also strived to democratise welfare provision by transforming 'those positioned as passive objects of welfare and development policy into active subjects, empowered to participate in democratic processes of need interpretation' (page 105). Finally, second-wave feminists expanded the meaning of justice beyond class and gender to take account of 'race', sexuality and nationality (Fraser, 2009).

Campaigning on these themes, second-wave feminism strived for a notion of citizenship as empowerment based on a rejection of economism, androcentrism, étatism and (to a lesser extent) Westphalian national sovereignty. Central to achieving citizen empowerment is distributive justice and 'strong political institutions capable of organising economic life in the service of justice' (Fraser, 2009, page 106). Rather than free markets from state control, second-wave feminists wanted to 'democratize state power, to maximise citizen participation, to strengthen accountability and to increase communicative flows between state and society' (Fraser, 2009, page 106). This contrasts, however, with the contemporary order of things where expectations of citizenship disproportionately fall on the least powerful – particularly disadvantaged young people – while the powerful increasingly withdraw from fulfilling their obligations to society (Lister, forthcoming) – that is the construction of the kind of support arrangements needed – economic, social and political – for active citizenship to flourish.

Summary and conclusions

Throughout the last three decades, there has been greater emphasis in British society on a model of citizenship emphasising behaviour, attitudes and duties rather than rights – especially toward young people and especially toward young people already disadvantaged by 'race', class, gender, sexuality, disability and poverty. As a consequence, social inequality and despair among young people in Britain has increased. Because of this, youth workers need to support young people to rediscover a discourse of citizenship that is emancipatory and recognises young people's capabilities to engage in dialogue about important political and social issues, as well as social action for positive social change.

ACTIVITY **7.8**

In your own youth work/training context, watch michael michael's podcast 'Critical Pedagogy in Action' and discuss the ethical implications of the message that children are not too young to handle the truth or talk about social issues in their own words.

vimeo.com/2560120

There is a need for youth workers to work with young people on restoring a rights-based, inclusionary model of citizenship, respectful of difference, diversity and social justice. There is a need to expose the irresponsibility of the powerful described by Richard Titmuss in the late 1950s when he wrote of the failure of government to fulfil its duties to society 'in a context of unacceptable levels of inequality' (Lister, forthcoming). In this circumstance, Titmuss suggested that 'in the decades ahead, we shall need all the social inventiveness, democratic skills and sense of responsibility which we can mobilise if we are to begin to close the gap of national inequalities' (cited in Lister, forthcoming) – a task that remains with us today.

CHAPTER REVIEW

- 'Citizenship' is a contested concept – one which can have inclusionary or exclusionary effects depending on how it is defined.
- Under neoliberalism, mainstream policy definitions in Britain have advanced a highly moralistic and conditional interpretation of 'citizenship', leading to the increasing marginalisation and pauperisation of the most disadvantaged young people in our communities.
- Because of this, it becomes even more incumbent for community and youth workers to embed emancipatory models of citizenship within their practice in order to support young people to engage innovatively and collectively in strategies of resistance to this assault on their wellbeing.

FURTHER READING

Fletcher, A and Vavrus, J (2006) *The Guide to Social Change Led by and With Young People*. Washington: CommonAction. Available online at www.commonaction.org/social-changeguide.pdf (accessed 18 March 2011). This guide offers a snapshot of the broadbased social movement of young people that exists today - part of a trend described as "The Multitudes" in which localised direct action is subtly, powerfully, having a global effect.

Huebner, A J (1998) Examining 'Empowerment': a how-to guide for the youth development professional. *Journal of Extension*, **36**: 6. Available online at www.joe.org/joe/1998december/a1.php (accessed 18 March 2011). This guide offers a toolkit for community development and youth work professionals.

Sazama, J and Young, K (2006) *15 Points to Successfully Involving Youth in Decision-Making*. Boston: Youth on Board. This guide offers examples of activities aimed at empowering young people to engage in community decision-making.

USEFUL WEBSITES

Citizenship Foundation: www.citizenshipfoundation.org.uk/index.php

The Commonwealth Youth Exchange Council (CYEC) – promotion of global youth work: www.cyec.org.uk/global-youth-work

Directgov – citizenship section for young people: www.direct.gov.uk/en/Nl1/Newsroom/DG_184821

Global Youth Work Project East Midlands: www.gywpem.org.uk/Default.aspx

Institute for Citizenship: www.citizen.org.uk/Home.htm

Chapter 8

Making sense of youth work

CHAPTER OBJECTIVES

This chapter will help you meet the following National Occupational Standards:

4.1   Establish and prioritise requirements for youth work.

4.2   Plan and implement youth work strategy.

4.3   Facilitate change.

4.4.   Monitor and evaluate the effectiveness of youth work strategy and planning.

It will also introduce you to the following academic standards as set out in the QAA youth and community work benchmark statement (2009).

5.1.1   Understanding, developing and managing their professional role: an understanding of and the capacity to apply and integrate theoretical frameworks and key concepts relevant to practice in youth and community work.

The starting point for this discussion of theoretical underpinnings is one of the ethical principles of the professional. In the guidelines *Ethical Conduct in Youth Work: A Statement of Values and Principles From the National Youth Agency* (NYA, 2004, page 6), it states that youth workers have a commitment to make a *contribution towards the promotion of social justice for young people and society in general through encouraging respect for difference and diversity and challenging discrimination*. What is meant by social justice and discrimination here? What would constitute a just society and how and why does discrimination exist and reproduce itself? The way individual youth and community workers answer this question is linked to their view of how individuals and society function and the framework used to explain this relationship.

Making sense of society

Major questions about the individual and society have preoccupied thinkers at all periods of history. The philosophers of Ancient Greece and Rome reflected upon the way society operated/should operate, and for centuries afterwards, social and political theorists and philosophers applied themselves to similar questions. But these 'philosophical' analyses of society are essentially based on speculations, on dubious and untested assumptions about the motives of human beings in their behaviour and on undisciplined theorising as there was no systematic analysis of the structure and workings of societies. In other words, philosophers and thinkers frequently constructed grand models about humans and their societies without looking at how societies actually worked.

ACTIVITY **8.1**

Spend a few minutes thinking about what you understand by society and culture.

Draw a picture (or a cartoon or diagram).

What is the relationship between society and the way people behave?

What do you think about the nature of individuals?

How would you evidence this?

Youth work is just common sense?

Common sense notions of the world involve individualist and naturalistic assumptions. An individualistic explanation of some event or phenomenon assumes that the event can be readily understood and explained solely through reference to the behaviour of the individual(s) involved in it. There is no attempt to understand or explain the phenomenon in terms of wider social forces. Naturalistic explanations of behaviour rests on the assumption that one can readily identify 'natural' (or sometimes God given) reasons for behaviour, such that, for example, it is only 'natural' that two people should fall in love, marry, live together and raise a family. Both types of explanation are rejected by sociologists: individualistic because it does not recognise the importance of wider social forces, acting on the individual whom she or he cannot control; naturalistic because it fails to recognise that behaviour patterns are not biologically determined but rather reflect social conventions that have been learned by individuals as members of social groups or, more generally, society. Prior to the Enlightenment pre-sixteenth century, the universe was seen as a closed world with the earth at the centre. The vast majority of medieval Europeans made sense of their everyday lives in what were essentially religious terms. Within this world view, the main concept used to explain particular events was that of God's purpose. Thus, questions like why do girls grow into women, heavy bodies fall to earth, fires rise from it and slaves serve masters were all answered in that it was their purpose, their natural potential, so to do. Similarly, health was seen as the 'natural state' of the human body. This way of thinking about nature and society gives one no control over them.

However, from the fifteenth, sixteenth and seventeenth centuries in Western Europe, important changes took place with regard to the development of the natural sciences, which, though essentially in their infancy, were beginning to develop systematic methods for studying the physical world. The resulting scientific and technological advances laid the foundations for the transformation from a predominantly rural, agricultural 'manual' way of life to an urban, industrial, 'mechanised' pattern of living, an industrial revolution that occurred in Britain.

Alongside the developments in science and technology, there were also extensive social, economic and political changes emerging from the French and American revolutions, which had profound effects. The changes produced by these revolutions produced societies, which in themselves produced wars between and within nations as well as internal conflicts, poverty, unemployment and so on. These changes resulted in new ways of thinking – understanding what we mean by knowledge. The emergence of the scientific tradition led to the replacement of religious explanations of social and physical phenomena by scientific explanations and posed the question, could science be applied to these human problems?

ACTIVITY **8.2**

Spend a few minutes thinking about a religious explanation of an event – it could be the act of creation.

How would science explain the same phenomenon?

If my car does not start in the morning, I look for an explanation from a diagram in the manual; I look for an explanation based on scientific theories. I might not understand the science but I know that there is some cause and effect explanation, which is rooted in reality.

What is the scientific method?

The method consists of

- observation and description of physical regularities;

- formulation of theories about these patterns and regularities;

- formulation of laws, which could then be applied to either natural or artificially created situations to predict their outcome and ultimately to control them.

The natural sciences, though essentially in their infancy, were beginning to develop systematic methods for studying the physical world and the individual's part in (and relation to) it, and they were being increasingly recognised and valued for providing this more 'certain' knowledge.

Thinking scientifically (about youth work?)

Of all seventeenth-century writers, it was the French philosopher Descartes who most clearly recognised the philosophical implications of this new way of looking. He agreed that the physical body could be understood as a machine but argued that there were other parts of the person that could not be explained in this way. He was concerned to separate out the passive functioning of the body (machine) from the active and rational deliberation of human minds. His main argument was that in almost every respect, the mind and the body possessed opposite characteristics.

Using social science (to theorise youth work practice?)

Sociology emerges against this background, and early sociologists were preoccupied with the problem of order and the causes of conflict. They wanted to get exact knowledge of the workings of society and, living in a period when the natural sciences were making real strides in knowledge, they felt that the application of natural science methods to the study of societies might produce similar advances in understanding social life. Thus, there was a stress on the adoption of the scientific method to the analysis of society, summed up by Auguste Comte's famous phrase: *To know, to predict, to control.*

Let us assume that we need to explore what is meant by a theoretical framework, beginning with the notion of theory. Take, for example, the theory of internal combustion. This theory can be outlined separately from its operation. In other words, we do not have to own a car or operate a car to understand the theory; it exists separately as an objective account of the application of fuel to motion. The different elements, for example, spark plugs, pistons and so on, that need to work together to achieve this purpose could be termed concepts. Thus, a series of concepts have to work together in a certain formation (formula) to operationalise the theory.

The origin of sociology is rooted in the idea that the same level of predictability can be achieved with individuals and society. The expectation from early sociologists was that the methods of the natural sciences could be used to produce theories of human behaviour and the requirements for a just, peaceful society and a vibrant culture. This approach to theory is sometimes labelled positivism and is exemplified through the work of Emile Durkheim. An equally strong approach in sociology takes a diametrically opposite view, sometimes labelled interpretative, demonstrated through the works of Max Weber. This approach uses the language of models and perspectives rather than theory and the starting point is that human beings are unpredictable and cannot be treated with the same methods as the natural sciences. A third approach is based on the works of Marx and Engels and developed by later writers; Marxism can be located on both sides of this debate as it depends on what kind of Marxism is used to investigate an issue or a problem.

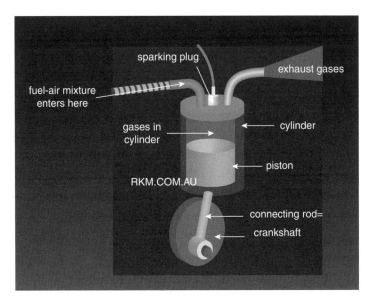

Figure 8.1 4–stroke engine model

What do we want theory to do?

Human beings operate with some kind of theoretical ideas, which may or may not be formed into a coherent framework. The point is that human beings attempt to understand and give meaning to personal problems and social issues. They may see some connections between these and perhaps place an individual problem in a wider social, political or economic context or not. An understanding of the variety of theoretical frameworks, which have and continue to influence policies affecting youth and community, can help workers to analyse practical issues and problems. If the ethics and professional demands of youth work as outlined by NYA/Banks (2004) are a central core of practice, then a worker has to draw from theory as there is a need to understand notions of social justice and equality.

Youth worker as educator

The first and second period listed above can be linked to the approach to the study of society, which is termed functionalism or a consensus model.

This approach has its roots in the history of the youth work movement itself (see Table 8.1). Youth work evolved out of a desire by the Victorian middle classes (philanthropic associations) and the Church to reinforce the existing social order and attempt to improve the conditions of the poor by influencing their attitudes and behaviour.

In the early periods of youth work, character building and cultural adjustment were shaped by this sociological approach, the basis of which can be found in the work of Emile Durkheim (1858–1917). Durkheim's major work *The Division of Labour in Society* (1893) springs from a concern with the problem of order, social

Table 8.1 A brief history of purpose in youth work

Period	Purpose	Worker	Young person
1870–1919	Character building	Role model	Follower
1920–1950	Cultural adjustment	Teacher	Role fitting
1950–1980	Personal development	Facilitator	Self-realisation
1980–1990	Empowerment	Activist	Group solidarity
2000–	Self-emancipation	Social critic	Change agent

Source: Adapted by Bamber and Murphy (1999, page 229) from Butters and Newell (1978).

Table 8.2 Forms of the division of labour

Organic solidarity		
Anomic character	Spontaneous	Forced character
Absence of regulation	Moral regulation	Coercive regulation
Moral anarchy	Just society	Repressive

Source: Eldridge (1973, page 79).

integration and social cohesion. He wanted to 'prove' that industrialisation was not a force for conflict, rebellion and revolution. The overriding emphasis in his work is what binds individuals together in a society. He believed that in simpler and more traditional society, solidarity is produced by the strong feelings people have of belonging to a group and that social cohesion is based on a similarity of values and life experiences, which he termed 'mechanical solidarity'. In contrast, industrial societies are characterised by 'organic solidarity', which is based on interdependence and industrial development.

By the anomic division of labour (see Table 8.2), Durkheim meant the failure of traditional societies, like Britain, to adjust completely to the changes in economic life brought about by industrialisation. The growth of the market economy meant that growth was relatively unregulated and that business involved considerable risk taking with the inevitable economic crises and failures. Also, the relations between employers and workers were altered, and their interests became more opposed. Workers were separated from their families, and their work became meaningless to them because they were regulated by machines and had no sense of purpose in their work. Durkheim did not see this situation as an inevitable result of the normal division of labour, as Marx did, for example, but as something that could be remedied.

Durkheim qualified his assertion that the division of labour resulted in organic solidarity by distinguishing another abnormal form of the phenomenon. Organic solidarity only resulted from the division of labour if it was a spontaneous development and not if it was forced: *labour is divided spontaneously only if society is constituted in such a way that social inequalities exactly express natural inequalities* (Durkheim, 1964).

A view of social justice from this perspective

In Durkheim's work there is a tension between the needs of individuals and the needs of society. As Anthony Giddens writes in his study of Durkheim,

> *The key to Durkheim's whole life's work is to be found in his attempt to resolve the apparent paradox that the liberty of the individual is only achieved through his* (sic) *dependence on society.*

(1972, page 45)

The paradox can be traced to Durkheim's view of human nature. Basically, he saw human beings as being a mixture – *homo duplex* – of good and bad. Restraint and moral regulation was needed in society, so that the negative aspects of human behaviour such as greed and selfishness can be modified if not eliminated. It was only through regulation and recognising the interdependence of each other, and groups, on the societal whole, that 'true' individuality could be achieved. The causes of conflict and social disorder, he regarded as 'abnormal forms of the division of labour' – forced regulation and anomie – and regarded the *economic structure of* 'laissez-faire' *society, with its powerful inducements to self-interested behaviour* (Lee and Newby, 1983, page 221), as a major source of alienation and disaffection. For Durkheim, social cohesion in industrial/capitalist societies can only be achieved by the 'spontaneous character' of the division of labour, which is based on equality of opportunity but not the elimination of inequalities. Education is the mechanism whereby young people are given opportunities to get their place in society, a system of meritocracy.

All individuals and groups should have the same freedom to choose their work and their employer, but this freedom of contract was not sufficient to ensure spontaneity if such things as the hereditary transmission of wealth occurred unchecked. Durkheim, then, was not advocating a laissez-faire situation but argued that social regulation was required to ensure a *just society* in which the spontaneous division of labour ensured organic solidarity. He did not believe that a society could exist without conflict but that social solidarity would moderate conflict.

Durkheim believed that socialisation, especially through the education system, was the key to establish social stability and social cohesion. Young people need to be socialised to the culture, traditions and ways of behaving in society. There is presumed to be a shared set of values in society, a consensus on culture, expectations and beliefs.

We unconsciously learn how to act and behave in the social world. We are taught to eat with a knife and fork because that is part of our culture. We are taught to dress and act in a certain way. For example, we don't go around picking our noses or pop on the number 8 bus naked because these things are seen as socially unacceptable. We are thus socialised into the norms and values of our society. So the fact that we use knives and forks instead of our hands to eat is part of our cultural inheritance.

What then do we understand by 'culture'?

- Culture refers to the organisation of experience shared by members of a community, a process that includes the standards and values for judging and thinking, for predicting and acting.

- Culture refers to the accumulated experiences, meanings, rule systems and forms of understanding of groups and societies

- Culture is that complex whole, which includes knowledge, belief, art, morals, law, custom and any other capabilities and habits acquired by human beings as members of society.

- Culture consists of models or patterns of thinking, feeling and behaviour, which have been socially learned.

There is clearly some overlap among these definitions, which can to some extent be explained by the fact that not all members of a society share the same culture. In one sense, of course, they do. To be a member of a society is to share in its language but regional differences, class differences, gender and ethnic differences means that coming up with a strict/clear definition of culture is difficult.

Role of youth work using a Durkheimian approach

The role of youth work in this model is that youth work complements the socialisation process of the family and the school. The aim is to prepare young people for their roles in society while instilling them with the shared moral values and beliefs. Youth workers would act as educators and as role models for young people. The participation of young people in decision making is thus limited by this view. If they are being trained, then decision making is almost always hierarchical, there is a clear distinction between adults and young people and it is adults who have power. Durkheim did not analyse power relations and thus ignored how structured social inequalities, not the division of labour, are the basis for the existence of alienated and socially excluded groups in society.

Levitas (1998, page 186) provides a detailed discussion of the relationship between Durkheim's ideas and New Labour's strategies on social exclusion. She states that

> *the problem with Durkheim's own argument … is that just as he represses the structural conflict of interest within society, so he simultaneously suppresses the question of whose interests are served.*

Her analysis of the contradictions and paradoxes thrown up by the Durkheimian underpinnings of Labour's 'third way' is well made as is her analysis that despite its limitations, the contradictions that emerge from social inclusion strategies could facilitate the posing of a debate on the extent to which capitalism can ever facilitate a stable, cohesive and equal society.

> *If we or future generations are to have any hope of living in a society which is built around our needs as persons … the question of alternatives to capitalism must be reopened. It may be countered that capitalism is the only game in town and there is no alternative; but humankind must sometimes set itself questions which it cannot immediately solve.*

(Levitas, 1998, page 189).

This quotation could be the foundation for critical youth work, but before this approach becomes an acceptable part of youth work practice, the emphasis shifts from the needs of society to the needs of the individual. Following the chronology provided by Butters and Newell (1978), there is a move to focus on the personal development needs of young people. This approach can be linked to the interpretative perspective in sociology. Through the work of Max Weber, this section introduces an alternative view of society and social theory to that discussed in the last section.

From socialisation to interpretation

German social science as opposed to German philosophy had been strongly influenced by Comte and Spencer as well as by the emerging Marxist intellectual culture, which occurred in 1890s. Under the leadership of Karl Kautsky and Eduard Bernstein, the German Social Democratic Party (SPD) in Germany at the time became the single most important Marxist political party in Europe, and it commanded widespread support from the German working class. The rise of and institutionalisation of German sociology effectively coincided with the development of this mass political party, committed to Marxism.

Weber's sociology developed as a response to both the evolutionary theorists of Comte and Spencer and Marxism (a particular version espoused by the SPD). So Weber's sociology was shaped by these currents. As with Marx, Weber's writings cover a wide range of topics. In addition to the methodology of the social science, which is the focus of the discussion here, he also wrote studies in economic sociology, political sociology (his work on bureaucracy) and comparative religions. So, his output was as great and varied as the works of Durkheim and Marx, and they are still of lasting importance and, of course, controversy in sociology. His starting point is very different to these writers. Rather than beginning with the structure of society, he begins with individual social action. For him, the aim of sociology is to understand the characteristics of social reality and how it differs from previous social realities. Social reality here is created by the social meanings given to social actions by individuals and groups. Society, for Weber, is made up of groups of individuals, acting meaningfully and oriented towards certain goals and values. Society, for Weber, is not this thing-like entity as it is for Durkheim; rather he sees society as being made up of groups of individuals, acting meaningfully and orientated towards certain goals and values.

Weber's approach to social science

Weber was much more concerned with causal analysis, rather than finding the 'laws' that governed society. One of the best ways to understand this perspective is Weber's study of the *Protestant Ethic and the Spirit of Capitalism*. For Weber, the origin of capitalism was linked with the emergence of Protestantism and, in particular, ascetic Protestantism and its associated religious sects such as Puritanism, Calvinism, Methodism, Pietism and various Baptist sects that developed towards the end of the sixteenth century. This Protestantism contained within it certain ideas and beliefs, which resulted in predisposing individuals to a particular rational ethic – a particular orientation to work – that produced a spirit of capitalism, which he relates to a particular structure of attitudes and beliefs towards life and eternal salvation. The religious practices stressed the need to be prudent and diligent, the avoidance of idleness, not wasting time, to be scrupulously honest in the repayment of loans and debts, to be frugal in consumption and so on. His main analysis focused on Calvinism and not just the writings of Calvin himself but the teachings of Calvinism towards the end of the sixteenth and into the seventeenth centuries.

For Weber, Calvinism was the notion of a world vocation or calling, the idea that individuals have a 'calling' from God to perform certain worldly tasks that should be carried out in a certain way – predestination. Whereas other religious thought may promote an 'other worldly' approach to life, stressing the life hereafter, Calvinism made individuals focus on their attention on life here and now, applying themselves to the fulfilment of duties in worldly affairs. Capitalism then is an unintended consequence of religious beliefs and the actions taken by groups of individuals and explains the change from simply spending wealth to attention being focused on the getting of it.

Why should people compulsively accumulate capital? Why the change from simply spending wealth to attention being focused on the getting of it? The ethics of Catholicism and most varieties of Christianity at that time urged people to give rather than accumulate. If you gave someone a loan, you did this out of human charity – you did not make money from another's misfortune. The opening sentence from Weber's text addresses this issue: what, he asks, is the significance of the fact that *business leaders and owners of capital, as well as the higher grades of skilled labour, and even more the higher technically and commercially trained personnel of modern enterprises are overwhelmingly Protestant?* (Weber, 1905, page 35). He saw religious ideas as having unanticipated consequences for the economic development of society.

The unintended impact of religious ideas on society

Business leaders then are following their 'calling'. This notion of 'calling' has to be viewed with another notion: that of predestination. This means that you were predestined by God either for salvation or for damnation. That is, you are fated, marked from the moment you were born and whatever you did in the world wouldn't affect whether or not you reach the kingdom of heaven. However, God created the world for his own glory, so whether or not you were predestined to see him it was still your duty to work for the glory of God and to try to live your life in a dutiful way.

Weber's argument is that it is precisely because the idea of predestination was so awful, causing such psychological inner loneliness that individuals attempted to prove to themselves that they were one of the 'elect', that is, one of God's chosen. They did this by being successful in their dealings, in this instance business dealing. This functions as a way of assuaging the fear of damnation and thus religion acted as a dynamic element in social changes.

The Calvinist, writes Weber, creates their own salvation or, more correctly, the conviction of it. Hard work and the moral pursuit of a calling, while not a guarantee of salvation, nevertheless functions as a sign and helps to assuage fear and psychological inner loneliness.

It was this rational calculating social action that has the unintended consequence of producing a spirit of capitalism. Weber is not arguing that these ideas on their own created capitalism, rather they are an element along with other components, very similar to those identified by Marx, which shaped the economic system. As he states,

> It is not my aim to substitute for a one-sided materialistic and one-sided spiritualistic causal interpretation of culture and of history. Each is equally possible, but each, if it does not serve as the preparation but as the conclusion of an investigation, accomplishes equally little in the interests of historical truth.

> (Weber, 1905, page 183)

There is a debate about Marx and Weber's view of capitalism, which we cannot consider here (see Hill, 1997; Marshall, 1982), but it is important to point out that while Marx's analysis is writing at the level of how the society is produced and reproduced, Weber's analysis is at the level of how individual differences are distributed. Weber's argument is about the methodology approach he adopts, which is against any reductionist, mono-causal explanation of social reality and directs social theory to the individual as an active agent in the shaping of society.

Interpretative perspective – a rational approach to youth work

Max Weber characterises this switch from 'religious' explanations to 'scientific' ones, as part of the rationalisation of the modern world. For Weber, modern society was above all, a society pervaded by rationalisation and an ever-growing commitment to action and activities based on rationality and reason. This means that the way we act is based on rational calculation, on predictability and using logical thought in social life as opposed to using custom or tradition.

For example, if I wanted to know the quickest way to work, I would calculate how long it would take me to go by car or bike or whatever, work out the shortest distance, predicting (if using a car, for instance) traffic hold ups and so on. This is instead of simply thinking 'I'm not going down that road because I will meet the devil or spirits', or 'I'm going this way because I have gone this way with friends and family for generations'.

More and more people orientate their lives to the idea of doing things efficiently, of achieving their ends by the most economical precisely calculated means. But as they become more and more rationalistic in this 'formal' sense, their actions progressively cease to be oriented to values or ideals. The means become the end. Rationality then is a problem for Weber, as it becomes irrational, signifies lack of spontaneity, of creativity, of magic and a retreat from ultimate values and ideals. Thus the ideology of science leads to the development of a supposed objective, rational, logical, account of the natural world and society. This method is the one that is seen as the only rational approach.

The role of youth work using this approach

The focus here is working with the individual and the contribution youth work can make by providing a range of opportunities for young people to acquire the skills necessary to take on the responsibilities of adulthood. The focus is on the personal development of the individual and the youth worker enabling a young person to reach their goals. Social justice in this model would mean helping each young person to determine their needs and goals in a rational and reasonable way. This approach differs substantively from the Durkheimian paradigm discussed previously. Here youth work is concerned with understanding the essence of the everyday world primarily from the viewpoint of the actions of those directly involved in the social process. Problem is that this mostly involves understanding rather than questioning the structures that perpetuate the social reality encountered by young people.

Critical social change model of youth work

Based on the works of Marx, key writers in this tradition would be Paulo Freire, Antonio Gramsci and Louis Althusser. The premise is that advanced capitalism is a complex and sophisticated social system that has used the organs of civil society very effectively in the service of the status quo, for example, the education system. It is precisely because a consensus has been created that it is able to resist and incorporate protest.

Introduction to Marx's theories

I would just like to outline some of the problems we face in studying Marx; first, there is the not inconsiderable problem of the large scale of Marx's work – he is not easily pigeonholed into being labelled as an economist, a sociologist, a philosopher, a political theorist or a historian – he was all of these. Indeed, Marx and Marxists reject the whole notion of this intellectual devision of labour. There is also the fact that Marx was not an academic commentator, content to mark out his thoughts in a contemplative manner. One of his most famous statements is, *philosophers have only interpreted the world, in various ways. The point, however, is to change it* [Thesis 11: *Theses on Feuerbach*]. He studied and wrote, argued and acted all his life, first to understand the world he lived in and then to change that world.

As Lee and Newby (1983) state, Marx is probably the single most intellectual figure in the history of ideas since Jesus Christ. As they point out, over a third of the world's population live in societies defined as 'Marxist'. Within existing capitalist societies, we read almost every day of the continuing activities of his followers (whether it be 'subversives' in the coal strike or the Peace movement or Catholic priests in Latin America who join together, within their 'theology of liberation', the ideas of Karl Marx and the life of Jesus Christ as part of their own struggle for a free and just society).

Therefore, it is very difficult, if not impossible, to approach Marx with a neutral view. People reading this text, despite different backgrounds and experiences, live together in a certain historical moment of time. Marx would have not been surprised to see capitalism today, on one hand, engaging in extraordinary space technology and also containing large sections of society living in poverty all under the umbrella of the same system.

So when you study Marx, you will be obliged to challenge your own views and experiences. The only proper way to know Marx is to read his writings and not to rely on other people's interpretations, including mine. Marx's favourite motto was 'Doubt everything' and I am sure you will be as rigorous as Marx was in applying that maxim.

Let us first of all place the young Marx in his historical context. He was born in 1818, in the German Rhineland, and brought up in a comfortable and fairly prosperous middle-class home. His father was a legal officer, and like many of his Rhineland contemporaries was a moderate liberal with a deep faith in the power of reason.

In l835, Marx went to University in Bonn to study law. Like his fellow students he got drunk, ran up huge debts, fought duels and on one occasion even spent a night in jail for brawling. In late l836, he moved to Berlin University where, after having a huge row with his father, he gave up law for philosophy, a crucial point in his development. German philosophy in the l830s and l840s was a highly political business. Germany itself was then a politically, economically and socially divided country, and its people were subject to the absolute power of local princedoms, which in turn were dominated by the powers of the Holy Alliance (so-called) of Austria, Prussia and Russia. Despite this, the country flourished intellectually, and the early nineteenth century was the golden age of German Philosophy.

First he was a philosopher who followed Hegel

The dominant figure in German philosophy was Hegel who at first had been an enthusiast for the French Revolution but who then became pessimistic and reactionary, advocating that the Absolutist Prussian State was the embodiment of reason. Thus, in the l830s and l840s, Hegel was to all intents and purposes the official Prussian philosopher, and his followers received appointments in the State controlled universities.

Increasingly, young German philosophers began to interpret Hegel's ideas in a more radical way, and this was related/reflected in a radical shift in their politics. Young Hegelians, as they were known (of which Marx was a prominent member), came into conflict with the Prussian State. Thus, Marx's apparent ambition to be a professional philosopher at a State University was denied and he threw himself into political journalism. At this time, Marx was little more than a radical liberal democrat who hoped to see in Germany a republic and universal suffrage; however, two experiences as a journalist were to prove vital to his future development – both led him to become very critical of 'private property'. The first was when he followed the local 'parliamentary' debates on the call for tougher penalties for theft of wood. Here, he saw how not only the old feudal landlords, who supported the Absolutist State, called for harsher treatment against the peasants who collected wood, but that the rising industrialists too were keen to defend private property. His second experience was that of seeing the miserable conditions of the peasants in the Moselle wine countries.

Hegel's method of looking at society and history provided Marx with a revolutionary conceptual tool – that is, the notion of dialectic.

The Greek Philosopher Aristotle codified traditional or formal logic. It was based on three fundamental laws:

1. The law of identity: A is equal to A: a thing is always equal to itself.

2. The law of contradiction: A is different from non-A. A can never equal non-A.

3. The law of exclusion: either A or non-A. Nothing can be either A nor non-A.

There is no in-between (conceptually re-enforcing the static nature of formal logic), that is, the acorn is an acorn.

If we just think about these three laws for a moment, we can see they're not as complicated as they may first seem. It's the codifying of what we would term the obvious – 'it's commonsense'.

We can see that we use this formal logic every day in our lives, but it has one major disadvantage – it has a static view of reality.

The key to Hegel's dialectical logic is that it takes into account the idea of motion, of change. The Hegelian dialectic is based on two assumptions:

1. That all things are *contradictory in themselves*;

2. That contradiction is at the root of all movement and life, and it is only insofar as it contains a contradiction that anything moves and has impulse and activity.

Let's use some examples to clarify what this notion of contradiction means. Consider the acorn and the oak. The acorn, in becoming an oak, has itself ceased to be. The oak is different from the acorn. The oak is not the acorn. Hegel would say that the oak is the negation of the acorn. Yet implicit within the acorn is the potential to become an oak. The acorn contains within itself its own negation and is thus contradictory. Hegel suggests that it is this contradiction and only this contradiction that allows it to grow.

Indeed, this sort of contradiction is present in everything; reality is the process through which, again and again, the negation within things comes to the surface and changes them. Reality is change.

Hegel develops this idea further: when something negates itself, it turns into its opposite. An example of this process is what Hegel called the transformation of quantity into quality. That is, a succession of small changes, each of which leaves the basic character of a thing unaltered, can lead, beyond a certain point, to its complete transformation. For example, gradually reducing the temperature of water will make no difference to it, until it reaches 0°C when it will freeze, changing from a liquid to a solid. Melt the ice and gradually raise the temperature of the water. Again no significant change will occur until 100°C is reached – boiling point – then the water will begin to evaporate, turning from a liquid into a gas. Thus, a series of changes in the quantity of temperature of water leads to a change in its quality. Quantity, says Hegel, becomes its opposite, quality.

But Hegel goes on to argue that beneath this apparent opposition is an underlying unity. For example, let us use another example to reinforce the point. A 70-year-old man is obviously very different from the week old baby he once was. Yet they are the *same* person. The old man was once that baby, and they share a basic identity despite the many changes that 70 years of living bring about.

So Hegel's broader argument is that if we merely concentrate on individual things, we see only the differences between them. Once we look at things from the perspective of the process of the dialectic, however, we see that they are all part of the same process. 'The truth is the whole'. Things acquire their real meaning only when we see them as moments in a process of change.

ACTIVITY 8.3

Have a rest, make a cup of tea.

While you are making the tea, look at the steam coming from the kettle. Note the change from water to steam. Look at the cup and the kettle. Note that there is a relationship between all these objects.

What is it?

They were conceived and made by human beings but not in conditions of their own making.

Hegel himself got terribly confused about how he used his ideas of the dialectic and instead of retaining the dialectic as a way of understanding the world, he elevated this way of thinking into the controlling factor itself. He claimed that his logical categories were *themselves* responsible for the life and movement of the real world. Thought created reality said Hegel, just as in the Bible we are led to believe that God created the world.

Marx described the predicament that Hegel got himself into in a famous passage where he said, *the dialectic is standing on its head. It must be inverted, in order to discover the rational kernel within the mystical shell* (Marx, 1875, preface).

It was Ludwig Feuerbach who cracked the 'mystical shell' in a devastating attack on religion in his book *The Essence of Christianity* (1841). Feuerbach argued that Hegel had turned something that is merely the property of human beings (the faculty of thought) into the ruling principle of existence. Instead of seeing human beings as part of the material world and thought merely as the way they reflect that material world Hegel had turned both human beings and nature into mere reflections of an all-powerful absolute idea.

Feuerbach's main achievement was that he re-instated the materialism of the French Enlightenment; but in cracking the mystic shell, he dismissed the notion of dialectic and replaced Hegel's idealism with his own inadequate materialism. In place of such concepts of as God and the Idea, Feuerbach put man, with an all-embracing capital big 'M'. Like the philosophers of the Enlightenment, Feuerbach still conceived human nature as something which did not change. He argued that it was love that was the cement and the motive force of human society and that all mankind had to do was to be educated into getting rid of superstitions and religious beliefs and discover their own essence. Rather like the hippies of the 1960s who claimed all you had to do was love each other.

Feuerbach's critique of Hegel had a very positive influence on Marx and indeed provided the starting point for the latter's own distinctive position. Having refined Hegel's concept of dialectic, Marx now precisely defined a materialist explanation as the basis of his conception of history.

> *It is not the consciousness of men that determines their being, but on the
> contrary their social being which determines their consciousness.*

(Contribution to the Critique of Political Economy, 1859)

The next formative step was when censorship in Prussia made work impossible and Marx moved to Paris and came into contact with a society undergoing rapid industrialisation and the emergence of a mass working-class movement that was inundated with all kinds of early anti-capitalist, proto socialist ideas. Marx begins to shift radically away from liberalism and begins to elaborate the role of the working class. Only a social revolution, which swept away private property, could offer 'human emancipation'.

In the *Economic and Philosophic Manuscripts of 1844*, Marx not only began to elaborate his critique of orthodox/classical economy but also further developed his alternative philosophical views to that of Feuerbach. Feuerbach saw 'love' as the native force in society, but for Marx, it was labour that was the essence of mankind and the basis of society. So instead of dealing with an historical, all-embracing notion of Man, Marx started to examine society and the economy from the perspective of men and women producing the means by which they will survive as a species.

This required the transformation of nature by human labour. Marx ridiculed the idea of an unchanging nature as much as he did that of an eternal human nature. He wrote of Feuerbach:

> *He does not see that the sensuous world around him is not a thing given
> directly for all eternity remaining ever the same, but the product of industry
> and of the state of society; and indeed (a product) in the sense that it
> is a historical product, the result of the activity of a whole succession of
> generations each standing on the shoulders of the preceding one.*

(Marx, 1845)

But, and note the influence of dialectical thinking, the labour of human beings not only transforms nature but also alters human beings themselves. Production is for Marx a social activity. Having defined production as the most fundamental human activity, it follows that Marx will now give most attention to the way in which production is organised. Thus, he was obliged to examine the nature of relationships within the organisation of production.

The dialectical method is displayed yet again when Marx concludes that if production is a social activity, then it follows that changes in the organisation of production will bring about changes in society, and therefore, since *the essence of man is the ensemble of the social relations* (Easton and Guddat, 1967, page 402; *Theses on Feuerbach: Thesis 6*) – which means human nature as such does not reside somewhere in us, like a spirit, but derives from the kind of *social relations of production* – changes in these means that there will also be changes in people's beliefs, desires and conduct.

163

The crucial point here is the absolute centrality of the economic system, for Marx. That is, the way people organise themselves to satisfy their material needs for food, clothing, shelter and so on determines their whole way of life. As long as each individual is not doing everything alone there exists a division of labour, and this will lead to divisions between skilled and unskilled workers, manual and non-manual workers, those who produce and those who provide services, those who give orders and those who do not, and most fundamentally between owners of capital and those with only their labour to sell. These social relations are *the real foundation on which legal and political superstructures arise and to which definite forms of social consciousness correspond*.

Thus, for Marx, work is the foundation of society upon which the superstructure of family, conjugal roles, religious beliefs, system of government, laws and so on are built. The work society undertakes constitutes the forces/means of production, the way people organise themselves to do it constitutes the relations of production; both of these together constitute the mode of production.

Remembering the quote earlier from Marx about social existence determining consciousness and not the other way around, let us try and pull this all together with an imaginary example. Imagine that this whole class is suddenly marooned on a desert island. To survive, you need food, but the only food available is a species of nocturnal rabbit. In the first instance, the forces and means of production will be hunting, and if everybody is required to hunt, your conventional pattern of living by day and sleeping by night must be reversed. Then, the way you decide to organise yourselves to catch the rabbits will produce the 'relations of productions' – who does what. Will everyone fend for themselves, or will there be a division of labour? If so, who will do what? Will the best numbers keep all they catch, or get the biggest share, or will the 'catch' be divided up equally? How will decisions be made? Will the most successful numbers become the leaders or have higher status? Will they develop more power? The answers to all these questions would describe the relations of production, but the answers depend on the forces and means of production plus the social relations of production which together constitute the mode of production.

So, a few people chasing rabbits to survive – and we see how incredibly complex the questions and issues are.

Imagine the position Marx finds himself in trying to explain a whole form of society. The development of his analysis first through criticism of other people like Hegel and Feuerbach provides him with the analytical tools to extend his ideas even further.

Marx then takes a scientific approach to radical social change

The previous section concentrated on the evolution of Marx's thought and, in particular, discussed how by revolutionising aspects of Hegel's thought he acquired a conceptual tool by which he could analyse humanity, society and production not as statistical entities but as processes forever in moments of change. This dialectical perception based on a materialist understanding of how human beings attempt to survive and live led Marx, as we saw, to develop a humanist philosophical critique of capitalism.

However, Marx's crowning achievement, indeed the centrepiece of his life's work, was *Capital*. Marx's object was, as he put it in the preface to volume 1, *to reveal the economic laws of motion of human society*. While previous economic thinkers had grasped one or other aspects of capitalism's workings, Marx sought to understand it as a whole.

The cornerstone of Marx's critique of capitalism is the Theory of Labour Value. The basis of every human society is the labour process, human beings co-operating to make use of the forces of nature, and during this to meet their needs.

The products of labour must therefore, before anything else, answer some human need. It must in other words be useful. Marx therefore calls it a 'use-value'. A product's value lies first and foremost in being of use to someone. The need met by a use-value does not have to be a physical need, for example, a book has a use-value because students need to read. Equally, the needs that use-values meet may be to achieve vile purposes. A murderer's gun is as much a use-value as a can of baked beans or a surgeon's scalpel.

Under capitalism, however, the products of labour take the form of 'commodities'; capitalism then is a system of commodity production. This is an entirely unique feature of capitalism, for pre-capitalist modes of production were concerned with the exchange of products only insofar as it is necessary to secure basic human needs; under capitalism, however, commodity production – production for the purposes of exchange – becomes an end in itself.

A commodity then, as Adam Smith pointed out, does not merely have a use-value but also an exchange value. Commodities are made, not to be directly consumed but to be sold on the market. They are produced to be exchanged.

Use-values and exchange values are different from each other. Again – to take an example of Adam Smith – the air we breathe is something of almost infinite use-value to human beings, because without it we would die; yet it has no exchange value. Diamonds on the other hand are of comparatively little use but have a very high exchange value.

Moreover, a use-value has to meet *specific* human need. If you are hungry, a book is no good. By contrast, the exchange value of a commodity is simply the amount it will exchange for other commodities. Exchange values reflect what commodities have in common, rather than their specific qualities – for example, a loaf of bread can be exchanged for a tin opener, either directly or through the medium of money even though their uses are very different. What is it that they have in common, what in other words permits this exchange to take place? According to Marx, the exchange value of commodities is determined by the average number of hours of labour, of average levels of skill, used directly and indirectly in the production of commodities.

In other words, Marx does not see questions of value relating to 'supply and demand' but to the amount of human labour expended in producing commodities. The value of a commodity is equivalent to the amount of labour expended in it.

Now the unique and distinctive feature of capitalism that Marx discovers is that, under capitalism, under this system of generalised commodity production, labour power is itself a commodity. *This point is crucial.* While pre-capitalist societies had been 'exploitative', that is, there was an exploiter and an exploited class, capitalism created a new form of exploitation.

In the past, under feudalism, for example, peasants paid taxes or produced goods (food products, etc.) for their masters. However, the vast majority of peasants had some control over producing their own means of subsistence, perhaps a strip of land for their own vegetables, or raising livestock on common pasture, and/or taking wood from common woods. Wage labour came into existence in the sixteenth and eighteenth centuries when large numbers of peasants were pushed off the land by landowners who took over the peasants land and the previously common-owned ground (the Enclosure Acts). As late as 1820, the Duchess of Sutherland dispossessed 15,000 tenants from 794,000 acres of land.

Peasants could no longer live and were forced to go to the growing cities where they found a commercial market-oriented economy. They could no longer produce or sell products as they had no access to the land or to the means of production. But as a worker, you had to buy commodities to live and you could not do this unless you sold something to acquire the money. Such a worker has only one sellable thing – capacity to labour. Under capitalism, the labourers sell their labour power for definite periods of times, the hour, the day or the week. The wage was the price the worker received for selling their capacity to labour for this period of time.

During this period of the working day, the labourer/the workers, however, do not receive the value of the labour. For in, for example, an eight-hour day, the worker produces more value – that is, what Marx called surplus value – than he or she receives back in the form of wages.

Example: shoe factory (loosely based on *The Ragged Trousered Philanthropists* by Robert Tressell – 1870–1911)

I earn £100 a week/£20 a day working in a shoe factory.

Each pair of shoes I make sells for £10.

In one hour, I make 1 pair of shoes = £80 in a day.

In one 40-hour week, I make 40 pairs of shoes at £10 = £400.

Surplus value = £300.

Take away cost of materials and so on, and the rest is PROFIT.

Surplus value is then the source of profit and not the equivalent of it. Surplus value refers to the exchange value of commodities, which the capitalist appropriates from labourers during the process of production. The rate of extraction of surplus value therefore determines the rate of exploitation of direct producers – workers. Put another way, under capitalism, the workers are involved in the creation of exchange value through their labour, but the capitalists retain part of this surplus value. From this surplus, the capitalist must find his investment in further constant capital (new machines, raw materials, etc.) retaining the remainder as profit. Thus, workers do not receive the full exchange value of the goods they produce.

Defining exploitation and how to achieve social justice

It is important to note that when Marx talks about 'exploitation' of the working class by the capitalist class, he is not using the word purely in an emotive or moral sense. He claimed that it was a precise scientific concept and took place whether an individual capitalist was good or bad tempered towards their workers. The reason for this is that according to Marx, workers spend part of the working time producing in order that the employer can pay their wages, so they can then purchase the means to live; for Marx, it is not relevant whether the worker is receiving high or low wages – she or he is still being exploited. For after working to acquire the value of their own upkeep, the worker carries on working – transforming through their own labour power the raw material into commodities. It is the additional labour which represents surplus value.

It is important to stress that for Marx capitalism wasn't merely an economic system that ran from 9–5 and then clocked off for the day. Furthermore, capitalism doesn't simply rely on the coercive organs of the state (army, police, law, etc.) – although Marx argued it would if necessary. Neither does it just rule by the dissemination of its ideas through institutions/agencies like the media, religions or educational systems – although again these ideological prize fighters of capitalism, as Marx called them, are vital components of a ruling class's capacity to rule.

What I want to concentrate on is Marx's analysis of what happens to human beings, and workers in particular, who are living within a capitalist mode of production.

People are social beings. As capitalism developed one of its key elements was the consistent need to revolutionise the division of labour. It is very rare for a worker to produce a whole product. They produce merely a part, which goes towards the final commodity. Also the division of labour separates intelligence, mental worker from manual worker – work on a production line needs only their hands not their brains. Marx states that this is part of the alienation experienced by workers under capitalism: *man becomes mutilated into a fragment of a man (degraded) to the level of an appendage of a machine in his direct productive activity* (*Capital*, Volume 1, 1906, pages 461–2).

> # Marx distinguishes four aspects of alienated labour:
>
> 1. *The relationship of the worker to the* product of labour *as an alien object that dominates them. Thus, the more the worker expends herself or himself in work, the more powerful becomes the world of objects, which she or he creates, the poorer she or he becomes in her or his inner life and the less she or he belongs to her or himself.*
>
> 2. *The relationship of labour to the act of production with the result that the work is external to the workers, that it is not part of their nature, and consequently, it does not fulfil them but denies them leaving a feeling of misery rather than well-being and does not develop freely their mental and physical energies but physically exhausts and mentally debases them. The workers, therefore, feel at home only during their leisure hours. Their work is not voluntary but imposed – forced labour. It is not the satisfaction of a need but the means of satisfying other needs.*
>
> 3. *The alienation of man (sic) from himself as a 'species being' from 'his own activity, which should be free – conscious activity'. Man is thus alienated from his own body – his mental life and his human life.*
>
> 4. *The alienation of humans from other humans: instead of relations between people as being that of individual to individual, under capitalism the relations of person to person are structured in terms of worker and capitalist, as farmer and landlord in feudalism.*
>
> *All these aspects of alienation are linked to production, for it is this sphere which shapes the way production is organised, which shapes a workers view of their work, their products and the institutions of their society and of other people and themselves. As Marx wrote,* the capitalist system perfects the worker and degrades the man *(sic).*

This theory leads onto another important concept of Marx, namely, 'Reification'. He said, 'It is not the consciousness of men that determines being but on the contrary their social being determines consciousness' (Marx and Engels, 1970, page 181). There is then, for Marx, a dialectical relationship in this – there is a mutual interaction between human ideas and the conditions they confront. Marx is careful never to stress one at the expense of the other. He is saying that human beings are conscious, acting, thinking human beings, which created the world even though they are also a product of the work.

On this idea of consciousness, Marx compares human beings to animal forms – a spider conducts operations that resemble those of a weaver, and a bee puts to shame many an architect in the construction of her cells. But what distinguishes the worst architect from the best of bees is this: that the architect raises his structure in imagination before they exist in reality. At the end of every labour process, we get a result that already existed in the imagination of the labourer at its commencement. They not only affect a change of form in material while they work but also many people in class society fail to realise what purposes could be realised other than the way they are at present. They fail to realise because human products become alien and independent of the control of most members of society – when this occurs there arises a corresponding structure of consciousness, reification.

This kind of consciousness divorces the act of work production from the people who made the work, human beings, and it is as though things made the world (i.e. technical inventions brought about industrial revolution rather than human beings). The human work is no longer conceived as social, as man-made. Human relations instead are seen as functions of relations between things. This characteristic of 'thing-hood' pervades our consciousness such that human beings can be perceived as 'things', for example, as a unit of production.

Remember the example about the Prussian landowners and the bourgeoisie calling for a clamp down on the theft of wood by the peasants. In this analysis, Marx shows how the theft of wood involved penalties, which denigrated a perversion of the relationship between human beings and things. Wood, a piece of inanimate matter, is seen as determining the relations of human beings to others, so that they are conceived not as human beings but either as, on one hand, owners of the wood or as thieves of the wood (they are conceived not as human beings but as functions of wood).

This reification of social relations can only occur in conditions where human beings do not act towards each other as human beings. The capitalist market, the present way we organise our needs and wants, is looked upon as a fitted unalterable entity to be obeyed; it takes on a super-human form. Its laws are not understood as the totality of the social relations that compose it – they are viewed and it is viewed as 'natural'. The market appears as beyond the conscious control of its participants – it therefore appears as self-sustaining; while Marx is severely critical of capitalism, he nevertheless at the same time recognised its unique qualities, its unique situation in human development. For the first time, the process of production harnessed inanimate sources of power to systematic techniques of production. Mankind (sic) has been freed as a species from its dependence upon nature. Capitalism made the abundance of goods and services potentially available to all. However, while capitalism has made the potential for such abundance available, the relations of production of capitalist society and the subsequent division of its surplus created conditions of scarcity for the majority.

Marx thus argues that with the revolutionising of the means by which people produce, there is now a potential for humanity to move on to a society based on co-operation and not competition. The only class that can bring such change about is the working class, and this would have to be done on an international level because capitalism exists as a world system.

It wasn't enough, Marx said, to be morally critical of capitalism and hope that one day it would fade away into a more humane society. History was nothing but the history of class struggle, he said, and in all previous epochs, the old ruling class had to be challenged/overthrown by the emerging new class. Thus, he said that the working class/proletariat would be forced to battle, whether it liked it or not, against capitalism, and indeed workers would fight over pay and conditions without realising they were fighting capitalism (it may be just their particular employer).

Marx argued that as workers struggled they would become more conscious of the generalised condition under capitalism and revolt. This class consciousness was of crucial concern for Marx, as he never predicted capitalism would collapse of its own accord. Instead, he talked about the dialectic unity of the objective and the subjective. The objective factors being a particular periodic crisis of capitalism with the subjective element consisting of how well organised and how high was the degree of class consciousness by the vast majority of workers. The class struggle took place irrespective of people's subjective desires. Even where an employer and their employees 'get on' the material well-being of either side depends on the distribution of the surplus.

Marx said that the working class, forced by economic necessity, would have to individually and collectively raise their consciousness to organise not only an economic battle but also a political struggle against the capitalist class – and this would mean not only individual employers but also the capitalist state apparatus. The approach taken here is to outline how Marx came to develop his method of analysis and then of what that analysis consisted. What is here remains just an outline. His theories and ideas are there to be disproved but what cannot be denied is the relevance of his theory. During his lifetime and in the 100 years since his death, critics have suggested that Marx's theories no longer apply or are no longer relevant – usually such critiques take place within/with the backdrop of a capitalist boom – only to be contradicted yet again by another slump or economic crisis (current examples: banks collapse and global recession 2008), in which the works of Marx are dusted off and brought back into circulation again.

Relevance for youth work

- The interests of dominant economic and social groups have the impact of marginalising young people and reducing their life chances.

- Equality for young people cannot be achieved until institutions are made to change their norms, rules and power bases.

- Empowerment of young people – how this is structured – will depend on the political consciousness, knowledge and understanding of the youth worker(s).

- The emphasis is on enabling young people to understand and reject existing social institutions as oppressive. Society is viewed as unequal and separated by 'race', class and gender. These inequalities are unjustifiable, psychologically and socially damaging to all, especially those who are oppressed.

- Ideology and hegemony are imposed rather than agreed and impede the personal development of young people.

- Marxism recognises that young people are victims of injustices in society.

- Youth workers must develop a deeper analysis of the causes of social disadvantage and produce a strategy for alternative interventions.

- Youth work has the positive intention of transferring power to young people.

- Relationship with young people is undertaken with a view to 'engaging' them as partners.

- Youth worker adopts the role of 'problem poser'.

- Young people actively involved in identifying, exploring and understanding issues of concern to them.

The shift from modernism to post-modernism

Post-modernists have a distinct way of seeing the world. The theoretical approaches discussed previously are referred to as modernist narratives, sometimes referred to as meta-narratives by post-modernists. A meta-narrative is a theory that tries to explain the whole of reality, a key example of which is Marxism. A key point about all the perspectives discussed thus far is that each of the theories contains the approach that society can be understood by using rational thinking and methods. For post-modernists, theories are 'texts' and meta-narratives are master texts that do not have an objective, logical and rational account of the world; rather each is a story and open to interpretation. These theories (meta-narratives) are used to legitimise social action and their authority stems from their attempted rigorous 'scientific' approach to explain social phenomena and their promise of reliable knowledge. For post-modernists the 'truth' or 'meaning' of a text is always relative and dependent on the perspective taken by the reading or viewing subject.

The Enlightenment had produced a scientific, rational, logical approach to the understanding of human beings, of a person (a self). So, for example, in each of these perspectives is the idea that it is human individuals who are the producers of knowledge and truth. As Zalewski explains,

> *If modernists think of the human subject like an apple, with a vital core, then postmodernists think of the subject more like an onion – peel away the layers and there is nothing there at the end or at the core.*

(Zalewski, 2000, page 23)

So, for post-modernists, identities are not fixed or stable, so using the terms 'young person' or 'youth' would be meaningless. Rather post-modernists would be interested in examining how discourses (stories, narratives) around young people get produced, and how they impact on young people. Thus, language and meaning are key elements of this approach.

A useful guide to these ideas is provided by Ferdinand de Saussure (1857–1913), a Swiss linguist who worked on structural linguistics and who is credited with the emergence of semiology (a 'science' of signs). Following semiology, the relationship of reality to language is not a given. What is essential to semiology is the arbitrary nature of the sign and the notion that where there are signs there is a system.

ACTIVITY 8.4

Play the semiology game

Close your eyes for a minute and imagine that someone has just come into the room in a boiler suit.

Exactly what image is conjured up?

The boiler suite indicates a particular life style, social role, social class and gender.

Think of another image.

Someone walks by in a bowler hat carrying a brief case, another indication of a particular life style, social role, social class and gender. There are two components of the sign: a signifier and a signified. Both together constitute a sign.

- 1. A Signifier

- 2. A Signified

- 1 + 2 = A SignSignifier + the word/image/sound

Signified = the idea it conjures up, the referent, indicating a particular lifestyle, social role or social attitude There are three different types of signs:

- *Icon: a sign which resembles signifier and signified (e.g. a portrait, an x-ray, a scale model)*

- *Index: causal relationship between signifier and signified*

- *Symbolic: the sign proper e.g. flag*

(Culler, 1976)

How is this useful?

If signs were natural, then there would be nothing to analyse. One would say that opening a door for a woman simply is polite, and that's all there is to it. But if one starts with the assumption that signs have meaning that pertain to a system of conventions (such as class and gender relations), then the man opening the door for a woman is saying something over and beyond the mere action. It can be read as signalling dominance, power and relations of subordination and inferiority. The relationship of language to meaning is beautifully complex and if you want to follow up these ideas, an interesting text would be Lakoff and Johnson (1980), which explores Derrida's techniques for deconstructing texts.

The meaning of a sign, a text, an object, a statement, an image, a picture, does not reside in the object but in its relationship (difference) from other signs. This is the only way we can give it meaning, and the only way we can understand the meaning. Linked to this idea that all meanings are arbitrary and that subjects (e.g. young people) are constructed through language and discourses, it follows that there is not one 'truth' about young people. 'Truths' are only an interpretation or a fiction, as knowledge does not produce 'truths' about the world. If a book is just as much the product of a reader as it is of an author, I cannot ensure that my intentions in writing this chapter will flow to you the reader in a straightforward way. Rather you will be constructing the meaning through your own viewpoints, interpretations, feelings, identities, knowledge and experiences.

ACTIVITY **8.5**

Ask all the individuals in a group to think of a pink elephant. And then go around the room asking them to present what the concept means to them. Each one will have a different interpretation of a pink elephant – guaranteed.

Yes, but then I as the tutor can tell people how *to interpret the concept 'pink elephant'.*

Foucault, for example, argues that our knowledge about young people (or women, or race, or society) is constructed though power relations. His concept of power is discussed in the first chapter on empowerment. There is a dominant meaning in the culture, and this dominance is enforced through power relations. Foucault's analysis of the relationship between power, discursive practices and subjectivity provides a number of conceptual tools from which to re-examine the contradictions of the experiences of young people. That is social relations are complex and unstable processes. Post-modernism seemed to offer some insights into these processes.

Post-modernism

- *Language does not simply* transmit *thoughts or meaning. Meaning is never fixed. Nothing has a stable, unambiguous meaning. Hence, the word 'woman' does not of itself mean anything. It is defined in relation to its opposite 'man' (which also has no fixed meaning) and means different things in different contexts. It can even refer to a man, as in the derogatory phrase 'old woman'.*

- *There is no fixed, unitary, rational subject. There is no essential self, which exists outside culture and language. Subjectivity is constituted through language and*

> culture and is fragmented and also in process. There is no place from 'outside' language and culture from which we can 'know' anything (including ourselves). Our identities and 'knowledges' of the world are products of the way in which we are positioned (or position ourselves) within knowledge and culture. (This is referred to as 'de-centring the subject'.)
>
> • There is no possibility of objective scientific 'truth', which exists out there waiting to be discovered. Knowledges are 'discursive constructs'. This idea comes from Michel Foucault for whom discourses (ways of thinking and talking about the world) produce objects of knowledge rather than describing pre-existing objects. (There is, in any case, no objective 'knower' standing outside the culture, nor is there a transparent language in which to convey some absolute truth.) Knowledges and discourses can be deconstructed – taken apart – in such a way as to reveal that they are not universal truths but rather discourses constructed from particular positions. This leads to the sceptical dismissal of grand theoretical 'meta-narratives', like Marxism, which purport to explain the social world. At its most extreme, this scepticism implies a denial of any material reality.

Relationship to youth work

Applying some of these ideas to youth work, we find that the worker would not operate with any fixed psychological or sociological theories in relation to young people. Their work would be premised on the view that there is no 'universal truth' about young people. All conceptual systems (according to Derrida) are misleading and distorting because they produce a hierarchy and a fixity to our way of thinking. So, for example, in modernist texts, something is true or false, natural or social and one thing or the other. We produce a category (young person, woman, man, parent, mother and manager) and then we fill these categories with values and ideas of what constitutes a 'good' woman, a 'good' or 'normal' young person. The idea of deconstruction derives from the work of Jacques Derrida (1976). In general, it means looking closely at any text, argument or assumption to reveal the inconsistencies and paradoxes which underpin it. Hence, statements that define what women are can be shown to contain contradictory assumptions. For example, we are told that femininity is 'natural' and yet women are constantly counselled to work hard at producing femininity – and the same for masculinity with men. This suggests that they are not natural but rather the product of specific discourses which define it.

These ideas enable an acceptance of contradictory situations and a variety of interpretations of experiences. An article by Krueger (2005) is a good example of a post-modernist approach:

> Consider, for example, a group of modern dancers whose performance is designed to portray a theme or themes. The goal is to create a mood, sense of struggle, or joy. A general direction for the dance is prepared (choreographed) in advance, but

then during the performance the dancers play off one another to the changing tempos of the music. Similarly, competent youth workers plan a shift, chore, meal, or recreation activity according to several themes in youth development, and then improvise as they move through the day with sensitivity to a multitude of factors that influence the nature and outcomes of their interactions.

Like modern dancers, competent workers study, practice, and develop the knowledge and skills that allow them to be in their experiences with youth in the most effective and responsive way. These workers sense, as well as know, when to intervene or not intervene, move close or farther apart, raise or lower their voices, and increase or slow the pace.

(Krueger, 2005, page 22)

Applying these ideas to anti-oppressive practice

The importance of these ideas can be shown by discussing them in the context of anti-oppressive practice. Just as one can trace the impact on youth policy and youth work by exploring the theoretical frameworks that shape practices; a similar process can be tracked with the concept of anti-oppression.

For example, rather than the notion that we know gender, sexuality, ethnicity, generation, that there is a 'fixed' truth about them, that is, women are oppressed; post-modernism points you to the shifting boundaries around these categories. There is no one way in which women are oppressed; rather there is a multitude of practices, which position some women in some situations as the oppressor of other women. Take, for example, a black American woman who employs a black American woman as a domestic cleaner. One cannot read off from the label 'black American woman' a fixed view of how oppression works. In other words, there is not one objective account of oppression in this instance that can be applied to both women. Such an objectivist account would be the notion of patriarchy or capitalism. Rather one has to take into account the subjective positions of both women both of which will be oppressed, but in different ways, and the differences are crucial.

Youth work – in striving for social justice and striving to create an equal and just society free from oppression, exploitation and discrimination – needs to understand how these practices operate in society. To challenge and understand how oppression operates on both an individual and an institutional level, all levels of youth work, from management to advisory committee, need to adopt a framework for anti-oppressive practice. The link between theory, practice and policy using a post-modernist framework means that one would avoid a fixed duality perspective of the oppressor/oppressed and also understand that the categories woman, gay and black do not tell us very much about the people who inhabit these categories. One can have an identity 'woman' but how that impacts on individual women will be related to their subjectivity – their experiences, feelings and desires. Máirtín Mac an Ghaill and Chris Haywood (1997) differentiate between anti-oppression and a 'differentialist position'. A 'differentialist' position uses some of the tools from post-modernism to explain the need for a more useful approach to the contradictions around oppression; the following critical event highlights the difference between the two approaches.

Do white working-class students have culture?

The first critical event occurred in an inner-city multicultural secondary school, where we were informed by white working-class students that the school was racist. They explained that the school favoured African-Caribbean and Asian students, while discriminating against whites. We raised the issue with their teachers, who responded that they were not surprised at these comments, as the white students were racist. In discussions with ethnic majority and minority working-class students, we began to engage critically with the impact of anti-racism on young people. We asked the head teacher what educational principles informed the school's anti-racist policy. She argued that it was very important in a multi-ethnic community that the curriculum addressed students' diverse cultural needs. We found evidence in the selection of curriculum material of positive representations of minority cultures, particularly that of African-Caribbeans and Asians. However, there appeared to be little awareness of the needs of other ethnic groups, including the high proportion of Irish students, who constituted the main ethnic group in the school. Equally significant, white working-class students' cultural needs did not appear to be addressed. We asked the teachers about this absence. They replied by asking us: have white working-class students got any culture?

(Mac an Ghaill and Haywood, 1997, pages 21–34)

C H A P T E R   R E V I E W

This chapter aims to outline a number of theoretical frameworks from sociology, which are then linked to the historical development of youth work. The emphasis is on the perspectives rather than the history. It may seem that these ideas have little to do with how youth workers go about their business (see Smith, 1988). However, the argument here is that these ways of thinking about the relationship between individuals and society, both consciously and unconsciously, shape practice. These are related to the way individual workers work with a view of youth, the type of activities that they set up for them, their view on how young people can participate in decision making and the efforts made to ensure social justice for all. Planning for youth work necessitates an understanding of purpose, and if the aim is a just society, then a rigorous understanding of how individuals and societies change is a necessary tool for practice.

Butler, C (2002) *Postmodernism: A Very Short Introduction*. Oxford: Oxford University Press.

Buchroth, I and C Parkin (eds.) (2010) *Using Theory in Youth and Community Work Practice*. Exeter: Learning Matters.

www.infed.org – the encyclopaedia of informal education organised by Mark Smith.

References

Adams, R (2003) *Social Work and Empowerment*, 3rd edition. Basingstoke: Palgrave Macmillan.

Addley, E (2010) With the clean-up comes the blame game. So who did start the violence? *The Guardian*, 11 December 2010. Available online at www.guardian.co.uk/education/2010/dec/10/student-protests-tuition-fees-violence.

Addley, E, Gabbatt, A and Dodd, V (2010) Police tactics at tuition fees protest questioned after further angry clashes, *The Guardian*, 10 December 2010. Available online at www.guardian.co.uk/education/2010/dec/09/police-tactics-tuition-fees-protest.

Althusser, L (1984) *Essays on Ideology*. London, Verso.

Andersen, NA (2003) *Discursive Analytical Strategies: Understanding Foucault, Koselleck, Laclau, Luhmann.* Bristol: Policy Press.

Arnstein, SR (1969) A ladder of citizen participation (reprinted from *Journal of the American Institute of Planners*, 35(4): 216–24).

Askheim, OP (2003) Empowerment as guidance for professional social work: an act of balancing on a slack rope. *European Journal of Social Work*, 6(3): 229–40.

Atkinson, PA, Martin, CR and Rankin, J (2009) Resilience revisited. *Journal of Psychiatric and Mental Health Nursing*, 16: 137–45.

Bamber, J and Murphy, H (1999) Youth work: the possibilities for critical practice. *Journal of Youth Studies*, 2(2): 227–42.

Batsleer, J (2008) *Informal Learning in Youth Work*. London: Sage.

Beck, D and Purcell, R (2010) *Popular Education Practice for Youth and Community Development Work*. Exeter: Learning Matters.

Bell, CR and Bell, BR (2003) Empowerment is a leadership trick! *Innovative Leader*, 12(10).

Bello, W (2002) *Deglobalization: Ideas for a New World Economy*. London and New York: Zed Books.

Belton, B (2010) *Radical Youth Work*. Lyme Regis: Russell House Publishers.

Bennis, W (2002) Becoming a tomorrow leader, in Spears, LC and Lawrence, M (eds) *Focus on Leadership: Servant Leadership for the 21st Century*. New York: John Wiley & Sons.

Bostock, J and Freeman, J (2003) 'No limits': doing participatory action research with young people in Northumberland. *Journal of Community & Applied Social Psychology*, 13: 464–74.

Boud, D, Cohen, R and Walker, D (1993) *Using Experience for Learning*. Maidenhead: Open University Press.

Boud, D, Keough, R and Walker, D (1985) *Reflection: Turning Experience Into Learning*. Oxon: Routledge.

Bourdieu, P (1991) *Language and Symbolic Power*. Cambridge: Polity Press.

Bourdieu, P (2002) 'The politics of globalisation'. *Open Democracy*, February, Available online at www.opendemocracy.net/print/283, pages 1–4.

Bowlby, J (1946) *Forty-Four Juvenile Thieves: Their Characters and Homelife*. London: Baillière, Tindall and Cox.

Bradford, S (2010) Modernising youth work: from the universal to the particular and back again, in Jeffs, T and Smith MK (eds) *Youth Work Practice*. Basingstoke: Palgrave.

Brake, M (1980) *Sociology of Youth Culture and Youth Subcultures: Sex and Drugs and Rock'n Roll?* London: Routledge and Kegan Paul.

Brookfield, S (1990) Using critical incidents to explore learners' assumptions, in Mezirow, J and Associates (eds) *Fostering Critical Reflection in Adulthood*. San Francisco: Jossey-Bass Inc.

Brunner, O, Conze, W and Kosselleck, R (eds) (1990) *Geschichtliche Grundbegriffe, Historisches Lexikon zur politisch-sozialen Sprache in Deutschland*. Stuttgart: Klett-Cotta.

Burden, T (1998) *Social Policy and Welfare: A Clear Guide*. London: Pluto Press.

Burden, T, Cooper, C and Petrie, S (2000) *'Modernising' Social Policy: Unravelling New Labour's Welfare Reforms*. Aldershot: Ashgate.

Butters, S and Newell, S (1978) *Realities of Training. A Review of the Training of Adults Who Volunteer to Work With Young People in the Youth and Community Service*. Leicester: National Youth Bureau.

Byrne, D (1999) *Social Exclusion*. Buckingham: Open University Press.

Byrne, D (2006) *Social Exclusion*, 2nd edition. Maidenhead: Open University Press.

Child Poverty Action Group (CPAG) (2009) *Child Well-being and Child Poverty: Where the UK Stands in the European Table*. London: CPAG.

Coles, B (2000) *Joined-Up Youth Research, Policy and Practice: A New Agenda for Change?* Leicester: Youth Work Press.

Collishaw, S, Maughan, B, Goodman, R and Pickles, A (2004) Time trends in adolescent mental health. *Journal of Child Psychology and Psychiatry*, 45(8): 1350–62.

Cooper, C (2002) *Understanding School Exclusion: Challenging Processes of Docility*. Nottingham: Education Now Books/University of Hull.

Cooper, C (2005) Places, 'folk devils' and social policy, in Somerville, P and Sprigings, N (eds) *Housing and Social Policy: Contemporary Themes and Critical Perspectives*. Abingdon: Routledge.

Cooper, C (2008) *Community, Conflict and the State: Rethinking Notions of 'Safety', 'Cohesion' and 'Well-Being'*. Basingstoke: Palgrave.

Cooper, C (2009) Rethinking the 'problem of youth': refocusing on the social and its interrelationship with dominant power structures. *Youth & Policy*, 103(summer): 81–92.

Cooper, C (2010) Responding to unhappy childhoods in the UK: enhancing young people's 'well-being' through participatory action research, in Greener, I, Holden, C and Kilkey, M (eds) *Social Policy Review 22: Analysis and Debate in Social Policy*. Bristol: Policy Press.

Cooper, C and Hawtin, M (eds) (1997a) *Housing, Community and Conflict: Understanding Resident 'Involvement'*. Aldershot: Arena.

Cooper, C and Hawtin, M (1997b) *Housing, Community and Conflict: Understanding Resident 'Involvement'*. Aldershot: Arena.

Covey, SR (2002) Servant-leadership and community leadership in the twenty-first century, in Spears, LC and Lawrence, M (eds) *Focus on Leadership: Servant Leadership for the 21st Century*. New York: John Wiley & Son.

Cox, A, Furlong, P and Page, E (1985) *Power in Capitalist Societies: Theory, Explanations and Cases*. Brighton: Harvester Press.

Culler, J (1976) *Saussure*. Brighton: Harvester.

Curtis, P (2010) Council budget cuts hit the most deprived areas, says study, *The Guardian*, 11 December 2010. Available online at www.guardian.co.uk/society/2010/dec/10/council-budget-cuts-poorest-areas

Curtis, P (2011) Big society plans raise concerns for parliamentary democracy, *The Guardian*, 22 January 2011. Available online at www.guardian.co.uk/politics/2011/jan/21/big-society-parliamentary-democracy

Curtis, P and Ramesh, R (2010) Local groups get right to take over services in "big society" bill, *The Guardian*, 10 December 2010. Available online at www.guardian.co.uk/society/2010/dec/10/local-groups-big-society-localism-bill

de Beauvoir, S (1949/1972) *The Second Sex*, translated by Parshley, HM. Harmondsworth: Penguin.

Deer, C (2008) Reflexivity, in Grenfell, M (ed.) *Pierre Bourdieu: Key Concepts*. Durham: Acumen.

Dentith, AM, Measor, L and O'Malley, MP (2009) Stirring dangerous waters: dilemmas for critical participatory research with young people. *Sociology*, 43(1): 158–68.

Department for Education and Skills (DfES) (2003) *Every Child Matters*. London: DfES.

Department for Education and Skills (DfES) (2005) *Youth Matters*. London: DfES.

Department for Education and Skills (DfES) (2006) *Youth Matters: Next Steps*. London: DfES.

Derrida, J (1976) *Of Grammatology*. Baltimore: Johns Hopkins University Press.

Dewey, J (1910) *How We Think*. Boston: D.C. Heath & Co.

Drysdale, J and Purcell, R (2001) *Reclaiming the Agenda: Participation in Practice*. Bradford: CWTC.

Durlak, JA (1998) Common risk and protective factors in successful prevention programs. *American Journal of Orthopsychiatry*, 68(4): 512–20.

Durkheim, E (1893, translated 1933) *The Division of Labour in Society*. New York: The Free Press.

Durkheim, E (1964) *The Division of Labour in Society* (1893). New York and London: Free Press/ MacMillan.

Easton, LD and Guddat, KH (trans and eds) (1967) *Writing of the Young Marx on Philosophy and Society*. New York: Anchor Books.

Eldridge, J (1973) *Sociology and Industrial Life*. London, Nelson.

Federation for Community Development Learning (FCDL) (undated) *Good Practice Standards for Community Development Work*. Sheffield: FCDL.

Field, F (2003) *Neighbours From Hell: The Politics of Behaviour*. London: Politico's Publishing.

Florida, R and Jonas, A (1991) U.S. Urban policy: the postwar state and capitalist regulation. *Antipode*, 23(4): 349–84.

Foucault, M (1979) *The History of Sexuality, Vol. 1, An Introduction*. London: Allen Lane.

Foucault, M (2005) *The Archaeology of Knowledge*. London: Routledge.

France, A (2007) *Understanding Youth in Late Modernity*. Maidenhead: Open University Press.

Frankl, V (1959) *Man's Search for Meaning*. New York: Simon & Schuster

Fraser, N (1989) *Unruly Practices: Power, Discourse and Gender in Contemporary Social Theory*. Oxford: Polity Press.

Fraser, N (2009) Feminism, capitalism and the cunning of history. *New Left Review*, 56: 97–117.

Freedom Writers (2007) Director: Richard LaGravenese.

Freeman, C, Henderson, P and Kettle, J (1999) *Planning With Children for Better Communities: The Challenge to Professionals*. Bristol: Policy Press.

Freire, P (1993, 1996) *Pedagogy of the Oppressed*. Harmondsworth: Penguin Books.

Frith, S (1984) *Sociology of Youth*. Ormskirk: Causeway Books.

Giddens, A (1972) *Capitalism and Modern Social Theory: An Analysis of the Writings of Marx, Durkheim and Max Weber*. Cambridge: Cambridge University Press.

Giddens, A (1998) *The Third Way: The Renewal of Social Democracy*. Cambridge: Polity Press.

Gilligan, R (2000) Adversity, resilience and young people: the protective value of positive school and spare time experiences. *Children and Society*, 14: 37–47.

Ginsburg, N (1992) Racism and housing: concepts and reality, in Braham, P, Rattansi, A and Skellington, R (eds) *Racism and Antiracism: Inequalities, Opportunities and Policies*. London: Sage.

Giroux, HA (2000) *Stealing Innocence: Youth, Corporate Power, and the Politics of Culture.* New York: St. Martin's Press.

Goleman, D (1985) *Vital Lies, Simple Truths.* New York: Simon & Schuster.

Gramsci, A (1971) *Selections From the Prison Notebooks.* London: Lawrence and Wishart.

Gutierrez, M (1990) Working with women of color: an empowerment perspective. *Social Work*, 35: 149–53.

Hall, GS (1904) *Adolescence: Its Psychology and Its Relations to Physiology, Anthropology, Sociology, Sex, Crime, Religion and Education*, 2 vols. New York: Appleton.

Hall, S and Jefferson, T (eds) (1976) *Resistance Through Rituals. Youth Subcultures in Post-War Britain.* London: Hutchinson.

Hardt, M and Negri, A (2005) *Multitude: War and Democracy in the Age of Empire.* London: Penguin Books.

Hart, R (1992) *Children's Participation: From Tokenism to Citizenship.* Florence: UNICEF.

Harris, V (ed.) (1994) *Community Work Skills Manual.* Newcastle: Association of Community Workers.

Hasan, R (2000) Riots and urban unrest in Britain in the 1980s and 1990s – a critique of dominant explanations, in Lavalette, M and Mooney, G (eds) *Class Struggle and Social Welfare.* London: Routledge.

Held, D and McGrew, A (2007) *Globalization/Anti-Globalization: Beyond the Great Divide*, 2nd edition. Cambridge: Polity.

Hill, C (1997) *The Intellectual Origins of the English Revolution Revisited.* Oxford: Clarendon Press.

Hock, D (1999) *Birth of the Chaordic Age.* San Francisco: Berrett-Koehler Publishers Inc.

Hoffman, J (2004) *Citizenship Beyond the State.* London: Sage.

Holland, J, Reynolds, T and Weller, S (2007) Transitions, networks and communities: the significance of social capital in the lives of children and young people. *Journal of Youth Studies*, 10(1): 97–116.

Hudson, M (2002) *Managing Without Profit: The Art of Managing Third Sector Organization.* London: Directory of Social Change.

Hutchings, K (2010) *Global Ethics: An Introduction.* Cambridge: Polity.

Jackson, B and Parry, K (2008) *A Very Short, Fairly Interesting and Reasonably Cheap Book About Studying Leadership.* London: Sage Publications.

James, A, Jenks, C and Prout, A (1998) *Theorizing Childhood.* Cambridge: Polity.

Jeffs, T and Smith, M (1999) The problem of 'youth' for youth work. *Youth and Policy*, 62: 45–66. Available online at www.infed.org/archives/youth.htm

Jones, G (1988) Integrating process and structure in the concept of youth: a case for secondary analysis. *Sociological Review*, 36(4): 706–32.

Kadushin, A (1992) *Supervision in Social Work*, 3rd edition. New York: Columbia University Press.

Kam, J (2010) 'Shocking: for police and me', *The Guardian*, 11 December 2010.

Katz, M (1997) *On Playing a Poor Hand Well: Insights From the Lives of Those Who Have Overcome Childhood Risks and Adversities*. New York: Norton & Company.

Kolb, DA (1984) *Experiential Learning Experience as a Source of Learning and Development*. New Jersey: Prentice Hall.

Krovetz, ML (1999) *Fostering Resiliency*. California: Corwin Press.

Krueger, M (2005) Four themes in youth work practice. *Journal of Community Psychology*, 33(1): 21–9.

Laclau, E and Mouffe, C (2001) *Hegemony and Socialist Strategy: Towards a Radical Democratic Politics*, 2nd edition. London: Verso.

Lakoff, G and Johnson, M (1980) *Metaphors We Live By*. Chicago: University of Chicago Press.

Ledwith, M and Springett, J (2010) *Participatory Practice: Community-Based Action for Transformative Change*. Bristol: Policy Press.

Lee, D and Newby, H (1983) *The Problem of Sociology: An Introduction to the Discipline*. London: Unwin Hyman.

Lerner, M (1988, 1991) *Surplus Powerlessness: The Psychodynamics of Everyday Life and the Psychology of Individual and Social Transformation*. New York: Humanity Books.

Levitas, R (1998, 1999) *The Inclusive Society? Social Exclusion and New Labour*. Basingstoke: Palgrave.

Levitas, R (2005) *The Inclusive Society? Social Exclusion and New Labour*, 2nd edition. Basingstoke: Palgrave.

Lewin, K, Lippitt, R and White, RK (1939) Patterns of aggressive behavior in experimentally created social climates. *Journal of Social Psychology*, 271–99.

Lister, R (1997) *Citizenship: Feminist Perspectives*. Basingstoke: Macmillan.

Lister, R (2010) *Understanding Theories and Concepts in Social Policy*. Bristol: Policy Press.

Lister, R (forthcoming) The age of responsibility: social policy and citizenship in the early 21st century, in Holden, C, Kilkey, M and Ramia, G (eds) *Social Policy Review 23*. Bristol: The Policy Press.

Liebau E and Chisholm, L (1993) Youth, social change and education: issues and problems. *Journal of Education Policy*, 8(1): 3–8.

Luhmann, N (1995) *Social Systems*, trans. by Bednarz, J and Baecker, D. Palo Alto, CA: Stanford University Press.

Lukes, S (1974) *Power: A Radical View*. London: Macmillan.

Luthar, SS (1991) Vulnerability and resilience: a study of high risk adolescents. *Child Development*, 62(3): 600–16.

Mac an Ghaill, M and Haywood, C (1997) The end of anti-oppressive education? A differentialist critique. *International Studies in Sociology of Education*, 7(1): 21–34.

MacDonald, R (ed.) (1997) *Youth, the 'Underclass' and Social Exclusion*. London: Routledge.

MacDonald, R and Marsh, J (2001) Disconnected Youth? *Journal of Youth Studies*, 4(4): 373–91.

Maguire, M (2009) *Law and Youth Work*. Exeter: Learning Matters.

Malik, S (2010) Schoolboy warned by police over picket plan at David Cameron's office, *The Guardian*, 11 December 2010. Available online at www.guardian.co.uk/uk/2010/dec/10/schoolboy-quizzed-cameron-office-picket

Malik, S and Townsend, M (2010) Officers 'tried to stop hospital staff treating injured protestor', *The Observer*, 12 December 2010. Available online at www.guardian.co.uk/uk/2010/dec/12/police-injured-protester-hospital

Marcuse, H (1964) *One-Dimensional Man*. London: Routledge & Kegan Paul.

Marshall, G (1982) *In Search of the Spirit of Capitalism: An Essay on Max Weber's Protestant Ethic*. Thesis. New York: Columbia University Press.

Marshall, TH (1950) *Citizenship and Social Class*. Cambridge: Cambridge University Press.

Marx, K (1845) *Theses on Feuerbach: Thesis 11*.

Marx, K (1875) Preface to the Second Edition of *Capital*.

Marx, K (1906) *Capital*, vol 1. Chicago: Kerr & Co.

Marx, K and Engels, F (1965) *The German Ideology*. London: Lawrence and Wishart.

Marx, K and Engels, F (1970) *Selected Works in One Volume*. London: Lawrence and Wishart.

Maton, K (2008) Habitus, in Grenfell, M (ed.) *Pierre Bourdieu: Key Concepts*. Durham: Acumen.

Mayo, P (2004) *Liberating Praxis: Paulo Freire's Legacy for Radical Education and Politics*. Rotterdam: Sense Publishers.

McAlister, S, Scraton, P and Haydon, D (2009) *Childhood in Transition: Experiencing Marginalisation and Conflict in Northern Ireland*. Belfast: Queen's University, Prince's Trust and Save the Children.

McDermott, E and Graham, H (2005) Resilient Young Mothering: Social Inequalities, Late Modernity and the 'Problem' of 'Teenage' Motherhood. *Journal of Youth Studies*, 8(1): 59–79.

McGhee, D (2005) *Intolerant Britain? Hate, Citizenship and Difference*. Maidenhead: Open University Press.

McSmith, A (2010) The Big Society: a genuine vision for Britain's future – or just empty rhetoric? *The Independent*, 20 July 2010. Available online at www.independent.co.uk/news/uk/

politics/the-big-society-a-genuine-vision-for-britains-future-ndash-or-just-empty-rhetoric-2030330.html

Mezirow, J and Associates (1990) *Fostering Critical Reflection in Adulthood: A Guide to Transformative and Emancipatory Learning.* San Francisco: Jossey-Bass Inc.

Milanovic, B (2006) *Global Income Inequality.* Working Paper. Washington DC: World Bank.

Miliband, R (1982) *Capitalist Democracy in Britain.* Oxford: Oxford University Press.

Miliband, R (1983) *Class Power and State Power.* London: Verso.

Mizen, P (2003) The best days of your life? Youth, policy and Blair's New Labour. *Critical Social Policy*, 23(4): 453–76.

Modood, T, Berthoud, R, Lakey, J, Nazroo, J, Smith, P, Virdee, S and Beishon, S (1997) *Ethnic Minorities in Britain: Diversity and Disadvantage.* Grantham Books.

Monbiot, G (2003) *The Age of Consent: A Manifesto for a New World Order.* London: Flamingo.

Morgan, G (1997) *Images of Organization*, 2nd edition. Thousand Oaks, CA: Sage Publications, Inc.

Morris, M and Patton, P (eds) (1979) *Michel Foucault: Power, Truth, Strategy.* Sydney: Feral Publications.

Mullard, M (2002) *Reclaiming Citizenship: Discourses on the Meaning of Citizenship.* Working Papers in Social Sciences and Policy, No. 7. Hull: University of Hull.

Murray, C (1990) *The Emerging British Underclass.* London: Institute of Economic Affairs.

Natiello, P (2001) *The Person-Centered Approach: A Passionate Presence.* Herefordshire, UK: PCCS Books.

National Crime Prevention (1999) *Pathways to Prevention: Developmental and Early Intervention Approaches to Crime in Australia.* Canberra: National Crime Prevention, Attorney-General's Department.

National Youth Agency (2004) *Ethical Conduct in Youth Work.* Leicester: National Youth Agency.

Natorp, P (1920, 1922), cited in Askheim, OP (2003) Empowerment as guidance for professional social work: an act of balancing on a slack rope. *European Journal of Social Work*, 6(3): 229–40.

New Economics Foundation (NEF) (2009) *National Accounts of Well-Being in Europe.* Available online at www.nationalaccountsofwellbeing.org (accessed 6 May 2011).

Newman, T and Blackburn, S (2002) *Transitions in the Lives of Children and Young People: Resilience Factors.* Interchange 78: Scottish Executive Educational Department.

Nieuwenhuys, O (2004) Participatory action research in the majority world, in Fraser, S, Lewis, V, Ding, S, Kellett, M and Robinson, C (eds) *Doing Research With Children and Young People.* London: Sage.

Noakes, L, Brecher, B, Rupprecht, A, Margree, V and Clewer, N (2010) Letters: violent policing and the student protests, *The Independent*, 13 December 2010. Available online at www.independent.co.uk/opinion/letters/letters-violent-policing-and-the-student-protests-2158589.html

Oakley, A (1972) *Sex, Gender and Society*. London: Temple Smith.

Office of National Statistics (ONS) (1999) *Regional Trends 1999: A Portrait of Britain*. London: ONS.

Packham, C (2008) *Active Citizenship and Community Learning*. Exeter: Learning Matters.

Page, N and Czuba, CE (1999) 'Empowerment: What Is It?' *Journal of Extension*, 37(5).

Parsloe, P (ed.) (1996) *Pathways to Empowerment*. Birmingham: Venture Press.

Patel, R (2010) Creativity and partnership, in Batsleer, J and Davies, B (eds) *What Is Youth Work?* Exeter: Learning Matters.

Payne, M (1997) *Modern Social Work Theory*. Basingstoke: Macmillan.

Pearsall, J (ed.) (1999) *The Concise Oxford Dictionary*, 10th edition. Oxford: Oxford University Press.

Perkins, DD and Zimmerman, MA (1995) Empowerment theory, research, and application. *American Journal of Community Psychology*, 23(5): 569–79.

Pilger, J (2002) *The New Rulers of the World*. London: Verso.

Podd, W (2010) Participation, in Batsleer, J and Davies, B (eds) *What Is Youth Work?* Exeter: Learning Matters.

Purvis, T and Hunt, A (1993) Discourse, ideology, discourse, ideology, discourse, ideology. *British Journal of Sociology*, 44(3): 473–99.

Quinn, JJ and Davies, PF (eds) (1999) *Ethics and Empowerment*. Basingstoke: Macmillan.

Raelin, JA (2003) *Creating Leaderful Organizations*. San Francisco: Berrett-Koehler Publishers Inc.

Rappaport, J (1984) *Studies in Empowerment: Steps Towards Understanding and Action*. New York: Haworth Press.

Ridge, T (2003) *Childhood Poverty and Social Exclusion: From a Child's Perspective*. Bristol: Policy Press.

Ritzer, G (1998) *The McDonaldization Thesis*. London: Sage.

Roberts, J (2009) *Youth Work Ethics*. Exeter: Learning Matters.

Roche, M (1992) *Rethinking Citizenship*. Cambridge: Polity.

Rutter, M, Giller, H, and Hagell, A (1998) *Antisocial Behavior by Young People*. New York: Cambridge University Press.

Rutter, M (2007) Resilience, competence and coping. *Child Abuse and Neglect*, 31(3): 205–9.

Rutter, M, Kreppner, JJ and O'Connor, TG (2001) Specificity and heterogeneity in children's responses to profound institutional privation. *British Journal of Psychiatry*, 179: 97–103.

Sawicki, J (1991) *Disciplining Foucault*. New York and London: Routledge.

Schön, DA (1983) *The Reflective Practitioner: How Professionals Think in Action*. London: Temple Smith.

Schubert, JD (2008) Suffering/symbolic violence, in Grenfell, M (ed.) *Pierre Bourdieu: Key Concepts*. Durham: Acumen.

Servian, R (1996) *Theorising Empowerment: Individual Power and Community Care*. Bristol: Policy Press.

Shukra, K (2010) Anti-racism to community cohesion, in Batsleer, J and Davies, B (eds) *What Is Youth Work?* Exeter: Learning Matters.

Smith, H (2010) Engaging in conversation, in Jeffs, T and Smith, MK (eds) *Youth Work Practice*. Basingstoke: Palgrave Macmillan.

Smith, M (1988) *Developing Youth Work: Informal Education, Mutual Aid and Popular Practice*. Milton Keynes: Open University Press.

Social Exclusion Unit (SEU) (1999) *Bridging the Gap: New Opportunities for 16–18 Year Olds*. London: The Stationery Office.

Solomos, J (2003) *Race and Racism in Britain*, 3rd edition. Basingstoke: Palgrave.

Spears, LC and Lawrence, M (eds) (2002) *Focus on Leadership: Servant Leadership for the 21st Century*. New York: Wiley & Sons.

Spooner, P (2010) *No Child Left Behind – A Study of the Interpersonal Impact Upon Young People Excluded From Mainstream Education in Hull*. Leeds: Children's Workforce Development Council. Available online at www.cwdcouncil.org.uk/assets/0001/0312/Microsoft_Word_-_PLR0910SpoonerLC.pdf

Staples, LH (1990) Powerful ideas about empowerment. *Administration and Social Work*, 14(2): 29–42.

Steger, MB (2009) *Globalization: A Very Short Introduction*. Oxford: Oxford University Press.

Such, E, Walker, O and Walker, R (2005) Anti-war children: representations of youth protests against the second Iraq war in the British national press. *Childhood*, 12: 301–26.

Tannenbaum, R and Schmidt, W (1973) How to choose a leadership pattern. *Harvard Business Review*, 51(3): 162–4.

Taylor, FW (2003) *The Principles of Scientific Management*. New York: Dover Publications Inc.

The Primary Review (2007) *Community Soundings: The Primary Review Regional Witness Sessions*. Cambridge: University of Cambridge.

The Young Foundation (2008) *Well-Being News Archive*. Available online at www.youngfoundation.org.uk (accessed 26 May 2011).

Thompson, N (2007) *Power and Empowerment*. Lyme Regis, Russell House Publishing.

Thomsen, K (2002) *Building Resilient Students*. California: Corwin Press.

Twelve Angry Men (1957) Director: Sidney Lumet.

Ungar, M (2004) *Nurturing Hidden Resilience in Troubled Youth*. Toronto: University of Toronto Press.

United Nations Children's Fund (UNICEF) (2007) *Child Poverty in Perspective: An Overview of Child Well-Being in Rich Countries*. Florence: UNICEF.

Valentine, J (2004) Personal and organisational power: management and professional supervision, in Tudor, K and Worrall, M (eds) *Freedom to Practise*. Ross-On-Wye: PCCS Books.

Wallerstein, N and Bernstein, E (eds) (1994) Special issue: community empowerment, participatory education, and health. Parts 1 and 11. *Health Education Quarterly*, 21(2/3): 141–419.

Watt, N (2010) Cameron finally reveals 'big society' vision – and denies it is just a cost-cutting measure, *The Guardian*, 20 July 2010. Available online at www.guardian.co.uk/politics/2010/jul/19/david-cameron-big-society-launch

Weber, M (1905) *The Protestant Ethic and the Spirit of Capitalism*, trans. by Parsons, T.

Weber, M (1947) *Theory of Social and Economic Organisation*. Glencoe, IL: Free Press.

West, A (1998) What about the children? The involvement of younger residents, in Cooper, C and Hawtin, M (eds) *Resident Involvement and Community Action: Theory to Practice*. Coventry: Chartered Institute of Housing/Housing Studies Association.

Wilkinson, R and Pickett, K (2009) *The Spirit Level: Why More Equal Societies Almost Always Do Better*. London: Penguin.

Williams, F (1998) Agency and structure revisited, in Barry, M and Hallett, C (eds) *Social Exclusion and Social Work: Issues of Theory, Policy and Practice*. Lyme Regis: Russell House Publishing.

Williams, F (2010) Group work, in Buchroth, I and Parkin, C (eds) *Using Theory in Youth and Community Work Practice*. Exeter: Learning Matters.

Wintour, P (2010) Councils that predict 140,000 job losses because of budget cuts are scaremongering, says minister, *The Guardian*, 26 November 2010. Available online at www.guardian.co.uk/politics/2010/nov/25/councils-huge-job-losses-scaremongering

Woodward, W (2006) Radical Muslims must integrate, says Blair, *Guardian Unlimited*, 9 December, Available online at www.guardian.co.uk/uk/2006/dec/09/religion.immigrationandpublicservices (accessed 17 March 2011).

Worley, C (2005) 'It's Not about race. It's about the Community': New Labour and 'Community Cohesion'. *Critical Social Policy*, 25(4): 483–96.

Wright, O and Taylor, J (2011) Cameron: my war on multiculturalism, *The Independent*, 5 February 2011. Available online at www.independent.co.uk/news/uk/politics/cameron-my-war-on-multiculturalism-2205074.html

Wright Mills, C (1956) *Power Elite*. London: Oxford University Press.

Wright Mills, C (1959) *The Sociological Imagination*. New York: Oxford University Press.

Wyn, J and White, R (1997) *Rethinking Youth*. St Leonards, NSW: Allen & Unwin.

Young, K (2006) *The Art of Youth Work*, 2nd edition. Lyme Regis: Russell House Publishing Ltd.

Zalewski, M (2000) *Feminism after Postmodernism: Theorising through Practice*. New York: Routledge.

Zimmerman, MA (2000) Empowerment theory: psychological, organizational and community levels of analysis, in Rappaport, J and Seidman, E (eds) *The Handbook of Community Psychology*. New York: Plenum Press.

Index